Is Medical School Your Goal?

FROM

HIGH SCHOOL

TO

MEDICAL SCHOOL

The Ultimate Guide to
BS/MD Programs

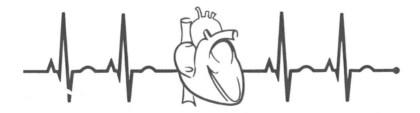

Rachel A. Winston, Ph.D.
Researcher, Professor, Admissions Expert, Motivational Speaker

ISBN 978-1-946432-03-2 © Copyright 2020 Lizard Publishing. All rights reserved.

Lizard Publishing® 7700 Irvine Center Drive, Suite 800 Irvine, CA 92618 *www.lizard-publishing.com*

This book was published in the U.S.A. Lizard Publishing is a premium quality provider of educational reference, career guidance, and motivational publications/merchandise for global learners, educators, and stakeholders in education.

Book Design by Michelle Tahan *www.michelletahan.com*

LIZARD PUBLISHING

ACKNOWLEDGEMENTS

There is never enough room to acknowledge every person who contributed to an individual's perspective, assisted in the development of a person's knowledge base, or taught indelible lessons that last a lifetime. In this book, I gratefully acknowledge Michelle Tahan, Jasmine Jhunjhnuwala, and Joe Klunder, as well as my family, friends, colleagues, and professors.

I would also like to thank the thousands of students I have taught, counseled, or tutored in my more than forty years of service in education.

Isaac Newton once said, "If I see so far, it is because I stand on the shoulders of giants." A few of those giants in my life whose shoulders have lifted me higher and helped teach me invaluable lessons include: Dr. John E. Roueche, Dr. Terry O'Banion, Dr. Sandra Savage, Dr. Arthur Levine, Dr. David A. Waugh, Dr. Annette Hartenstein, Dr. Zenobia Miro, Malka Mirvis, Michael Ortell, Riki Kucheck, Dennis/Charlene Ashendorf, Gary Crisp, Batzi Heger, Mike/Lola Knicker, John Smart, Raymond Hunter, Steve/Debby Kurti, Samantha Mann, Joey/Ricky Hanzich, Jacqueline Xu, Chelsea Lee, and Robert A. Helmer.

> *"If I see so far, it is because I stand on the shoulders of giants."*
> *– Isaac Newton*

Lizard Publishing creates, designs, produces, and distributes books and resources to provide academic, admissions, and career information.

Our mental process is fueled by three tenets:
- » *Ignite the hunger to learn and the passion to make a difference*
- » *Illuminate the expanse of knowledge by sharing cutting edge thinking*
- » *Innovate to create a world that makes the transition from dreams to reality*

We work with academic leaders who transform the educational landscape to publish relevant content and advise students of their educational and professional options, with the aim of developing 21st-century learners and leaders. We also work with students to publish their books and present widely diverse ideas to the college/graduate school-bound community. With headquarters in Irvine, California, Lizard Publishing works virtually with authors to edit, publish, and distribute both hard copy and paperback books.

ABOUT THE AUTHOR

D r. Rachel A. Winston is a tireless student-advocate. She has served the educational community as a university professor, college advisor, statistician, researcher, author, motivational speaker, publishing executive, and lifelong student. As one of the leading experts in college counseling and an award-winning faculty member, Dr. Winston has spent her lifetime learning, teaching, mentoring, and coaching students.

She started college at thirteen and graduated from college programs in such widely ranging disciplines as chemistry, mathematics, educational computing, liberal arts, international relations, business administration, higher education leadership, interpreting, college counseling, and publishing. Throughout her education, she attended Harvard, UChicago, NYU, GWU, Syracuse, Maryland, UCLA, UCI, CSUF, CSUDH, Cal Poly, ASU, Claremont Graduate University, Pepperdine, and USC among other colleges.

Her position working in Washington, D.C. on Capitol Hill and with the White House in the 1980s took her to approximately a hundred universities training campaign managers at colleges from Colorado to California, thoroughly dotting the western states. Later, she led college tours with students and their families on road trips throughout the United States. She has taught or counseled thousands of students over her career and speaks at conferences and academic programs throughout the world.

As a professor and avid writer for numerous publications, she won the 2012 McFarland Literary Achievement Award and numerous other awards, including Faculty Member of the Year, Leadership Tomorrow Leader of the Year, and college service and leadership awards. Studying Human Capital at Claremont Graduate University, she was a scholarship recipient at the Drucker School of Management. She was also elected to the statewide Board of Governors for the Faculty Association for California Community Colleges, where she served on their executive committee.

She served as a faculty member for the UCLA College Counselor Certificate Program, the Director of Mathematics at Brandman University, and a professor at Embry Riddle Aeronautical University, Chapman University, Cal State Fullerton, and a handful of California Community Colleges, including Cerro Coso College where she also served as the Academic Senate President and retired in 2016. Over her career, she taught mathematics online, on television, live interactive satellite, telecourses, and in large and small lecture halls.

Rachel A. Winston, Ph.D.
Researcher, Professor, Admissions Expert, Motivational Speaker

---

"Knowledge has to be improved, challenged, and increased constantly, or it vanishes."

AUTHOR'S NOTE

Y ou are reading this book because you are considering a medical school education. Whether you choose to pursue the BS/MD, BS/DO, premedical route, or apply to different types of programs with the goal of deciding later, you are in the right place. Right now, you need to gather information to make informed decisions. While many people offer advice, suggestions differ. Friends will tell you the 'right' way or the way their neighbor was accepted.

You should graciously accept this anecdotal information while you commit to learning more. This is your future. Dig deeper to consider both expert and current information from counselors who have worked with hundreds of BS/MD students. Changes in programs, curricula, requirements, and links happen each year. Double-check each program's specifics yourself. This guide is current as of April 2020 with each school's website information. However, in researching this book, a few programs have been discontinued. A few of these include BS/MD programs at the University of Miami (not just for UM undergrads) and Lehigh (discontinued since 2017, though they still have BS/DMD and BS/OD), UTSA Health, and UT Rio Grande Valley.

> *"We are what we think. All that we are arises with our thoughts. With our thoughts, we make the world."*
> *— Buddha*

There are a few good books on BS/MD programs written by talented and experienced counselors. I admire and cheer on their efforts. This guide is different in that it provides maps, lists, timelines, and unique ways of organizing the information. I hope you find this information valuable.

Your job is to begin early by assembling information for the schools you are considering, creating a road map, and setting yourself on a clear path. If you see an error in this book or even a suggestion for a future edition, please write to me and let me know at *collegeguide@yahoo.com*. I will fix the entry with the next version I print.

All of that said, this book was written for you in mind. There is a wealth of information on the Internet with free downloads, FAQs, testimonials, and offers to help you with your applications. Some of these advisors are knowledgeable and could help you. Students and parents hunt around the web searching for a tremendous number of hours seeking the information they need. This book was designed to make your search easier.

For now, though, I will assume that you are reasonably confident that you want to attend medical school and are exploring this avenue as a possible way to take advantage of a program that will get you on your way toward your goal. I will also assume that you are a highly academic candidate who is willing to work very hard. You may have a fascination with the human body, passion for medicine, or a commitment to serve others selflessly. These are virtually prerequisites for BS/MD programs.

As you investigate colleges, you might find that some schools call these programs BS/MD, BA/MD, BS/DO, BA/DO, direct med, early acceptance, or early assurance programs. Applying to and writing essays for each application will require research. While you might have in your mind that BS/MD programs are relatively similar, each program's nuances make them very different. While these small differences may seem confusing, my goal with this book is to demystify the process.

CONTENTS

Part 1

The Road to Medical School

Part 2

Research and Preparation for BS/MD Programs

Part 3

The Application Process

Part 4

Choosing the BS/MD Program For You

Part 5

Lists and Worksheets

GLOSSARY AND ACRONYMS

A FEW ACADEMIC AREAS

Biological Sciences: biochemistry, biomedicine, cell biology, conservation, ecology, genetics, human biology, microbiology, pathobiology, and physiology

Humanities: ancient/modern foreign languages, art, dance, English, film, history, law, literature, music, philosophy, politics, and religion, theater

Math and Statistics: actuarial science, computational science, cryptology, data science, econometrics, statistics, operations research, and population genetics

Physical Sciences/Engineering: astronomy, chemistry, engineering, geology, meteorology, physics

Social Sciences: anthropology, criminal justice, economics, geography, history, international relations, political science, sociology, and psychology

Specialized Health Sciences: dietetics, gerontology, kinesiology, nursing, nutrition, occupational therapy, public health

ACRONYMS

AAMC – American Association of Medical Colleges www.aamc.org

AMCAS – American Medical College Application Service®

AOA – American Osteopathic Association

Bacc – Bachelorette programs lead to B.A. or B.S. degrees

Bachelor of Arts (BA) vs. Bachelor of Science (BS) degrees

CCHE – The 'Colorado Commission on Higher Education' index score is no longer used by the University of Colorado Denver School of Medicine.

http://catalog.ucdenver.edu/mime/media/14/1137/admission_index1.pdf

DO – Doctor of Osteopathy

EAP – Early Assurance Program

MD – Medical Doctor

MPH – Master of Public Health

Ph.D. – Doctor of Philosophy

Post-Bacc – These programs are designed for students needing additional preparation after college and before they apply to medical schools. Some post-bacc programs are strictly for non-science majors, some offer masters degrees while completing preparatory coursework, and some offer the top candidates spots in their medical school upon completion.

SLOs – Student Learning Objectives – Classes commonly have a list of student learning objectives the teacher is expected to teach and the student is expected to learn.

PROGRAM ACRONYMS

EAP – University of South Alabama's 'Early Acceptance Program'

EMSAP – The University of Alabama at Birmingham's 'Early Medical School Acceptance Program'

GEMS – University of Louisville School of Medicine's 'Guaranteed Entrance to Medical School'

GPPA – The University of Illinois at Chicago College of Medicine's 'Guaranteed Professional Programs Admissions'

HPM – University of Miami's 'Health Professions Mentoring' Program (Their HPME program no longer exists)

HPME – Northwestern University's 'Honor Program in Medical Education'

JAMP – Texas University's 'Joint Admissions Medical Program'

JAS – University of Minnesota's 'Joint Admissions Scholars' Program

MSP – University of Miami's 'Medical Scholars Program' – Dual-Degree Program in Medicine and Rice/Baylor 'Medical Scholars Program'

NEOMED – 'Northeast Ohio Medical University'

PLME - Brown University's 'Program in Liberal Medical Education'

PPSP – Case Western University's 'Pre-Professional Scholars Program'

REMS – University of Rochester's 'Rochester Early Medical Scholars' Program

RHOP – Chadron State College, Wayne State College, & Peru State College ' 'Rural Health Opportunities Program' w/the University of Nebraska Medical Center (UNMC)

SPiM – University of Colorado at Storrs' 'Special Program in Medicine'

PART ONE

THE ROAD TO MEDICAL SCHOOL

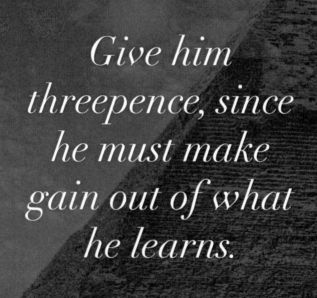

Give him threepence, since he must make gain out of what he learns.

— *Euclid of Alexandria*

CHAPTER ONE

THERE IS NO ROYAL ROAD

Euclid of Alexandria (~365 BCE – ~300 BCE), a mathematician who was thought to be a student of Plato, wrote one of the most widely read collection of books in all of history called *Elements*. This series of thirteen texts rigorously lays the foundation for mathematics, proofs, and spatial representations. The books emphasize deduction, logically constructed from explicitly stated assumptions. Although much of the contents were known long beforehand, Euclid systematically organized the definitions, abstractions, and proofs in a comprehensive set of texts.

Proclus Lycaeus (412 AD – 485 AD) wrote that when Ptolemy 1 was studying *Elements*, he struggled with the concepts. Ptolemy 1 asked if there was an easier way to learn the material. Euclid responded to the future ruler of Egypt (323 BCE – 283 BCE), "There is no royal road to geometry."

Similarly, there is no royal road to BS/MD programs. The road is long, difficult, and not designed for those who want an easy path. Fortunately, for some programs, the MCATs are not required when seeking admission to medical school, and students are guaranteed admission. If they keep up their grades, their saving grace is the peace of mind that if they learn the required material, they will not have to sweat another grueling and very competitive admissions process with no assurance of admission. After all, Harvard Medical School has a 3.8% chance of acceptance.

In another anecdote, a frustrated student asked what he would get out of studying geometry. Euclid, in a sarcastic reply, told his servant, "Give him threepence, since he must make gain out of what he learns." Admissions representatives are keenly aware of students who complete only the minimum community service requirements for their high school to 'look good'. Euclid might say, "Must you get credit or 'make gain out of what you learn' or are you so passionate about your chosen activities that you would do them anyway?"

There is another saying that goes, "Do what you love, and the money will come." Relating this to your current pursuit might translate to, "Do what you love, and you will enjoy your life no matter what happens in the future." Undoubtedly, both attitudes are recognizable during interviews.

STEM teachers and athletic coaches remind students that disciplined learning is often not easy. Effort and practice are required for mastery. This is particularly true for coursework in pursuit of medical school since 'failure is not an option'. Students must be committed and passionate about the subject matter they study as well as their career path.

You may not know the reason for studying theoretical concepts that may seem too abstruse or abstract to be necessary or relevant. Nevertheless, there are many reasons for learning and mastering difficult concepts, not the least of which are logical reasoning and rigorous analysis of assumptions. There are no short cuts to medicine or 'royal road' that will smooth out your path. However, with persistence, diligence, and serious study, you will find that the result is worth the effort.

Allow your passion to become your purpose, and it will one day become your profession.

— Gabrielle Bernstein

CHAPTER TWO
THE RIGHT AND WRONG REASONS

The journey to and through medical school is long, but the reward is worth the effort. "No pain – no gain," as the saying goes, is the appropriate mantra. No matter how smart you are or how little you had to study to excel in the toughest classes in high school or college, the medical field will demand much of you mentally and physically – more than you expected. You must be disciplined in your study habits and organized in your thinking to prepare for medical school, even in a direct med program.

There are dozens of reasons why you might believe that the medical field is inspiring, rewarding, and/or appealing. A few that come to mind include:

» *To serve.*

» *To support.*

» *To care.*

» *To save lives.*

» *To diagnose.*

» *To treat.*

» *To resolve.*

» *To learn.*

» *To collaborate.*

» *To research.*

» *To empathize.*

» *To reassure.*

» *To help families cope with death.*

» *To persistently seek cures.*

» *To extend compassion.*

» *To work with a team of professionals.*

» *To improve other people's lives.*

» *To immerse yourself in patient care.*

» *To fix a broken system.*

» *To provide healthcare for the underserved.*

» *To follow a rewarding path.*

» *To make a difference.*

» *To understand the human body.*

» *To always be fascinated.*

» *To connect to your curiosity.*

» *To be intellectually stimulated.*

» *To get paid to do what you love.*

These are all good. The medical school journey, though, is arduous—many quit. The time you invest while studying can be long. However, the hours working day and night as an intern can be even longer. Real-life medicine is not like the popular medical shows on television like *Chicago Med, ER, House, Grey's Anatomy, The Good Doctor, Scrubs,* or *Code Black.* Even if you have the stamina, the field of medicine demands attentiveness to responsive caring for fellow humans who have families, loved ones, and people who count on them.

Pursue medicine for the right reasons. Otherwise, you are likely to hit a roadblock very hard if you are pursuing this course of study for the wrong reasons. There will be times when you do not understand a concept, you have been working on a chemistry assignment for too long, or you are simply exhausted. You might be deliriously ill, or your computer may crash after you have completed the twentieth page of a twenty-five-page paper due the next day. An internal engine with a booster shot of adrenaline can kick in at the last minute if you are certain where you are headed.

Patients count on you. They put their lives in your hands. Medicine is not the field for people who want to be a hero, show off their intelligence, or gain a prestigious reputation in the community. Many students feel the pressure to pursue medicine because their parents were doctors, or their family is urging them to go into a field where they can make a lot of money. Others simply feel that becoming a doctor will make their parents happy or proud. One or more of these wrong reasons may resonate with you, but do not let the wrong reasons be your driving force.

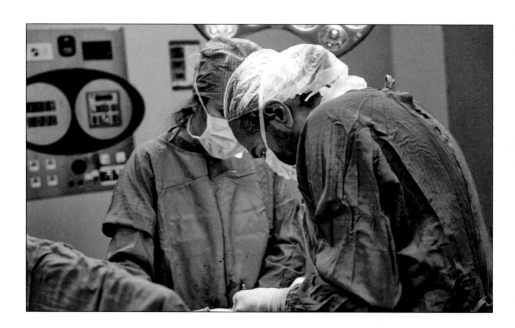

Strong people stand up for themselves, but stronger people stand up for others.

— *Unknown*

ZENELY PHOTOGRAPHY

CHAPTER THREE
PREPARING FOR THE JOURNEY

Your academic choices in middle school and high school determine your trajectory. Although you can often catch up with additional math and science courses later, starting early is helpful. Depending upon the school, frequently, you cannot take one science class without taking the prerequisite math class, or you cannot take an AP science class unless you take the CP or Honors science class beforehand. In some cases, you must have a specific grade or recommendation from the teacher in order to proceed to higher levels. Find out the requirements and procedures for the school you attend at the outset.

Academics are important, but they are not everything. There are lots of students who study seemingly 24/7 and have high grades. Yet, they do not participate in school activities, clubs, athletics, or leadership. Some have never served in the community or shadowed a doctor.

Get involved! There are many reasons for this. In order to understand the world around you and the people you will serve and treat, you need to learn more about all kinds of people. Tutor underprivileged kids. Volunteer at a retirement home. Help at a homeless shelter. Cut up vegetables at a soup kitchen. Take a leadership role in Girl Scouts, Boy Scouts, National Charity League, or the National League of Young Men. These and many others, like coaching soccer, working with the disabled, and volunteering with refugee organizations are excellent ways to know more about the people who live in your region.

Discover activities you can do to support groups of people in your community.

»	*Old*	»	*Gang Members*
»	*Young*	»	*Rural Community Members*
»	*Homeless*	»	*Farmers*
»	*Disadvantaged*	»	*Disabled*
»	*Rape Victims*	»	*Hospitalized*
»	*Refugees*	»	*Veterans*
»	*Immigrants*	»	*Victims of Domestic Violence, etc.*

If you cannot drive to another location or you are quarantined, volunteer to take phone orders for food deliveries or collect donations of supplies from people in your neighborhood. You could write thank you letters/e-mails to the people who are important in your life; send care packages to veteran's homes; sponsor a drive to provide necessities to older or disabled people who cannot leave their residences.

Due to the coronavirus pandemic, we all have a heightened consciousness of the challenges and opportunities of doctors, nurses, and other health professionals. We have heard or watched stories of the many vulnerable people who live on the streets each day with chronic conditions and limited access to healthcare. Those who live from paycheck to paycheck must choose between paying their rent or buying food. Some do not have the money for a dental appointment or a physical.

What can you do to make their lives better? How can you improve the health of others? You do not have to wait until medical school to make a difference in the mental or physical health of people in your community. This concept is the basis of community service – helping the people in your community. Figure it out. Find a unique way to serve. Do not wait for a program to ask you to join them. Start one. There are many needs of people within a few miles of wherever you live.

Preparing for the journey is as much about being part of your school and regional society as it is about your education. Getting involved in high school is a good indicator of whether or not you will get involved in college and take an active role in the BS/MD community. Even if you cannot stay after school for sports, debate, theatre, MUN, Mock Trial, or clubs, you might find other ways to participate in student government, musicals, artistic groups, or volunteer service. You might find it easier to get involved in weekend events, community service, research, or hospital activities. By taking part in your school and community, you gain a better understanding of the field of medicine, collaboration with others, and the critical state of people, old and young.

Life is a matter of choices, and every choice you make makes you.

— John C. Maxwell

CHAPTER FOUR

IS THE BS/MD ROUTE OR THE TRADITIONAL PREMEDICAL PATH RIGHT FOR YOU?

You probably already know that Direct Med BS/MD programs are highly competitive. The most popular programs, like Brown's PLME (Program in Liberal Medical Education), Northwestern's HPME (Honors Program in Medical Education), Boston University' Seven-Year Liberal Arts/Medical Education Program, and George Washington's Seven-Year Dual BA/MD Program have low acceptance rates and are highly selective. You will need more than the minimum requirements.

The most competitive schools only accept the very best math and science students. Many valedictorians are rejected. Students with perfect test scores are set aside for more well-rounded students or those who fit the school's residency or diversity requirements. Now is the time for you to gain medical experiences, school leadership, serve the community, conduct research, and build your resume.

You have probably 'received the memo' that says you should take four years of the highest level of AP/IB science classes and mathematics at your school (through AP Calculus, if it is offered). You will need to take the SAT I or ACT and possibly the SAT II Subject Tests in math and science. These testing requirements may be relaxed during the pandemic but are essential indicators of aptitude and, in the case of the subject tests, knowledge.

Of course, you need both high grades and high test scores. When you see a minimum GPA listed, those are the lowest possible scores the school will even consider. Admitted students to BS/MD programs have significantly higher average scores. Additionally, the requirements colleges list on their website simply get you to the starting plate to swing the bat. The goal is to hit a home run. Lots of students begin their journey to medical school and arrive at first, second, or third base with decent successes along the way. Yet, they miss the homerun.

IS THE PRE-MED TRACK BETTER FOR YOU?

If you are a highly academic student who is certain medical school is in your future, an option you should consider is the BS/MD track. If you are unsure that you want to pursue medicine, the BS/MD avenue is the wrong road. You have other options. You can go to college, major in a field of your interest, take the required premedical courses, and apply to medical school after your four years of study.

If you head in this direction, you should know that a degree in biology or chemistry is not required to enter medical school. You can major in any field provided you take the required science course work and the MCAT. You will discover in the attached chart that some alternative majors have a higher acceptance rate.

Following the pathway toward medical school, while gaining medical training, scientific research, and service experiences, you will learn more about yourself and your specific career interests. There are many avenues where you can translate your interest in medicine into a related field. You might consider dental school, vet school, or pharmacy school. Maybe you would prefer to be a physician's assistant, nurse practitioner, or medical researcher. You might find mental health, public health, or community medicine more appealing. By choosing to pursue the premedical pathway, you will navigate college while continuing to discover what subjects and activities you enjoy the most. Maybe you will find that medicine is not right for you.

Most students take the longer road to medical school through undergraduate school because this avenue is more flexible. You can take the opportunity to explore majors and consider alternative career paths. For many students who want to attend medical school, this is the most appropriate. Students can choose any major while taking premedical requirements.

LOOKING AT THE DATA

The following is a table from the AAMC website that offers 2019-2020 statistical data of GPA, MCAT, and majors for students who applied and those who matriculated. The AAMC website provides tons of valuable information. Check it out. While you are not yet applying to medical school, it is valuable to keep your eye on the prize. Look at where you are headed to make good decisions now as to how to get there.

Table A-17: MCAT and GPAs for Applicants and Matriculants to U.S. Medical Schools by Primary Undergraduate Major, 2019-2020

The table below displays MCAT scores and GPAs for applicants and matriculants to U.S. medical schools for 2019-2020 by primary undergraduate major. MCAT scores and GPAs are displayed by mean or median and standard deviation (SD). Please email datarequest@aamc.org if you need further assistance or have additional inquiries.

Applicants	MCAT CPBS		MCAT CARS		MCAT BBLS		MCAT PSBB		Total MCAT		GPA Science		GPA Non-Science		GPA Total		Total Applicants
	Mean	SD	Mean	SD	Mean	SD	Mean	SD	Mean	SD	Mean	SD	Mean	SD	Mean	SD	
Biological Sciences	126.4	2.7	125.8	2.7	126.8	2.7	127.1	2.7	506.0	9.2	3.49	0.41	3.74	0.27	3.59	0.33	30,693
Humanities	126.6	2.6	127.0	2.6	126.9	2.6	127.6	2.5	508.1	8.8	3.44	0.45	3.71	0.29	3.58	0.33	1,678
Math and Statistics	128.0	2.6	127.0	2.7	127.7	2.7	127.9	2.8	510.5	9.4	3.56	0.38	3.70	0.27	3.61	0.32	344
Other	126.1	2.8	125.7	2.8	126.3	2.8	126.9	2.9	505.0	9.6	3.46	0.44	3.71	0.28	3.58	0.34	8,754
Physical Sciences	127.6	2.6	126.5	2.7	127.2	2.6	127.5	2.6	508.9	8.8	3.56	0.39	3.70	0.29	3.61	0.32	4,937
Social Sciences	126.0	2.8	126.1	2.7	126.2	2.8	127.5	2.7	505.7	9.3	3.38	0.47	3.65	0.33	3.52	0.35	5,001
Specialized Health Sciences	125.5	2.9	125.2	2.8	125.7	2.9	126.4	3.0	502.8	10.1	3.43	0.45	3.70	0.30	3.57	0.34	1,964
All Applicants	126.4	2.8	125.9	2.7	126.7	2.7	127.1	2.7	506.1	9.3	3.49	0.43	3.72	0.28	3.58	0.33	53,371

Matriculants	MCAT CPBS		MCAT CARS		MCAT BBLS		MCAT PSBB		Total MCAT		GPA Science		GPA Non-Science		GPA Total		Total Matriculants
	Mean	SD	Mean	SD	Mean	SD	Mean	SD	Mean	SD	Mean	SD	Mean	SD	Mean	SD	
Biological Sciences	127.7	2.2	126.9	2.3	128.2	2.0	128.5	2.1	511.1	6.5	3.67	0.30	3.82	0.21	3.73	0.24	12,484
Humanities	127.8	2.1	128.1	2.1	128.1	2.1	128.9	1.9	512.9	6.1	3.63	0.31	3.80	0.22	3.72	0.23	780
Math and Statistics	128.9	2.2	128.0	2.1	128.5	2.1	129.0	1.9	514.8	6.4	3.70	0.26	3.77	0.22	3.72	0.23	163
Other	127.6	2.1	127.0	2.1	127.8	2.0	128.5	2.1	511.0	6.4	3.65	0.31	3.80	0.21	3.74	0.23	3,371
Physical Sciences	128.7	2.0	127.5	2.3	128.3	2.1	128.6	2.0	513.1	6.5	3.70	0.28	3.78	0.23	3.73	0.24	2,355
Social Sciences	127.6	2.2	127.4	2.2	127.8	2.1	129.0	1.9	511.7	6.2	3.60	0.33	3.75	0.25	3.68	0.26	1,995
Specialized Health Sciences	127.4	2.2	126.8	2.3	127.6	2.1	128.3	2.2	510.1	6.7	3.65	0.30	3.83	0.19	3.74	0.23	721
All Matriculants	127.8	2.2	127.1	2.3	128.1	2.1	128.5	2.0	511.5	6.5	3.66	0.30	3.81	0.22	3.73	0.24	21,869

To get a clearer picture of the applicant's majors and their matriculation, here is a condensed version of the percentages.

ACADEMIC FIELD	MATRICULANTS	APPLICANTS	PERCENTAGE
Biological Sciences	12,484	30,693	40.67%
Humanities (Phil., Rel., Lit., etc.)	780	1,678	46.48%
Math & Statistics	163	344	47.38%
Other	3,371	8,754	38.51%
Physical Sciences	2,355	4,937	47.70%
Social Sciences (Psych., Soc., Anthro...)	1,995	5,001	39.89%
Specialized Health Sciences	721	1,964	36.71%

Notice, the academic field with the highest probability of matriculating to medical school is the Physical Sciences. This is followed by Math & Statistics and the Humanities. The lowest was Specialized Health Sciences, followed by Other, Social Sciences, and Biological Sciences. Most students believe that the chances are higher in the Biological Sciences, but this is not the case. The problem-solving skills of the Physical and Mathematical Sciences are fundamental in medical school. Students more often get stuck along the road in physics, chemistry, and mathematics classes and not in biology or social sciences. While that knowledge is valuable, medical schools want to be sure you can succeed in the most academically challenging classes.

BS/MD VS. EARLY ASSURANCE PROGRAMS

Traditionally, BS/MD and BS/DO programs are direct-to-medical school pathway programs, although many still require students to take the MCAT and/or apply through AMCAS. When the AMCAS application is required, (1) some schools offer an automatic admit upon achieving the requirements, (2) others require candidates to apply to the affiliated medical school through the AMCAS binding Early Decision option, (3) and still others allow students to complete the first four years and attend another medical school upon completion. There is no consistency between programs.

However, there are other options, called Early Assurance Programs or Early Acceptance Programs (EAPs). With EAPs, students are accepted to their undergraduate college and then apply to the direct med program. These programs typically allow students in their first two years of college to apply for a specialized premedical pathway that guarantees admission provided the student achieves the requisite grades and MCAT scores or at least prioritizes these students in the medical school admissions process. Some of these programs require students to take the MCAT and/or complete the AMCAS; some do not. This book does include some programs of this type since you should know these exist so you can plan accordingly.

Finally, some college's BS/MD programs are connected to the same university's medical school. Alternatively, at other schools, students complete four years at one university and then finish their last four years at another university's medical school. A pathway agreement is made to take candidates who have successfully completed all of the requirements, like the Medical Scholars Program (MSP) between Rice University and Baylor College of Medicine.

There is no elevator to success. You have to take the stairs.

— Zig Ziglar

CHAPTER FIVE

THE FIELD OF MEDICINE AND AFFILIATED MEDICAL CAREERS

MEETING THE NEED FOR HEALTHCARE WORKERS

According to the Bureau of Labor Statistics (BLS), the healthcare industry is expected to grow faster than the average for all other occupations. With a projected increase of 14 percent from 2018 to 2028, approximately 1.9 million new jobs will be available for those interested in medicine. The demand for healthcare will only increase in the post-pandemic environment. However, increases are anticipated due to the aging population in a demographic shift sometimes referred to as the "gray tsunami."

According to the U.S. Census Bureau, baby boomers, born between 1946 – 1964, are turning 65 at a rate of about 10,000 per day. By 2030, when the next census is taken, all baby boomers will have crossed that threshold. This information is critical to understanding all careers in healthcare and is the key reason why the healthcare profession will have a surge of jobs. Hospitals, emergency services, home healthcare, nursing homes, and mental health services will require professionals to meet the rising need. Wages are likely to rise in the next decade.

WHAT MEDICAL PROFESSION IS RIGHT FOR YOU?

When students ponder the pursuit of medicine, they tend to consider medical school as the quintessential career and life objective. No doubt medical school is the right pursuit for many students. Yet, there are many rewarding options and there is more than one road to get to your goal.

In the 1990s, a Harvard interviewer asked one of my very talented Hispanic students why she would want to attend a liberal arts school if she wanted to pursue nursing. My student answered the question without hesitation, explaining that her mom had a DNP but always wished she had started her road with a rigorous liberal arts education. However, I never stopped thinking about that question. Sure, specialized undergraduate nursing education is a more direct pathway and this route would extend her timeline, but she was committed to expanding her knowledge base. After we talked, I came to understand her long-term objective. She did not get accepted to Harvard, but she did attend Columbia and she is now a nurse practitioner.

There are numerous possibilities for students who find medicine, healthcare, and human biology fascinating. Popular choices for those who complete graduate school include allopathic medicine (MD), osteopathic medicine (DO), podiatrist (DPM), dentist (DDS), veterinarian (DVM), pharmacist (PharmD), psychologist (M.A., Ph.D., Psy.D.), psychiatrist (MD), optometrist (OD), chiropractor (DC), physician's assistant (PA), physical therapist (PT), speech pathologist, nurse practitioner (MSN, DNP), occupational therapist (MSOT, DOT), nurse anesthetist (MSN).

OCCUPATION/DEGREE	ASSOCIATIONS, CERTIFICATION ORGANIZATIONS	BUREAU OF LABOR STATISTICS DATA (2018)
Medical Doctor (MD) Allopathic Medicine – AMCAS - 154 accredited colleges in the U.S.; 17 in Canada	*American Association of Medical Colleges (AAMC) *American Medical Association (MDs & DOs)	Median Annual Salary – $208,000 Number of Physicians & Surgeons (2018) – 756,800 Projected Job Change (2018 – 2028) – 7% inc. Job Openings (2018 – 2028) – 55,400
Physician (DO) Osteopathic Medicine – AACOMAS - 36 accredited colleges in the U.S.	* American Association of Colleges of Osteopathic Medicine (AACOM) *American Osteopathic Association (AOA) *Bureau of Osteopathic Specialists (BOS) *Certifying Board Services (CBS)	Median Annual Salary – $208,000 Number of Physicians & Surgeons (2018) – 756,800 Projected Job Change (2018 – 2028) – 7% inc. Job Openings (2018 – 2028) – 55,400
Podiatrist (DPM) – CPME - 9 accredited colleges in the U.S.	*American Association of Colleges of Podiatry Medicine (AACPM) * Council on Podiatric Medical Education (CPME)	Median Annual Salary – $129.550 Number of Podiatrists (2018) – 10,500 Projected Job Change (2018 – 2028) – 6% inc. Job Openings (2018 – 2028) – 600
Dentistry (DDS) – ADEA AADSAS – 67 ADA accredited dental schools in the U.S.; 10 in Canada	*American Dental Education Association (ADEA) *American Dental Association (ADA)	Median Annual Salary – $156,240 Number of Dentists (2018) – 155,000 Projected Job Change (2018 – 2028) – 7% inc. Job Openings (2018 – 2028) – 11,600
Veterinary Medicine (DVM) – VMCAS - 30 accredited veterinary medical schools in the U.S.; 5 in Canada	*Association of American Veterinary Medical Colleges (AAVMC) *American Veterinary Medical Association (AVMA)	Median Annual Salary – $93,830 Number of Veterinarians (2018) – 84,500 Projected Job Change (2018 – 2028) – 18% inc. Job Openings (2018 – 2028) – 15,600
Pharmacist (PharmD) – PharmCAS - 144 full or candidate accredited pharmacy schools in the U.S.	*Accreditation Council for Pharmacy Education (ACPE) *American Pharmacists Association (APhA)	Median Annual Salary – $126,120 Number of Pharmacists (2018) – 314,300 Projected Job Change (2018 – 2028) – 0% inc. Job Openings (2018 – 2028) – (-100)
Psychologist (MA, Ph.D., Psy.D) – numbers vary by type	*American Psychological Association (APA)	Median Annual Salary – $79,010 Number of Psychologists (2018) – 181,700 Projected Job Change (2018 – 2028) – 14% inc. Job Openings (2018 – 2028) – 26,100
Psychiatrist (MD)	See MD	Median Annual Salary – $208,000 Number of Physicians & Surgeons (2018) – 756,800 Projected Job Change (2018 – 2028) – 7% inc. Job Openings (2018 – 2028) – 55,400

OCCUPATION/DEGREE	ASSOCIATIONS, CERTIFICATION ORGANIZATIONS	BUREAU OF LABOR STATISTICS DATA (2018)
Optometrist (OD) - 23 accredited optometry schools in the U.S. and 2 in pre-accreditation	*Association of Schools and Colleges of Optometry (ASCO) *Association of Optometrists (AOP)	Median Annual Salary – $111,790 Number of Optometrists (2018) – 42,100 Projected Job Change (2018 – 2028) – 10% inc. Job Openings (2018 – 2028) – 4,000
Chiropractor (DC) - 20 chiropractic schools in the U.S.	*Association of Chiropractic Colleges (ACC) *American Chiropractic Association (ACA) *Council on Chiropractic Education	Median Annual Salary – $71,410 Number of Chiropractors (2018) – 50,300 Projected Job Change (2018 – 2028) – 7% inc. Job Openings (2018 – 2028) – 3,700
Physician's Assistant (PA) - 254 ARC-PA accredited PA programs in the U.S.	*Accreditation Review Commission on Education for the Physician Assistant (ARC-PA) *American Academy of Physician Assistants (AAPA)	Median Annual Salary – $108,610 Number of PAs (2018) – 118,800 Projected Job Change (2018 – 2028) – 31% inc. Job Openings (2018 – 2028) – 37,000
Physical Therapist (PT) - Over 400 CAPTE accredited PT schools	*American Physical Therapy Association (APTA) *Commission on Accreditation in Physical Therapy Education (CAPTE)	Median Annual Salary – $87,930 Number of PTs (2018) – 247,700 Projected Job Change (2018 – 2028) – 22% inc. Job Openings (2018 – 2028) – 54,200
Speech Pathologist – 230 accredited programs	* *American Speech–Language–Hearing Association (ASHA)	Median Annual Salary – $77,510 Number of Speech Pathologists (2018) – 153,700 Projected Job Change (2018 – 2028) – 27% inc. Job Openings (2018 – 2028) – 41,900
Nurse Practitioner (NP) MSN, DNP - Approximately 400 NP programs	*American Association of Colleges of Nursing (AACN) *American Association of Nurse Practitioners (AANP)	Median Annual Salary – $113,930 Number of NPs (2018) – 240,700 Projected Job Change (2018 – 2028) – 26% inc. Job Openings (2018 – 2028) – 62,000
Occupational Therapist (MSOT, DOT) - 37 fully accredited DOT programs	*American Occupational Therapy Association (AOTA) * Accreditation Council for Occupational Therapy Education (ACOTE)	Median Annual Salary – $84,270 Number of Occupational Therapists (2018) – 113,000 Projected Job Change (2018 – 2028) – 18% inc. Job Openings (2018 – 2028) – 23,700
Nurse Anesthetist (MSN)	See NP	Median Annual Salary – $113,930 Number of NPs (2018) – 240,700 Projected Job Change (2018 – 2028) – 26% inc. Job Openings (2018 – 2028) – 62,000

ALLIED HEALTH PROFESSIONS

The medical profession would not be able to serve the public without the talented and dedicated service of allied health professionals who support, assist, record, evaluate, and rehabilitate patients. From intake and testing to nutrition and maintenance, if it 'takes a village', the village that is needed to treat patients is multifaceted, multilingual, and multitalented. These careers often require interpersonal skills in communication and listening along with recordkeeping, problem solving, and critical thinking. In addition to healthcare administrators, managers, and insurance professionals, the following presents a list of some of the many professionals in the medical support community.

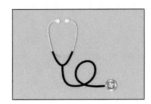

» *Athletic Trainer*

» *Audiologist*

» *Cardiovascular Technologist*

» *Clinical Laboratory Technician*

» *Clinical Laboratory Technologist*

» *Diagnostic Medical Sonographer*

» *Emergency Medical Technician*

» *Exercise Physiologists*

» *Dental Assistant*

»

» *Dietician (RD, RDN)*

» *Dispensing Optician*

» *Genetics Counselors*

» *Health Information Technician*

» *Home Health Aide*

» *Kinesiologist*

» *Massage Therapist*

» *Medical Assistant*

» *Medical Records Assistant*

» *Medical Transcriptionist*

» *Midwife*

» *MRI Technologist*

» *Nuclear Medicine Technologists*

» *Nursing Assistant (CNA)*

» *Nutritionist*

» *Occupational Therapy Assistant*

» *Orderly*

» *Orthotists*

» *Paramedics*

» *Pharmacy Technician*

» *Phlebotomist*

» *Physical Therapy Assistant*

» *Prosthetists*

» *Psychiatric Aide*

» *Recreational Therapist*

» *Radiation Therapists*

» *Radiologic Technologist*

» *Registered Nurse (RN, BSN)*

» *Respiratory Therapist*

»

» *Ultrasound Technician*

» *Veterinary Assistant*

» *Veterinary Technologist*

A mind that is stretched by a new experience can never go back to its old dimensions.

– Oliver Wendell Holmes, Jr.

CHAPTER SIX
COVID-19 & THE MEDICAL SCHOOL PIPELINE

A tsunami is transforming healthcare education caused by a quake of global magnitude. The rollout and repercussions could not have been predicted because society was not in the mindset of planning for an unprecedented medical catastrophe. Enhanced 'virtual clinical training' and 'ethics in telehealth procedures' were immediately conceptualized and established in some fields at the height of the pandemic to allow students to progress. Adjusting medical programs to compensate for missed learning and experiences has been difficult on all levels. Medical education is particularly precarious because the patient relationship and specific technical knowledge cannot be left out of the curriculum without devastating consequences related to science foundation coursework, medical training, and board exams.

The medical school pipeline will continue to bring in new students, but challenges presented by the coronavirus pandemic has left numerous questions in its wake. There is no question that COVID-19 and the pandemic of 2020 has and will impact medical education in general along with the number and types of students drawn to the healthcare profession throughout the subsequent decade. Medicine has come a long way since the Spanish Flu of 1918-1920 which terrified the world for three years and killed nearly fifty million people. Yet, while the death toll is not as high, the fear today is palpable. The consequences permeate the lives of everyday people as they come to grips with their mortality and sense death around them. Even if a medical solution is resolved, more research is necessary to combat and thwart future medical catastrophes and more planning is needed to mitigate the challenges to the medical education pipeline.

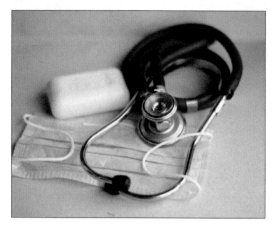

The world's population has been awakened to the fact that the human body is not resilient to new and virulent microbes. For lay people, this idea has remained dormant in some undisturbed subterranean sector of our subconscious. Movies like *Contagion* left lingering reminders as they dramatized the possibility of global health emergencies. Yet, many did not want to believe a global pandemic was possible. Few in academia were prepared for how they might transcend a tumultuous ride. As the tremors shook across the Pacific Ocean, the threat was too far away in January and February of 2020 to feel that an eruption of our lives was not too far behind.

Like the rippling effect of foreshocks to an earthquake that had not yet released its energy, most people in the academy did not plan for 'the big one' even as it began to rock Europe. Information from China had been cut off, so quantitative and qualitative data from the epicenter could not be accumulated. However, doctors in Italy were not silent. Deaths mounted. Hospitals and clinics were unprepared. Supplies were needed. Protection was limited. Nobody was immune - young, old, educated, skilled. From the garment worker to state leaders, COVID-19 passed through cities with its destructive

force. Money could not stem the tide as people sang from their balconies and vehicles bearing coffins rolled down the streets. Accounts from nurses and physicians sent up flares lighting the sky and warning all that this pernicious menace was headed their way.

Schools, heading the siren, acted quickly, though the consequences of stopping in-person school meant an abrupt change from classroom education to online chaos. Some schools were more prepared, but others languished with students who had no computers, tests that could not be proctored, and school lunches that would no longer be provided. The challenges did not just rest with K-12 education as colleges and medical schools struggled to determine how they would deliver lectures, hold labs, and support the thousands of students who were asked to leave their dormitory rooms. International students had nowhere to go, with flights grounded to their far away homes and, even when they could get to their home country, they had limited connectivity to the online resources they had grown accustomed to accessing not to mention having to manage disturbances like 'Zoom bombing'.

Faculty who had never taught online or used virtual classrooms were caught off-guard. Student expectations exceeded the ability for faculty to deliver. Communication and feedback were awkward as they were unable to recreate the classroom in the online environment. Everyone from the students to faculty and administrators needed to adapt to the enormous shakeup that has erupted life along the medical school pathway. Everyone from high school to residency education needed to be seamlessly migrated online, which was a tall order.

Those on their undergraduate or graduate pathway toward a medical degree were forced to rethink their education and discover new ways to learn the material in a self-advocating, efficient manner despite the other obstacles they faced. OChem labs could not be completed, lectures were interrupted, and collaborative projects needed a fresh lens to view project development and delivery. Students toward the end of applying to BS/MD programs and medical school were unable to interview in some cases or visit their prospective schools in others. Their final decisions had to be made with significantly less information.

As students struggled to make decisions, parents became more protective and cautious. Many parents started to make choices, preferring that their children stay closer to home. This change in demographics impacted the geographic diversity of many colleges across the county. While this shift may only be a one or two-year change, the consequences of the 2020-2021 decision-making process may last much longer. Decisions, decisions. Those in admissions continue to search for ways students can be connected to their university while realizing that some international students faced the very real possibility that they would not be able to renew their visa to attend in the fall.

Prospective undergraduate or graduate students may be even more dedicated to their pursuit given the focus on medicine, health, and curiosity about knowing more about the human body. Some might have a renewed drive to help others, serve their communities, and prevent the possibility of death from overshadowing life. Their determination to study and hunger to learn may inspire them to seek a greater understanding of diseases and their impacts on anatomy and physiology. To be sure, the pandemic's cloud over the population clarified the real need to understand the pathophysiology of diseases.

Students in the medical pipeline faced challenges to present themselves in the best light. Academically, they may not have been able to complete required classes, learn critical information, take summer advancement opportunities, or participate in valuable training. Other impediments blocked thoroughfares. Research projects were discarded, disbanded, or postponed. Presentations at conferences, acceptance of papers, and delivery of proposals were put on hold or canceled altogether. Volunteer medical experiences and service projects to demonstrate leadership and   were hindered. Prestigious research grants were held up, not to mention the stoppage of academic travel or programs vital to service, learning, and funding.

Without being able to present a strong academic background, community service, dedicated hospital experiences, and teamwork through collaborative activities, students may have decided their prospects to enter BS/MD programs or medical schools were limited. Some counted on their SAT, ACT, or MCAT they had been studying for throughout the year to send a strong signal that they were prepared. Yet, these tests were canceled. Their pathway disrupted, many had to rethink how to move forward with their goal.

Others may have changed course entirely, dissuaded from pursuing medicine due to the deaths of healthcare workers and doctor's lack of safety and protection. Those whose heart was not into the selfless service of medicine may have changed their minds. Some witnessed their parent's medical practices that were virtually shut down for months when non-necessary procedures slowed their patient appointments.

Telemedicine, while having some promise, did not make up for the number of patient appointments lost that medical professionals once had.

Quick thinking innovators, though, emerged from the smoke and rumblings of COVID-19's eruption. Their previous rigorous, but planned, course was set. They were nimble in their life choices and determined to be flexible and adaptable. 'Necessity is the mother of invention' as the saying goes, and creative acts of kindness, support, service, and healthcare during the pandemic show tenacity and persistence. 'Walk the walk' resonates better when demonstrated rather than crafted on a personal statement.

Medical education, from pre-training in high school and skill development in college through medical school, will be different in the future. All involved in education will be more prepared. Proactive thinking will be common on all levels. Some students will stay the course and pursue their passion with every breath in their body. Some will not. Technology will be better integrated into the curriculum. Resilience will be a sought-after attribute. Experiential learning through medical practice, only moderately replicable at home, will have to suffice for the near term. However, there is no substitute for live patient care. Some medical services will adapt along with previously held mindsets about how to care for patients while also being personally safe and healthy. Handshaking may be an anachronism of a bygone era.

For many years after the coronavirus pandemic's tentacles have been severed, there will continue to be widespread mental and physiological recuperation. Still, we will survive and be better off for the transformation. We have all stared in the face of death and have been reminded of our mortality. Medical education from high school to residency will continue, along with the necessary adjustments needed to acclimate to the new normal. Rigorous education and methodological training are both necessary and powerful tools to shape talent and hard work into skills. Some may say learning is the most valuable tool we have to plant the seeds of our new generation of physicians, fertilize them with the pandemic's dose of humility, and unite physicians, scientists, and inventors to uncover the mysteries of the human body yet to be revealed.

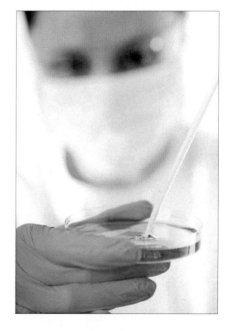

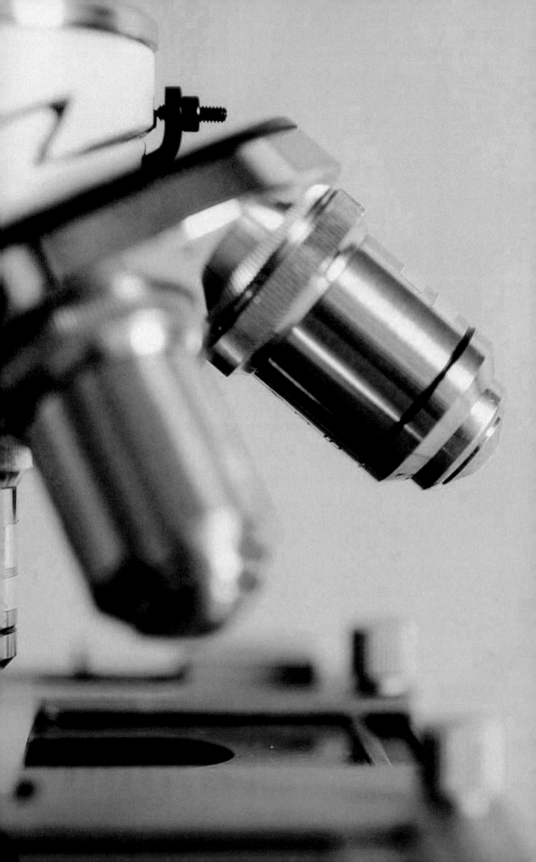

PART TWO

RESEARCH AND PREPARATION FOR BS/MD PROGRAMS

By failing to prepare, you are preparing to fail.

— Benjamin Franklin

CHAPTER SEVEN
COURSEWORK AND GPA

A dose of pragmatism is required in formulating an academic plan. You will need four years of high school science. More is better, whether that means taking two in a year or taking science at a college in the summer or during the school year. Math is required. Four years is typically the minimum, although some students take an extra math class outside of school at a college to get ahead. Other students exhaust their high school's math course options earlier in their curriculum.

Science and math classes are essential components of a student's schedule. Why? Frequently, students begin their freshman year of college taking General Chemistry and Calculus. When graded on a curve, these classes tend to 'weed' students out who have not taken AP Chemistry or AP Calculus. Imagine taking General Chemistry in college next to a student who has had two years of high school chemistry and being told that only half of the students in the class will earn an A or a B. This is not uncommon.

I always say, "A college does not reject you because they don't like you. They reject you because they do not know enough about you to accept you." Alternatively, "A college does not reject you because they don't want you. They reject you because they do not want you to fail, particularly if you are less prepared than other candidates, and you might feel overwhelmed."

Most applicants to BS/MD programs have taken AP Calculus AB. Some have also taken Multivariable Calculus, Linear Algebra, and/or Differential Equations. Eighth graders are often allowed to take an algebra class at a community college, though some students take Precalculus during the summer along the way to get to AP Calculus AB or BC as a junior or senior. Note: Since BS/MD programs are highly competitive, applicants frequently have higher credentials than those who plan to pursue the traditional premedical route. Many students will have completed AP Biology, AP Chemistry, and AP Physics as well as AP Calculus BC (if offered) by the time they graduate.

INVESTIGATE MEDICAL SCHOOL REQUIREMENTS EARLY

It is essential to keep in mind your future college curriculum pathway. BS/MD programs may allow students to choose from a wide variety of majors, although they will still need to take a set of standard requirements that could include a year of biology, genetics/microbiology, anatomy/physiology, general chemistry, organic chemistry, biochemistry, physics, English, psychology, statistics, and calculus.

Check the medical schools to which you plan to apply to see their specific requirements early enough to ensure that you are not missing a critical course. It does not hurt you to research college and medical school academic requirements while you are in high school, well before you start college so that you have a game plan. Certainly,  you will want to seek counsel from your BS/MD or premedical advisor, but the due diligence to know what is required is on your shoulders. Taking responsibility to create an organized and manageable plan will help you better choose your course of action.

The three toughest classes for students are often, but not always, Organic Chemistry, Biochemistry, and Physics. This is why medical schools want to know how students fair in individual courses across a challenging curriculum rather than a high overall GPA that may be stacked with easy classes. General Chemistry, Organic Chemistry, and Biochemistry must be taken in that order, and physics is tough stacked alongside a biology and a chemistry class, especially if you have not taken AP Physics in high school.

KEEP ONE EYE ON THE MCAT

Keep an eye on your future. You may need to take the MCAT. The MCAT takes 7 hours and 30 minutes, including 6 hours and 15 minutes of testing and the rest in breaks and test administration. The scaled score has a minimum of 472 and a maximum of 528 comprised of four section scores, each ranging from 118 to 132.

Students are not penalized for wrong answers. For the 2018-2019 application year, the AAMC states that the mean score was 505.6 while the score for those who matriculated at U.S. medical schools, the mean was 511.2.

THE FOUR SUBSECTIONS ARE:

» *Biological and Biochemical Foundations of Living Systems (59 questions)*
» *Chemical and Physical Foundations of Biological Systems (59 questions)*
» *Psychological, Social, and Biological Foundations of Behavior (5 questions)*
» *Critical Analysis and Reasoning Skills (53 questions)*

FOR ONE EXAMPLE, HERE IS 2018-2019 DATA FROM NYU'S SCHOOL OF MEDICINE:

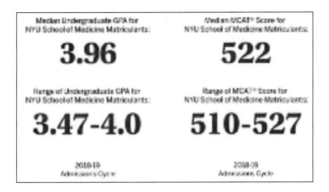

Medical school requirements should matter to you while you are in high school because you want to be mentally and academically prepared for this type of curriculum before you get into college. Since you are likely to have to take three years of college chemistry, AP Chemistry is extremely valuable. Especially at universities where classes are graded on a curve, you are likely to fall behind and have a difficult time reaching the higher end of the curve when most of your classmates already have a year or two of high school chemistry. This is especially true for physics.

COMMUNITY COLLEGE CLASSES

High school students often take community college classes. Sometimes this is to get ahead, and other times it is to complete lower-division social science or humanities requirements before attending college. Either reason is fine, though some colleges state in their admissions profile that students cannot have more than a specific number of college credits before attending a BS/MD program. UMKC comes to mind. Check out any restrictions ahead of time.

Whether or not you earn credit in an AP or college class in biology, chemistry, or physics, you should strongly consider retaking that class as a freshman in college.

Chalk the credits up to experience. Yet, these classes are fundamental to your future and critical components of the MCAT. You want to learn the material well – even better than you learned it the first time. If you are confident about the material, then, earning an A by taking the class over will not hurt you. It is very possible that your future university science classes cover material you did not learn before. Jumping ahead will only put you at a disadvantage with your classmates. There are no awards for bravery and precociousness. Steady your boat and dive into the material again for mastery. Tutor other students in your class if you feel you have learned all of the concepts.

During college, some students consider taking physics at a community college to 'dodge' a more competitive university class, finish course requirements in the summer, or choose a less expensive alternative to university classes. While the difference in material or difficulty of the tests may not always be disparate, many times community college classes, taken in required science classes, are viewed by medical schools as a red flag.

Classes taken at a community college in non-science classes could simply be used as GPA boosters since a student's undergraduate GPA is vitally important. Remember that a low GPA, particularly in a student's most challenging science classes, could thwart your plans for medical school. Be prepared by taking more challenging courses in high school.

Note: When you apply to medical school, the medical school application service, AMCAS, will calculate a separate science GPA, called BCPM (Biology, Chemistry, Physics, and Math), which is very important for admissions. Thus, you want to be extra prepared by taking more challenging courses in high school and entering with knowledge you need so that the classes you take or the competition you face does not overwhelm you. If you can manage this, you could even take two sciences in your last two years to lay a stronger foundation for what you will face ahead.

POST-BACC PROGRAMS

For those premedical students who choose not to pursue the BS/MD and do not complete the required classes during their undergraduate program, or want to bolster their application, there are options like Post-Baccalaureate Medical Programs or post-baccs. In these programs, students complete the required curricular courses after they graduate from college. This allows them to complete or supplement their academic credentials. These programs are sometimes seen as second chance opportunities.

Post-bacc programs create a gap between college and medical school and allow you to bridge your education. Advising and mentoring opportunities can help you better plan and prepare for medical school and alternative healthcare options. Some advisors may become role models as they help you navigate volunteer work, clinical opportunities, and networking. For those who work in a paid or volunteer position, some post-bacc programs offer part-time programs and accelerated options.

Though the post-bacc does extend your education, the intensive boot camp-type classes often include test preparation. If you take one year to complete the missing science prerequisites and study for the MCATs, a second-year would be required to apply. There is no guarantee you would be admitted. On the other hand, some universities have 'linkages' with a medical school so that graduates who satisfy all requirements and are at the top of their class are automatically admitted. Since the percentages of admits are often low, entering the program does not guarantee you will be accepted to medical school.

Review the courses, rules, and class make-up. You may find that some are designed for students from low socioeconomic backgrounds, underrepresented groups, or educationally disadvantaged families. Others only take students who already have high MCAT scores. Some offer master's degrees; some are only

bridge programs. Some accept none of their students into their medical schools and some have relatively high acceptance rates. The University of Alabama at Birmingham did an excellent job creating a list of these programs broken down by type available at *https://www.uab.edu/medicine/home/images/List_of_Post_Baccalaureate_Programs_Around_the_Nation.pdf*

While you might be better served by completing requirements while you are in college, a master's degree program in an affiliated area might be helpful. A two-year stint in graduate school might offer you an MPH (Master of Public Health) or an MS (Master of Science) in a biochem related area, or the study of allied health fields. Other gap or bridge options include conducting research in the interim while gaining medical experiences. These offer alternative career options in case you are not admitted.

DEBT BURDEN

A drawback to these post-bacc programs is that they can be costly. An extra year or two in college could add $20,000 to $140,000 to the cost of your education. Medical school is already expensive. Medical school tuition and living expenses for four years can range from $200,000 to $400,000. The American Association of Medical Colleges (AAMC) website in April 2020 states that the median debt for medical students is $200,000.

Some schools like NYU and Columbia have relieved the debt burden to some or all medical students, which is a major step. Furthermore, since some specialties like surgery and orthopedics require years of additional training, research has shown that this easing of debt encourages students to pursue areas where salaries are often double the average salary of a general practitioner.

Additional options include the Public Service Loan Forgiveness (PSLF) program, which provides debt relief for doctors who choose to pursue public service. This incentivizes physicians to serve in areas where there is the greatest need. Other choices for debt relief include service with the Department of Veterans Affairs, the National Institutes of Health, the Indian Health Service, and the U.S. military.

With the motto, "Learning to Care for Those in Harm's Way," the Uniformed Services University is affiliated with the U.S. military. Located in Bethesda, Maryland, at Walter Reed National Military Medical Center, the Uniformed Services University is not only free, but students are paid $70,000 or more for their medical training in exchange for paid service upon graduation. Since the program is year-round, students gain more than 700 hours of additional training beyond what is offered at traditional medical schools.

Behind every brilliant performance, there were countless hours of practice and preparation.

– Eric Butterworth

CHAPTER EIGHT
TESTING

Due to the coronavirus, the admission years 2020-2021 and 2021-2022, may have some testing flexibility regarding when to take the tests and which tests will be required. Scores may be de-emphasized in the near term, which may allow more candidates to be considered for interviews. BS/MD programs use the tests to demonstrate mastery and provide a bar for students to reach. Additional study may be required for students who have not learned the tested objectives. Khan Academy and practice tests can be beneficial, though there are many private organizations that assist with test preparation. Prepare, prepare, prepare!

HERE IS A USEFUL PLAN:

1. Purchase practice test books.

Official tests are best straight from the testing agency. However, most of the major test publisher's materials are also worth getting. You do not need a book on how to do algebra questions since the test is intended to test what you learned. On the other hand, you do want the explanations at the end of the test to be fully explanatory in case you missed the question and want to know why. An answer of "c" is not good enough.

2. Establish a study schedule that you are willing to keep.

Everyone's life is different. Course requirements vary. Clubs, sports, leadership, service, etc. take time. You know what will work for you.

3. Plan to take 6 – 10 full practice tests.

Your personal program should include taking 6 – 10 full practice tests. Go over each one carefully to see where you made a mistake. Space out your personal test prep schedule so that you complete as many of the ten practice tests as you can. This means that if the test is ten weeks away, plan for one a week. If the test is 20 weeks away, plan for one every two weeks. Starting early makes this process easier. If you are good at math or English, do not skip the practice test in that area since you want to get a very high score and not miss any of those questions.

4. Time yourself.

You only need to take two of your practice tests as full timed tests. The others you can clock one section at a time. Sometimes you only have one hour. If so, take that one hour and do a section and check your answers. Just make sure that by the end of that week or two-week period, you have finished the entire practice test.

5. Highlight and tape flag questions you miss.

After you finish taking each full test or subsections, highlight and put a tape flag where you missed a question. You can color-code these with blue the questions you did not know how to do or you skipped. Green for the ones in which you missed the questions and you have an idea of why it is wrong, but you need to review the concept. Finally, put a yellow where you made a 'careless' error, and you want to remember the rule that you forgot when you took the test. Whatever method you choose, make sure you identify the topics you need to review. Sometimes a pad of paper with the rules you need to remember is fine or a computer file or a sticky-note.

6. Test prep classes can be helpful.

If you do not practice, though, test prep is very time consuming and inefficient. You have very little time if you are actively involved in school. Figure out what makes sense so that you do not sacrifice your classwork. It is not the cost for test prep that is as much of a problem as driving back and forth on a schedule that does not always fit.

Additionally, with test prep classes, you often listen to lectures on the material you already know. In other cases, the test prep company has someone time you while you take a test. You can really do that at home with a stopwatch or timer. However, if you choose to study on your own, you may find that after every test you take, you may want to hire a private tutor for an hour or two to go over the questions you missed.

Delaying the test-taking until the fall of your senior year is unwise unless absolutely necessary. Yet, you should not take a test in which you are unprepared or not in the test-taking mindset. The best time to take a subject test is along with the final exams of that subject. Thus, if you are a sophomore and you took AP Biology, the May or June date of your sophomore year is the best time to take that subject test. The end of your junior year is likely to be challenging with multiple AP tests, SAT, ACT, and subject tests. Pace yourself. You need to take the tests, but this is not a good time to cram for the exam. Try to spread apart your preparation and test-taking.

SAT I, ACT, AND SUBJECT TESTS

Almost all schools profiled in this book require either SAT or ACT testing. Some, like Northwestern, Brown, and George Washington, require subject tests. Typically, when subject tests are required, the colleges request Math II and a science, though check whether they prefer chemistry. Note that subject test scores above 700 are nearly a requirement on each of these tests.

Higher than average test scores are required since these programs are designed for

the best and brightest students. Some programs have lower requirements for entry, particularly those whose focus is on attracting students who want to work in rural areas or with disadvantaged communities. However, for the most competitive programs, students who matriculate have SAT ERW+M scores higher than 1400, though 1500 or higher is standard for those who are competitive in the admissions process. An ACT of 34 or higher is expected.

Minimum scores are often given so that students do not spend considerable time working on an application in which they have virtually no chance of being accepted. There must be some cut off for applicants to evaluate the best candidates who have applied.

For example, Brown's 2019 entering class had 2,641 applicants, 94 offers of admission, 20 ED candidates, 74 accepted RD. Of those, 61 matriculated to Brown (20 ED + 41 RD with 22 males, 3 females). Their average SAT ERW was 742 and SAT M was 770. The average ACT composite was 34.

While super-scored tests are common in admissions processes that consider standardized testing, it is less common for BS/MD programs. Since super-scoring is not done in medical school admissions for the MCAT, in general, medical schools would prefer to see a test score in one sitting.

AP TESTS

AP test scores are rarely used except to determine mastery and only sent to colleges after the admissions process. They are often put on the application along with the AP tests you are planning to take. Most students applying to BS/MD programs have taken six AP or IB tests by the end of their junior year and have four planned for their senior year. Of the six, one is typically a science, and the other is either AP Calculus AB or AP Calculus BC. On the other hand, official scores are not requested before submitting the application.

STUDENTS JUST SELF-REPORT WHAT THEY EARN AND POSSIBLY STATE WHETHER THEY ARE:

AP Scholar (3 AP scores with three or higher)

AP Scholar with Honors (4 AP scores with three or higher & an average score of 3.25)

AP Scholar with Distinction (5 or more AP Scores with three or higher & an average score of 3.5)

State AP Scholar (one male, one female student in each state with the highest number of tests with a 3 or higher and highest average score of all students for that year)

National AP Scholar (8 or more AP scores of 4 or higher & an average score of 4 in all AP exams)

DoDEA AP Scholar (one male, one female student attending a Dept of Defense Education Activity school with a 3 or higher on all exams and the highest average score on the highest number of exams)

International AP Scholar (one male, one female student attending a school outside of the U.S. or Canada with a 3 or higher on all exams and the highest average score on the highest number of exams)

Seminar and Research Certificate (3 or higher in both AP Research & AP Seminar)

Capstone Diploma (earn a 3 or higher in AP Research, AP Seminar, & 4 additional AP exams)

Success is not the key to happiness. Happiness is the key to success. If you love what you are doing, you will be successful.

—Albert Schweitzer

CHAPTER NINE
HIGH SCHOOL AND COMMUNITY ACTIVITIES

C olleges look at much more than just grades and test scores. A holistic review is particularly true to BS/MD programs. In part, this stems from the small group of students chosen to work together collaboratively and foster relationships throughout the program. Yet, another major factor is that students in these programs are the elite class of top students at the university and are looked to as leaders. Their habits are likely to be emulated by other pre-med hopefuls. Thus, school involvement and leadership are considered highly in the application process.

If you cannot join a club or a club is defunct, take responsibility for its resurgence or start a new one. Many students will say that they quit a club because nobody is doing anything. That is a red flag. When people are no longer participating, and there are no activities planned, it takes leadership to get the club up and running again. If you were working on a team project and your elected group leader got sick, would you quit? If the leader of your group project did not respond to e-mails, would you decide not to finish the assignment and fail to deliver your class presentation? If your club is inactive, breathe life into the group. Find a list of members, invite new members, and revive the heart of these activities.

Getting involved in student body leadership on a school-wide scale is valuable too, since running for an elected office as a representative is likely to identify those who may pursue student body leadership in college as well. Furthermore, the role of a doctor in a clinic or hospital is, in many ways, a leadership position. Thus, whether you are the leader of a club, sport, student group, or team, you are demonstrating the skills needed to progress as a leader in the healthcare industry.

Community service is essential to understanding the world around you. There are dozens of places to serve with a host of public and private organizations. Tutoring kids at a local elementary or junior high school, volunteering at the YMCA, coaching a kids camp, helping build homes in Mexico, or spending a week at Vacation Bible School are just a few of the many volunteer opportunities with children. You can work with the elderly at a nursing/retirement home or at a soup kitchen or homeless shelter. Some in admissions consider the absence of community service a deal-breaker.

RESUME OR CURRICULUM VITAE (CV)

You will want to create a one-page resume that summarizes your academics (school, GPA, test scores), awards, research, publications, activities, service, employment and leadership. Two pages are possibly okay. Remember though, people rarely read the second page. Organizing the information clearly on one page has a higher probability of being read. Consider it this way; if someone hands you a resume, you will only see the first page. If you decide to flip through the pages, that is all you will do is flip through them. *LinkedIn.com* states that the average time a person looks at a resume is six seconds. How much can you read in six seconds? The goal is to make it visually easy to read.

People hand me resumes that have four or five pages thinking that I will be impressed. I put the resume down, look at the top page, and then ask them questions. It is just too hard when there is little time to read through more than one page. If you handed a reviewer a four-page personal statement, they are unlikely to read that either. This is why personal statements are typically one page – two if double-spaced. There are no bonus points for long resumes or essays. Furthermore, admissions representatives may not think you will be able to get to the point or succinctly convey your message to them or your patients.

Professional resumes are unadorned without distracting features. Organize the information neatly so that sections or types of information are together. Start making a 'working resume' as soon as you read this and then continue to add to the sections every time you add a new activity.

The best way to find yourself is to lose yourself in the service of others.

— *Mahatma Gandhi*

CHAPTER TEN
SCIENCE AND HEALTHCARE EXPERIENCE

RESEARCH

Experience with scientific research allows you to better understand not only the scientific method but the process scientists undergo to understand the complexity of the human mind, body, and behaviors. Whether you are involved in stem-cell research, neuroscience development, virus testing, or demographic study of disease spread, you have embarked on uncovering problems yet to be resolved. Knowing how this process works in university or private laboratories provides you with a deeper understanding of the field of medicine.

Some universities place a high priority on students who have experience in research and pursued labs where they were selected to be a part of a study or even developed their own research projects like the Siemen's competition which has a top prize of $100,000 and $50,000, and finalists receiving $25,000. This scholarship is only for high school students. Another science competition for high school students that gives out $3.1 million dollars each year with a first-place prize of $250,000 is the Regeneron Science Talent Search. Although the March 2020 award event was not held due to the coronavirus pandemic, those who submit applications by November 2020 will receive a t-shirt, laptop sticker, and one-year subscription to Science News magazine just for entering. There are other competitions as well, though, to be sure, research in your local university lab or corporate research center is also valuable.

SUMMER RESEARCH PROGRAMS (THIS IS A SUBSET OF SOME EXCELLENT OPTIONS):

RIBS - University of Chicago's Research in the Biological Sciences

COSMOS - The University of California's California State Summer School for Mathematics & Science

MIT'S RESEARCH AND APPLIED SCIENCE PROGRAMS:

MITES – Minority Introduction to Engineering and Science - 6-week intensive (free – 80 students)

RSI – Research Science Institute - 6-week theory, research, applied science (free – 70 students)

WTP – Women's Technology Program – 4-week hands-on engineering labs/ projects (60 students)

SSP – Summer Science Program – 6-week program

SIMR – Stanford Institutes of Medicine Summer Research Program – 8-week intensive for rising junior or senior

RISE – Boston University's Research in Science & Engineering – 6-week practicum or internship track

SAMS – Carnegie Mellon's Summer Academy for Math & Science – 6-week residential program

MMSS – Michigan Math and Science Scholars (MMSS) – 2-week research program

RABS – Cornell University's Research Apprenticeship in Biological Sciences – 6-week medical/research program

UCLA – Applications of Nanoscience Summer Institute – 2-week residential research program

HSHSP – Michigan State University's High School Honors Science/Engineering/ Mathematics Program – 7-week intensive summer research program (MI residency not required)

Clark Scholars Program – Texas Tech's 7-week research program comes with a stipend

SPARK - Cedars Sinai's CIRM (California Institute of Regenerative Medicine) Summer Program to Accelerate Regenerative Medicine Knowledge (SPARK) Program – Summer Stem Cell Research Internship – 7-week mentorship program for high school juniors starts in June (8 students chosen)

Research-oriented universities are looking for talented students who will bring their curiosity and research skills to their projects. This is not a requirement, though some creativity may land you a clinical or academic research opportunity. If you do pursue a research project, be able to explain why you got involved, the lab procedures, what the study aims to discover, and what you learned from the experience.

CLINICAL

Volunteer healthcare service demonstrates five qualities: (1) Empathy, (2) Care, (3) Awareness, (4) Commitment, (5) Passion. It takes more than intellect and knowledge to be an excellent physician. It takes a large dose of humanity. Selflessness is an essential ingredient as well. During the coronavirus pandemic, physicians went to work compassionately treating patients, even though their lives were in jeopardy.

Many doctors died just to save their patients. Service is a mindset. Altruism is highly valued.

Thus, clinical experiences are essential to the learning experience. BS/MD admissions decision-makers want to know if you are serious about medicine. Remember, accepting you is their promise to support you through this process on some level.

This is both a commitment and an investment. They could choose someone else. Admissions decision-makers also want to know that you are dedicated to helping people and passionate about serving your community.

Experiences working in a hospital, clinic, or some other type of healthcare facility offers the chance to know whether you enjoy helping the weak, challenged, ill, or dying. More extensive, sustained experiences show a consistent commitment. The primary underlying reason is for you to learn more about healthcare and whether or not you are a good fit for this field, its demands, and the importance of empathy and compassion for those whose health and possibly life is in question. Many students who apply have 50 – 100 hours of clinical experience.

Volunteering in a hospital or clinic helps you learn more about the field and determine your commitment. You will develop a reasonable expectation of what you might experience in the medical field. BS/MD admissions officers want to select students who fully demonstrate their determination to pursue medicine through service and describe this commitment in an interview.

SHADOWING

Shadowing a doctor or two is central to your experience in the medical field. The physician you shadow could be with your doctor, family friend, or parents if they are medical professionals. You want medical experiences not just to demonstrate to BS/MD programs your commitment, but to get a sense of the practice of medicine. You should witness the day-to-day physician-patient experience and immerse yourself in the whole of the healthcare process. Ask the doctors questions. You are likely to be asked in your interviews to tell about a situation that left an impression upon you.

The specialty does not matter. You might start with a doctor who you know well and then, either ask that doctor or a family friend if they know of another person you might shadow. Diverse experiences are helpful as well since a sample of one rarely provides a wide-ranging perspective.

Shadowing a doctor is not a ticket to gain admissions into a program, but it is an excellent way to know whether you want to pursue the long haul to and through medical school. While you may choose to shadow a doctor in a specific area of your interest, you might want to shadow a second doctor in another area to gain a broader understanding of the field. First, the life of a general practitioner can be very different from the day-to-day experience of a pathologist or surgeon. Second, while the idea of medical discovery is fascinating, there is a great deal more to helping patients. Seek practical insights into a physician's concerns, commitment, responsibility, and ethical practices.

You will interview at some point. During that interview, you can point to the understanding you gained from your shadowing experiences. Ask yourself these questions.

1. What experiences left an impression on you?

2. What did you learn from the doctors you shadowed?

3. What challenges and opportunities do you believe physicians face?

4. What specific formative experiences led you to be sure medicine is your future?

> *If your actions inspire others to dream more, learn more, do more, and become more, you are a leader.*

— John Quincy Adams

CHAPTER ELEVEN
DESIRED QUALITIES

B S/MD programs are more than training grounds for our best and brightest science-minded college students and future physicians. These intellectual arenas with their dedicated staff cultivate the character, ethics, and expertise in young people who persevere through demanding schedules while helping others who are struggling. As opposed to pre-med programs that can sometimes be a hotbed of competition, the goal of BS/MD programs is to encourage students to be considerate and supportive by taking away the rankings and zero-sum, winner-loser effect.

The goal is to create humanitarians who care for the sick and work collegially with fellow doctors to investigate and diagnose diseases that are potentially life-threatening. Talent is developed through academics and research, but colleges also want to complement their love for learning with a hunger to serve that is bigger than themselves. The needs are significant in rural areas and with those who are underprivileged. This is why some students choose to go on medical

missions, volunteer with Doctors without Borders, or participate in school-sponsored service trips to Latin America, South America, and Africa.

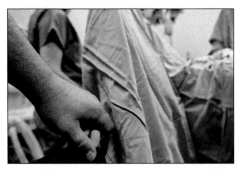

Healthcare is about compassion, integrity, and responsibility. Medical doctors need to be thoughtful and proactive, always thinking ahead to what patients might need or want. Sometimes they must be take-charge, leadership-minded advocates, and authorities. Admissions professionals have a strong desire to identify those personalities through the essay and interview process who have a sense of maturity and emotional intelligence.

This is why many medical schools require that students take the CASPer (Computer-Based Assessment for Sampling Personal Characteristics), which is a type of psychological test, called a situational judgement test, that determines a student's behavioral tendencies in realistic, hypothetical scenarios.

Along this challenging academic highway, students must be self-aware, secure, and respectful. Pre-medical students often need to advocate for themselves, ask for help when they are stuck or behind, and progress through the rigor of their coursework. Knowing yourself and what you need is essential throughout the journey to medical school and in medical practice. Similarly, support for patients means empowering them to make crucial decisions about their healthcare choices. The first of the many desired qualities of a physician is to know yourself and, as such, manage your personal emotions, health, and needs.

A FINAL NOTE ON PREPARATION

UMKC's BS/MD section had a note posted that read, "Despite COVID-19 restrictions that may impact standardized testing and obtaining healthcare experiences, all current admissions deadlines and requirements currently stand as indicated below. The Office of Admissions will continue to monitor the situation, should changes need to be made to our process. Please contact us if you run into difficulties meeting admissions

requirements or with additional questions you may have." This is unsurprising but underscores the importance of the due diligence required in reviewing the websites and their requirements as well as getting on their mailing list.

The programs and their policies are in an upheaval as with many aspects of higher education at this moment. Premedical programs, including BS/MD, BS/DO and other accelerated programs may change and have alternative dates and requirements

Some programs may be discontinued. These decisions continue to unfurl. The coronavirus pandemic's ramifications to higher education are likely to ripple through the academy, leaving a wake. From the precocious student who was accelerated at an early age, to the student who cannot afford not to work, to the adult returning to college envisioning a different career path, to the international student who cannot get a visa, every current and potential student will emerge with a different perspective.

With these various considerations, administrators must re-envision higher education at their campus without the same type of coordination seen before. There are likely to be disparities, discord, and calendar alterations that cannot be predicted at the time of writing this book. Furthermore, considerations regarding the length, breadth, and impact of COVID-19 will institute new transformations.

Some schools may not be listed here that should have had a place in this text. The consideration of whether to include any BS/DO programs and which ones to include meant that some were left out. Links may be broken. Please let me know of any changes or additions at *collegeguide@yahoo.com*.

PART THREE

THE
APPLICATION
PROCESS

The natural healing force within each of us is the greatest force in getting well.

— *Hippocrates*

CHAPTER TWELVE
ALLOPATHIC VS. OSTEOPATHIC MEDICINE

BS/MD OR BS/DO – WHAT IS THE DIFFERENCE BETWEEN ALLOPATHIC AND OSTEOPATHIC MEDICINE?

People often ask me about the differences between allopathic, MD, programs and careers and osteopathic, DO, programs and careers. Allopathic schools are those we typically call medical schools, though both train physicians. Their educational pathways and focuses are slightly different. Osteopathic programs also produce trained doctors who practice medicine, often in the same hospitals and clinics as their MD counterparts. So, if they are both considered doctors, and they both treat patients, and they both prescribe medicine, and they both work together, then what is the difference?

Osteopathic medical schools are more touch-oriented, practicing Osteopathic Manipulative Medicine (OMM). One component of their total approach to diagnosis, treatment, and preventive therapy for illnesses or injuries includes Osteopathic Manipulative Treatment (OMT). Some health problems, osteopathic physicians contend, like musculoskeletal conditions, require more than pharmaceutical treatments or surgical options. Surgery is not necessary for many conditions. They are well-served by applying gentle pressure along with using stretching techniques and resistance. This hands-on approach is a whole-body approach. Allopathic medical schools rely more on diagnostic procedures, like lab results and x-rays, to review and evaluate the body and diagnose patients.

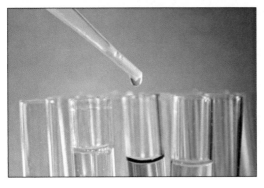

Both types of medical education, Doctor of Medicine (MD) and Doctor of Osteopathic Medicine (DO) are rigorous 4-year programs. Both are competitive to enter, though GPA and test scores are slightly lower for DO schools. Students who are applying to medical school should consider DO programs. Physicians who graduate from a DO school can practice medicine like an MD. However, some consider the more hands-on treatment inappropriate, and there are students who refuse to even consider the DO pathway. That is a personal choice, often backed up by mentors they had who believe there is a stigma associated with DO practitioners.

Some hospitals and clinics do have a preference for MD over DO or DO over MD, depending upon how they view medical practice. The intellectual difference is found in the statement some say, "If the body can heal itself, as DOs contend, then there must be more natural solutions or alternative approaches to healing than medications and surgery." Again, this is a preference, and both types of doctors are trained to understand the body thoroughly.

In the 'whole person approach', DOs are more focused on a body's interconnectedness. Environmental, personal, nutritional, and other factors interplay in the development of pain and disease. On the website of Western University's College of Osteopathic Medicine of the Pacific there is an explanation.

"Doctors of Osteopathic Medicine (DO) see patients, prescribe medications, perform surgeries and deliver babies in hospitals, medical centers, and offices across the United States and overseas. Whether they are primary care providers or specialists, DOs use all the standard tools of modern medicine, but also have additional therapeutic modalities with which to care for their patients."

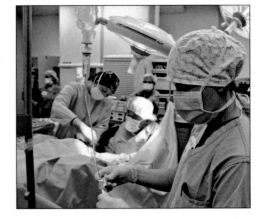

Medical doctors often perceive the practice of medicine through scientific lenses. Doctors of osteopathic medicine see themselves as viewing the bigger picture, while also resolving conditions through a more holistic approach. Both MDs and DOs consider themselves excellent practitioners, even though they look through the prism of human science differently.

The science foundation of MD and DO programs are similar. While data show that more DOs choose primary care than MDs, some do pursue specialties. The drawback is that DOs often pursue specialties where there are more DOs simply for the ability to share a common experience and expertise while working with those who have the same type of training.

Applicants for MD schools apply through AMCAS while applicants to DO programs apply through AACOMAS. Both complete residencies after medical school. For more information, look at the American Association of Medical Colleges (AAMC) and American Osteopathic Association (AOA) websites.

Wherever the art of medicine is loved, there is also a love of humanity.

— *Hippocrates*

CHAPTER THIRTEEN
APPLICATIONS – WHERE TO APPLY?

N o doubt, with so many students wanting to attend medical school, applying to BS/MD admissions is competitive. Acceptance rates are often less than ten percent. Some only accept one or two out of a hundred. There are BS/DO programs as well with slightly higher acceptance rates. Both types of programs require a high GPA, challenging curriculum, and high test scores. However, I always say you should not look back and wonder, "What if...?" The reality is that you are here now.

Some interviewers ask the question, where do you plan to be one year from now? Five years? Twenty years? Fifty years? Often people do not ponder their future more than creating a bucket list or wish list. Many students don't stop long enough to fully think through and figure out their intentional goals. They live in some dream state – a place where they say, "It would be nice if..." However, they do not go much further, because to go further demands work, persistence, and sacrifice. It is much easier to consider the effort too stressful. Next time you ask yourself where you will be a year from now, consider taking a half hour to write down your goals, commitments, and steps you will take to get there. You owe it to yourself to move from a dream state to reality.

If becoming a physician is where you are headed and what you truly want, the worst case scenario is that you are rejected by a BS/MD or BS/DO program and you follow the four-year pre-med path and knock on the door to medical school with more information, knowledge, and experience.

If you are committed to healthcare, apply, so that you have no regrets. Sure, there is competition, but there is more competition on a higher level when you apply to medical school and only the cream of the crop submits applications with high MCAT scores. If you are accepted, then the BS/MD is one of your college choices. You can turn down the BS/MD program option if you change your mind months down the road.

BS/MD programs often have minimum GPA and standardized score requirements. Students must meet these minimum GPA and test score standards. Also, since there are so many applicants, review committees can and do set lower bounds on different variables in the process like – students with a C on their transcript will not be considered, no students without AP or IB courses will be considered (unless they are not offered at the school), students from out-of-state or out of the country will not be considered, or SAT/ACT test scores must be higher than 1450 ERW+M or ACT of 31 during that cycle.

While class rank has been eliminated at many schools, when a percentile or decile rank is provided by a high school, few students are accepted that are below the 90th percentile or below the top 10% of their high school class. Acceptance is even tough for students in the top 1% of their high school class.

> *Join the mailing list for these programs early so that you can receive more information and receive regular updates. You may want to make a separate e-mail address from your personal address so that you can easily find the information you need.*

FUNNELING DOWN CHOICES

Begin by narrowing down the list of BS/MD, BS/DO programs to 10 schools you will investigate more thoroughly.

1. Eliminate colleges that require in-state residency.
2. Eliminate the schools where your GPA and scores, including subject tests if required, are below their minimum.
3. Check to see if you have met their course requirements.
4. If you are only considering BS/MD programs, eliminate the BS/DO schools from your list.

5. Decide whether you are willing to consider schools where the application process is during your freshman or sophomore year or you are only looking for those programs that accept you as an incoming freshman. Remember that Early Assurance Programs (EAP) are not the same as BS/MD programs.

6. Decide whether you want a program that guarantees admission if grades and requirements are met or if you must take the MCAT, complete the AMCAS, and go through the entire medical school admissions process during your program. After all, one of the primary advantages of these programs is that you apply and commit out of high school and do not need to repeat the entire test preparation and application process again in four years.

When you are done, you should find about five schools. The BS/MD application process is longer than traditional applications, so you may not want to select more than five schools. You will need to apply to pre-medical programs as well and the probability of entering these programs is generally lower than the most competitive colleges in the country. Another criterion some people use is to check the number of people accepted or the number of people accepted from out-of-state. Actually, you may find that if there are only five people accepted from out-of-state, few out-of-state students will apply, so your chances may improve.

Some students want to pursue a gap year, Fulbright, Peace Corps, or other volunteer opportunities. Others want to earn an MPH or hone their skills after their undergraduate program. If you do, you want to select a program that offers you some flexibility. Since every program has different expectations, you might want to make a list of the questions you want to ask when you visit or at your interview so that you know your responsibilities and opportunities.

If possible, visit the BS/MD programs ahead of time and tour their laboratories, lecture halls, pre-health facilities, and local hospitals where you might volunteer. BS/MD programs allow you to develop relationships with the medical school, doctors, and facilities before you begin. This is an advantage. Ask questions when you visit. This is your future. You want to make the best decision possible, particularly if you are going to spend four to eight years at the school. In the end, you are looking for a school where you fit and offers the experiences you seek.

Don't be afraid…
Science is light…
and it is through
science that we
will find a way
out of this.

— Luiz Henrique Mandetta
Brazil's former Health Minister

CHAPTER FOURTEEN
ADMISSIONS AND RECOMMENDATIONS

You will need to complete a preliminary application like the Common Application, , ApplyTexas, or Institutional Application (on the school's website). You will probably need to complete a supplemental application that is either part of one of the applications or a separate application on the BS/MD program's website. These applications may include additional items like essays, short answers, explanations, resume, activity list, unofficial transcript, recommendation requests, photograph, and short questions specific to the college. Read these thoroughly because they have specified processes and formatting.

TIMING MATTERS

Program administrators monitor the numbers of applications as they flow into the system and are being cataloged and inputted into their process. Some schools consider students on a rolling basis, while others have stages of consideration for binding ED, non-binding EA, and regular decision RD applicants. The earlier you apply, the better off you are in most cases, despite your possible desire to wait so you will have better essays, tests, or a stronger application.

This does not mean that you need to apply ED. First, you can only apply to one ED school, so that decision must be made based upon your absolute commitment to attending. Second, finances need to be considered when choosing an ED school since you are making a commitment to pay for the program without knowing what financial aid you will receive. ED may make sense to you and your family, though it may not. Explore this further.

(EA), though, when offered has many benefits since you finish your application early, the school knows you are interested, and you can complete one stage of the admissions process. Remember that in BS/MD programs, there are often three stages: (1) the preliminary application, (2) a supplemental application, and (3) interviews. Applying late may take you out of consideration or minimize your otherwise excellent chances.

APPLICATION PROCESS

In addition to applying to the university's undergraduate program, most BS/MD programs have additional steps you must complete. Typically, you will apply early to the university, gain admission, complete secondary applications before or after admission, and ensure that there are no additional forms required. If you are applying for financial aid and scholarships, those forms and requirements must also be completed in the fall of your senior year.

Most schools have an interview process on their campus, though a few schools will interview online. In part, they want to meet you in person and show you the school while also introducing you to other people with whom you will interact. You will often have a second interview with medical school admissions' representatives where you will tour their facilities on the same visit. These activities take time. You need to be able to manage your schedule along with your academic, extracurricular, and family responsibilities.

RECOMMENDATIONS

If you have not gotten to know your counselor, this is a good time. Your counselor will need to write one of your letters of recommendation, even if you have never met him or her. Either way, you will need to help them get to know you. Frequently, this is facilitated by a counselor packet that requires you to complete a set of questions and fill in general information about you and your interests so they have a better idea of how they can help you the most and provide a better letter of recommendation on your behalf.

Note: If you are required to submit a counselor recommendation packet, take this seriously. I realize that there are too many essays asked and the requirement seems unreasonable to put tons of effort into, but it is essential so you can get the best recommendation possible. Many counselors have 400 to 700 recommendations. To make each one interesting and unique is difficult. Rushing through this defeats the purpose of you attempting to get the best reference possible. If or when this is requested, get on it. Your counselor's thorough and informed recommendation depends upon it.

This is also a good time to think about what teachers may be the best recommenders for you. Typically, schools are looking for a math, science, or humanities teacher. Some require three teachers – math or science, English, and language or social science. This is a wide spread of subjects, so you want to be the best version of yourself in each of your classes, demonstrate your excellent study habits, test preparation skills, interest in the material, teamwork, and support for your classmates. Sometimes schools require teacher recommendation forms to be completed ahead of time as well. Finally, ask early. Some teachers have a limit on the number of recommendations they are willing to write. If you ask too late, you may not make their list.

*Have the courage
to follow your heart
and intuition. They
somehow know
what you truly
want to become.*

— Steve Jobs

CHAPTER FIFTEEN

ESSAYS

Probably the most important factor that you can control in the admissions process is your personal statement and additional essays on the supplements. When an essay is compelling, reviewers can give the applicant a second look, even when they may have been put on the "probably not" pile. Passion, empathy, humility, and resilience can resonate with admissions officers.

First rule of thumb is to be authentic. Tell your story. Since everyone's story is different, look back at pivotal moments in your life. Tell those short stories that impacted your decision to pursue medicine. Capture the reader's attention with the clarity and detail that brings them into your life and reveals the humanity and compassion you have for people. Who were the people who inspired you along the way?

Be respectful, vulnerable, and thoughtful. What experiences show your best qualities, core values, and character? Connect anecdotes seamlessly so that the flow is easy for the reader to follow. Do not be afraid to share a moment where you questioned your decisions, wondered if you were headed along the right path, or worried about how you might approach a patient with news about cancer or the possibility of death.

The most difficult essays to read are the ones that are blatantly boastful. Most students do not do this intentionally and do not realize how arrogant they may sound. Their goal was to tell how proud they were of their successes and tell those in admissions that they were a winner. However, what comes across is not what they may have intended.

Difficult decisions, tough choices, challenges, and hopelessness are part of life and show that you realize that medicine does not always have a positive outcome and you may not always turn out to be the hero of the story. What sacrifices did you make? What did you prioritize? What is important to you? Reveal your true self and your commitment to medicine.

Those tidbits of advice seem wise and encouraging. However, when you are ready to incorporate them into your essay, you sit back and ask, how can I turn the story of my life into an eloquent personal statement? How will my story be seen as one that is as good as someone else's story?

Here is my advice. Write down five pivotal moments in your life. What did you learn from each? Write down five moments where you had any experience with medicine. These could be personal experiences or those with family members or through your volunteer service. Again, what stuck out as being meaningful to you? Finally, since this is a personal statement, name five attributes that you believe define you. Why are these important to you and your pursuit of medicine? This exercise will help you hone your story into episodes so you can select from those that resonate the most with you and show the body of your character.

Rarely will you only submit one essay. Most often you will have a personal statement on the Common Application or the Coalition Application and a Why Medicine essay (or two or three) on a supplement. For some schools you will have short answer questions which are 50 to 350 words. You do not want to say the same thing in each essay. Think about how you can describe a broader vision of who you are by separating your experiences on your life's canvas. Maybe your personal statement will be on your identity, heritage, challenges, or lessons from your upbringing. Your 'Why Medicine" essay will cover swatches of science, research, medical work, nursing homes, and shadowing. Most importantly, you want the committee to understand how you came to want to be a physician and a glimpse into your future in medicine.

You can do this. You just have to take some time and think through the five moments, five medical experiences, and five attributes. If you are worried about how your writing will sound, record your voice telling short versions of your stories and then transcribe them. Some students come to me and say they cannot make their essay profound, or their life was "vanilla," or they do not have a tear-jerking phenomenon, or they are worried that the stories will not fit. Yet, they do not worry when they tell their friend or family member stories that they find intriguing or experiences they had that were profound. Try telling your story to someone else. People are often better at telling their stories verbally because they do not worry so much about the grammar. You can edit your personal statement later.

When you write your essay, do not fill it with stories, that is not the point. The question is to describe how your life purpose came to be and how it revealed qualities in your character that showed up as a result. Cherry-pick one that threads through your life. Who you are is perfect. Each piece fits like a jigsaw puzzle piece. There was a reason you made certain decisions, and you are here today applying to pursue medicine. Nobody has your story. Show the committee who you are.

"

*Nothing we do is
more important
than hiring and
developing people.
At the end of the day,
you bet on people,
not on strategies.*

Former COO of General Electric

CHAPTER SIXTEEN
INTERVIEWS

I f you have gotten to the point where you are offered an interview, you are halfway there. Plus, you must have done something right! Getting to the interview is a leap forward. You only have one hurdle left. The committee has already reviewed your application, essays, and resume. From all they can tell so far, you seem to be a good fit. Now, they must determine whether you are.

This upcoming interview is the defining juncture. If your personality, presence, and professionalism are in line with their vision of their ideal candidate, you will be offered a spot. There are a few steps along the way. You need to

1. Respond
2. Plan
3. Prepare
4. Interview

First, acknowledge whether you will accept the interview quickly and respectfully. For certain reasons, you may not want to follow through with the interview process. If the interview comes late enough in the process, you may decide that you no longer have that school prioritized. You may have changed your mind and decided to pursue the pre-medical route, or you may have applied and been accepted to a binding Early Decision school. On the other hand, you may have been offered other interviews that conflict and do not have the time or money to fly to each of the schools.

Second, you need to schedule the day and time of your appointment. Most BS/MD programs interview on set days and times. Thus, you may not have many choices. Managing your schedule may mean that you must rearrange your commitments. Traveling to schools that are out of state or a significant distance will require that you make reservations and plan transportation and lodging. In some cases, the university will fly you out on a specific day from a specific airport like the University of Nevada, Reno. Be on time or early! Being late can be a deal breaker.

Now that you have taken a deep breath, the door is open for you to prepare to present yourself. The BS/MD program only has a few spots. However, since you have researched the program, you have considered how you would fit into the university's culture and have a decent sense of how you could contribute to the specific program. You presented an articulate description of your academic and personal background. As you prepare, reread what you wrote in your essays.

Remember that you have made it to the next to the last cut. Interviewing gives the university a chance to get to know you a bit better. They need to determine if the picture and stories you presented in your application match the person they meet and if the person they meet will be the best for the program. They will determine this during the interview process.

Before you thoroughly practice the interview questions, take some time to think through three basic questions that you should have no problem answering.

1. Tell me something about yourself.

2. What activity is most important to you and why?

3. What experiences led you to the field of medicine and why are you committed to attending medical school?

These fundamental questions are designed to put you at ease. You might find the first question deceptively difficult. Try to describe yourself and your life in four to five sentences. After all, there is so much to say. Where do you start? Family? Community? Background? Education? Health? Siblings? Successes? You need to ask yourself how you want to be defined. Prepare.

The university already knows quite a bit about you from what you have submitted. Here is a chance to clarify, expand, and present. Sadly, some applicants lie or tell half-truths on their applications. This is wrong morally and ethically and can have serious consequences, including expulsion. Students accused of falsifying their application or resume can be disciplined by being put on probation or expelled. Since ethics is such a high priority in medicine, if it is determined that you did not tell the truth, there are unlikely to be second chances.

Asking about the most important activity gives the interviewer an opportunity to learn about your passions with your own voice, expressions, and personality. What excites you about your chosen activities, and what fostered this commitment? Was it the people with whom you interacted, the activity itself, or maybe a link between that activity and a personal experience in your life?

The people you meet can be inspired by your effort, commitment, and love. You might truly enjoy being around eldery people or kids. The activity itself could be a love of reading books to kids in a library, coaching little league, or playing bingo with your favorite friendly seniors. Maybe you want to mentor or tutor kids because you remember struggling when you were just starting. Or possibly the people in the old folks' home remind you of your favorite grandmother or grandfather who passed away too soon.

Additional questions are designed to determine your level of commitment, persistence, and desire to pursue medicine. While the questions undoubtedly vary from interviewer to interviewer or program to program, they are likely to focus on the school's mission, vision, and values. Questions are often developed by a committee so that they are the same from individual to individual, though interviews are likely to be conducted by a single person. Don't be surprised if you have more than one interview.

In some cases, you are invited to come to the campus for a tour, meetings, and interviews. Dress appropriately. Typically, men wear suits and women wear professional-looking suits or dresses. If you do not have a suit, there are often decent suits available at Goodwill, Salvation Army, American Cancer Society, Ticktocker, and Assistance League. Your goal is to portray the image of professionalism they desire of their graduates. What will you look like when you represent the university in their programs? While you should not feel uncomfortable when you tour the school or meet with representatives, you want to be confident in becoming a medical professional.

Some accoutrements to your clothing and attire that present your individuality like multiple piercings, spiked hair, and very long eyelashes or nails may not be enthusiastically embraced by the committee. If possible, choose conservative colors. Political pins, national flags, or organizational symbols are looked at differently by those who come from different faith, ethnic, gender, or political positions. While colleges embrace diversity, faculty and admissions officers are human and have biases.

One school administrator admonished a student for her tattoos. Another said, "We have enough white men." Still, another said in front of a group of students, "We need to make sure we choose enough African Americans," while a fourth said, "Students will need to leave their exotic behaviors at the door." Know that these people were well-intentioned, but they approached the world from their own unique perspective. You are not interviewing to show off your individuality but to be part of a cohort of scholars who will humbly, empathetically, and graciously care for others. No flair is needed.

RESUME?

Some students ask me if they should bring a copy of their resume. Sure. People who go to interviews typically have a one-page resume, two at the max. They will not have time to skim more than a page - if they even want your resume at all. If you bring a resume, do not rely on the resume or read from it. Interviewers may not look at the resume, although they are likely to ask you what is on your resume since they have a file of your activities. Be prepared to address anything on your resume.

Should you hand them a resume at the start? Since it is more respectful to let the interviewer lead, you can say at the outset if you like, "I have brought a resume if you would like to see it." If they do, they will say yes. If not, then keep it in your folder or padfolio. During the time you are at the university, there may be a person with whom you might want to share your resume.

PREPARATION

Be prepared. If you have not practiced for the interview, you may not have considered some of the questions they may ask. You will not be able to anticipate every question, but you should be prepared for the commonly asked questions. If you are unable to answer their questions, you may be tossing aside your golden opportunity. Know why you are committed to a career in medicine. Know why you like science. Know about your activities, commitments, research, hobbies, favorite books, classes, grades, people who inspired you, and your reasons you want to attend that school.

While your interview may not be as rigorous as it might be for medical school, the interviewer could challenge your thinking or ask you pop questions.

HERE ARE TWENTY QUESTIONS TO PREPARE AHEAD OF TIME:

1. Tell us something about yourself.
2. What activity is most important to you and why?
3. Why are you interested in pursuing medicine?
4. Is there someone who inspired you?
5. What is your favorite hobby and why?
6. What experiences have you had with medicine?
7. What would you do to improve healthcare in the US?
8. What recent books have left an impression on you and what was your takeaway?
9. What has been your greatest challenge?
10. What opportunity did you jump at taking?
11. How did the coronavirus epidemic impact your life?
12. Describe an ethical challenge you faced and how did you handle the situation?
13. Who is your role model?
14. What is your greatest strength? Weakness?
15. What was your most interesting volunteer experience?
16. When did you realize you wanted to be a doctor?
17. When have you exhibited leadership?
18. Describe a time when you embraced teamwork?
19. What do you enjoy about science and math?
20. Why is this BS/MD program right for you?

Listen intently. These are not empty questions. There is a reason why they ask each. Interviews can be very informative. If they have enough time, they would want to get to know you more. Their commitment to you and their program is partly why the visit is a day-long event, and you interact with a dozen different people along the way. The interview is not the only time you should make a good impression.

Be mindful of the time. Do not take too long to answer one question. Your response is not supposed to be a description of your life story. Also, you do not have to try to look smart. A few sentences suffice for each question. If they want to know more, they will follow up with another question.

HERE ARE FIVE QUESTIONS YOU MIGHT ASK AN INTERVIEWER IF GIVEN THE OPPORTUNITY:

1. What is the biggest challenge BD/MD students face during the program?

2. What clinical opportunities can students pursue?

3. Are there physicians who work directly with students in the program?

4. Do all students in this program succeed? If not, what could fellow students do to support their classmates and prevent them from dropping out?

5. What do you think are the three highlights of the program?

These questions are critical to your decision-making. There may be some other questions as well that you need to know to make a good decision. You want to determine whether this university is the right one for you to attend. After all, you have, undoubtedly, applied to other universities. If you interview at more than one school, you might find that two of them seem very similar. What nuances of the program will sway you to their school? Often, the dealbreaker is scholarship money, but there may be other reasons as well. You want to make useful comparisons.

Most BS/MD websites are vague, though there are a couple that are very thorough with FAQs, scholarship information, and detailed specifics about the program. Since most have only one page of information, you will need to do more research. This interview is your chance to interview them – not challenge them – to get more information. Be respectful. After all, you just want to know more about the program, and this is an important decision you must make.

If you have very high grades and scores with leadership, service, awards, and school activities, you may be choosing between colleges that have offered you full scholarships. Other choices might include schools like Harvard or UChicago. Certainly, these schools are different. Ultimately, though, you need to make a choice. Furthermore, all roads could lead to medical school. Asking questions is not bad. Think of five questions to ask schools so you can learn more. Add to this list with your own questions.

Here are some topics you might consider:

»	*Research*	»	*Performance Requirements*
»	*Summer Programs*	»	*Guidelines*
»	*Limitations*	»	*Dress Codes*
»	*Paid Work Experience*	»	*Meetings*
»	*Roles and Expectations*	»	*Study Locations*
»	*Collaborative Projects*		

Communicate candidly. Interviewers are looking to see how you think, react, and present yourself. Some questions may be staccato in nature – role model, pet peeve or favorite food, book, movie, quote, inspiration, hobby, type of music, city you have visited, or place to study. These types of questions are helpful in determining what comes off the top of your head and how quickly you can think. There are no right and wrong answers. They are not evaluating your favorite ice cream flavor or pizza topping. They just want to know if you can answer questions on the spot.

Other questions are designed to determine your actions, challenges, or ethical framework. Interviewers want to see how you will handle complex situations that are unique, unexpected, or challenging. After all, in the emergency room, you could get twenty-five people who are seriously injured from a bus accident and then get two people who were shot followed by someone who has a knife running through their leg. You have to be able to think clearly and quickly in very diverse situations.

SOME MORE CHALLENGING QUESTIONS MIGHT INCLUDE:

1. Describe a moral challenge you faced in school and how did you handle it?

2. Describe a time when you were criticized. What did you do?

3. When did someone else get credit for a project you did? How did you approach the situation?

4. When did you witness a classmate cheat? What did you do?

5. What mistakes do you regret? Why was it memorable?

The interview process varies by program. For example, at the University of Nevada, Reno (UNR), the students they select to interview are notified by February 1. Then, interviews are scheduled for February 13th and 14th on the UNR campus. The School of Medicine will arrange flights for Southern Nevada applicants from Las Vegas to Reno early so the candidates can return on the same day.

The University of Colorado at Denver also requires on-campus interviews and does not hold phone or Skype interviews, though this might be different over the next year or two if the pandemic persists. CU-Denver's interview process lasts from 8:00 – 4:00 pm and includes two separate 30-minute interviews.

Most colleges would prefer the process to take place on their campus. The main reason why is because they want you to see and experience the campus first-hand, particularly if you have never been there before. Second, they want to introduce you to each person with whom you may work. Third, they want you to experience the facilities. After all, you will be there for many years and you want to know what to expect.

Make a chart of the interview processes and dates. You can do this for all schools to which you apply, including non-BS/MD programs. Schools to which you are applying pre-med have different policies. Some contact you to interview. Some will not give you an interview until you contact them. Some allow you to interview on campus, while others interview remotely. Others have a grid of interview times on their website where you choose a convenient time. Since there are many different procedures, a chart is very helpful.

Finally, do not stress about the interview. The committee only wants to meet you. Prepare, smile, and show the committee who you are.

We all have dreams. But in order to make dreams come into reality, it takes an awful lot of determination, self-discipline, and effort.

— Jesse Owens

CHAPTER SEVENTEEN
FINANCIAL AID AND SCHOLARSHIPS

P aying for college may seem insurmountable, but financial aid and merit scholarships are offered in many programs to those who are chosen. You should know that at most schools more than half of the students receive financial aid. Furthermore, the price a student pays at a private school is rarely the price listed on the school's website as the cost of attendance. In fact, 50 – 80% of the students at private colleges receive some type of grant that does not need to be paid back.

Do not let the cost of attendance (COA) scare you off. Colleges are generous. They strive to find ways to help you cover the costs. Making your dream of attending a reality is a central mission of financial aid offices. Work with them. Do not feel bad about asking for financial aid and exploring your options. Financial aid officers want to help when they can – even at the end of the process.

During the coronavirus pandemic, most financial aid offices went into overdrive as they attempted to support families where the parents were suddenly unemployed, lost their businesses because they could no longer pay the rent without customers, or depleted all of their savings to survive and never thought they would ever have to fill out a FAFSA. Many families financial position changed within months. After losing their jobs, the stability and certainty of their incomes no longer existed. Colleges know what is at stake for you and for them.

It always seems impossible until it is done.

— Nelson Mandela

CHAPTER EIGHTEEN
WAITING AND DECLARING

Waiting to hear whether you got an interview and later waiting to hear the final decision is tough. The road to get to BS/MD is long, and you put in considerable time. You have persisted through more than a decade of school. Through sweat and uncertainty along the way, you put in hard work to get to this moment. Will they see who you are and why you are committed? Will your efforts be worth the time you put into this pursuit? Will they want you?

It is natural to ask these questions, particularly as you wait, day after day, to hear the result.

> *"Winter will thaw, and spring will bring both showers and flowers."*
>
> *– Rachel Winston*

It is unlikely that you will get accepted to every school to which you apply. The showers will rain on your parade. However, if you have applied to safeties, target schools, and reaches along with your BS/MD programs, you will be accepted and will move forward with your pursuit of medical school one way or another. You are likely to have a few choices. With these, you will make the best decision possible with the best information possible at the time. All roads can lead to medical school, provided you follow a well-constructed path.

While the National Candidate Reply Date is May 1. Know this. Some BS/MD programs have earlier deadlines. Be aware of these. Either way, you will decide, put down your deposit and prepare for the next step of your journey. After high school graduation, your road will head toward orientation. Use your summer wisely and prepare ahead of time for your classes. Undoubtedly, universities will provide you with GPA requirements you must satisfy. Reviewing all material for your courses and program before you begin is wise and well worth the effort.

Best wishes!

4
Regions

89
Programs

PART FOUR

CHOOSING THE BS/MD PROGRAM FOR YOU

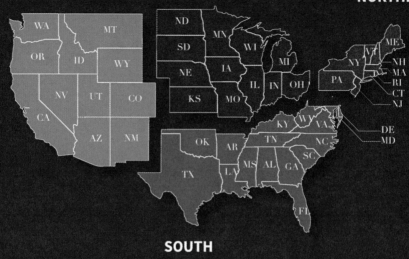

BS/MD PROGRAMS BY REGION
U.S. CENSUS BUREAU CLASSIFICATIONS

REGION 1 – NORTHEAST

Connecticut, Maine, Massachusetts, New Hampshire, New Jersey, New York, Pennsylvania, Rhode Island, and Vermont

REGION 2 – MIDWEST

Illinois, Indiana, Iowa, Kansas, Michigan, Minnesota, Missouri, Nebraska, North Dakota, Ohio, South Dakota, and Wisconsin

REGION 3 – SOUTH

Alabama, Arkansas, Delaware, District of Columbia, Florida, Georgia, Kentucky, Louisiana, Maryland, Mississippi, North Carolina, Oklahoma, South Carolina, Tennessee, Texas, Virginia, and West Virginia

REGION 4 – WEST

Alaska, Arizona, California, Colorado, Hawaii, Idaho, Montana, Nevada, New Mexico, Oregon, Utah, Washington, and Wyoming

CHAPTER SEVENTEEN
LIST OF BS/MD AND BS/DO PROGRAMS

The programs listed in the following pages include BS/MD, BS/DO, GAP (guaranteed admissions programs), EAP (early assurance programs), DAP (dual acceptance programs), and accelerated medical programs. Following this list, this book provides lists of MD, DO, dental, PharmD, vet schools, since many students interested in medical school are also interested in healthcare. There are many facets of the healthcare world. One of these other areas might be a good option for you.

Medical school is not for everyone.

Thus, this book aims at providing you with a more comprehensive set of lists so that you can explore your options. Keep the book handy. You may find that even after you begin college, if you choose a traditional pre-med path, you may find the list of additional programs in the back a good option for you.

Lists are often tedious to find and take a while to pull together. These lists were gathered to help you with this task.

Descriptions of the college programs, tuition, requirements, and deadlines are accurate as of April 2020. Requirements may have changed somewhat due to the pandemic, but all of this information is a great place to start!

Note: To simplify the text and fit information into the charts and descriptions, abbreviations were used as well as shortened sentences and acronyms.

REGION ONE

NORTHEAST

CONNECTICUT

MAINE

MASSACHUSETTS

NEW HAMPSHIRE

NEW JERSEY

NEW YORK

PENNSYLVANIA

RHODE ISLAND

VERMONT

12 Programs	CONNECTICUT
4 States	MASSACHUSETTS
	NEW JERSEY
	RHODE ISLAND

20 Programs	NEW YORK
1 States	

10 Programs	PENNSYLVANIA
1 States	

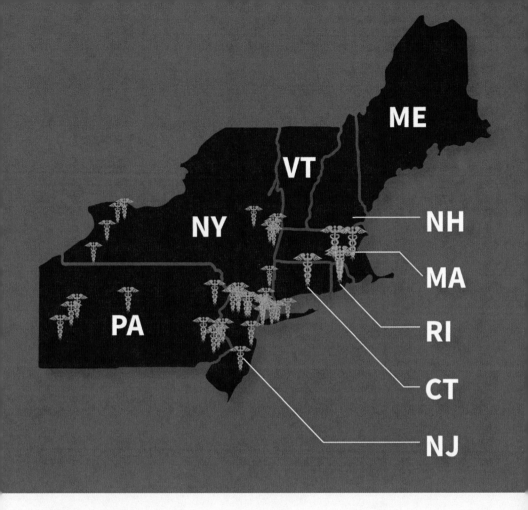

42 Programs | **9** States

1. CT – University of Connecticut (8-year)
2. MA – Boston University (7-year)
3. MA – Tufts University Early Assurance (8-year)
4. NJ – Caldwell BA/MD w/ St. George's (7-year)
5. NJ – College of St. Elizabeth (8-year)
6. NJ – Monmouth University (8-year)
7. NJ – Montclair University BS/MD (7-year, 8-year)
8. NJ – Rutgers University (7-year)
9. NJ – Stevens Institute of Technology (7-year)
10. NJ – Stockton University BS/DO (7-year)
11. NJ – New Jersey Inst of Tech w/ St. George's (7-year)
12. NY – Adelphi University w/ Upstate BS/MD (8-year) & BS/DO
13. NY – Albany College of Pharmacy and Health Sciences (8-year)
14. NY · Brooklyn College BA/MD (8-year)
15. NY – CUNY/CCNY Sophie Davis (7-year)
16. NY – Hofstra University BS-BA/MD (8-year)
17. NY – New York Institute of Technology BS/DO (7-year)
18. NY – Purchase College (8-year)
19. NY – Rensselaer Polytechnic Institute (7-year)
20. NY – Rochester Institute of Technology (8-year)
21. NY – Siena College with Albany Med (8-year)
22. NY – St. Bonaventure University (8-year)

23. NY – Stony Brook BA/MD Scholars Program (8-year)
24. NY – SUNY Geneseo BS/DO (7-year)
25. NY – SUNY New Paltz BS/DO (7-year)
26. NY – SUNY Old Westbury BS/DO (7-year)
27. NY – SUNY Polytechnic Institute (8-year)
28. NY – Union College Leadership in Medicine (8-year)
29. NY – University at Albany SUNY (8-year)
30. NY – University of Rochester REMS (8-year)
31. NY – Yeshiva University (8-year)
32. PA – Drexel University (8-year)
33. PA – Duquesne University PMHPP (8-year)
34. PA – Lehigh University (7-year) BS/DMD **BA/MD discontinued
35. PA – Penn State University Accelerated Med (7 year)
36. PA – Rosemont College Dual Degree (7-year, 8-year)
37. PA – Temple University Health Scholars (7-year, 8-year)
38. PA – University of Pittsburgh, Guaranteed Admissions (8-year)
39. PA – University of the Sciences with LECOM (7-year, 8-year)
40. PA – Washington and Jefferson College (8-year)
41. PA – West Chester University (8-year)
42. RI – Brown University PLME (8-year)
    * St. George's University affiliation (in Grenada) (7-year)

DIRECT MED PROGRAMS
Connecticut, Massachusetts, New Jersey, & Rhode Island

Connecticut, Massachusetts, New Jersey, & Rhode Island

12 Programs | **4** States

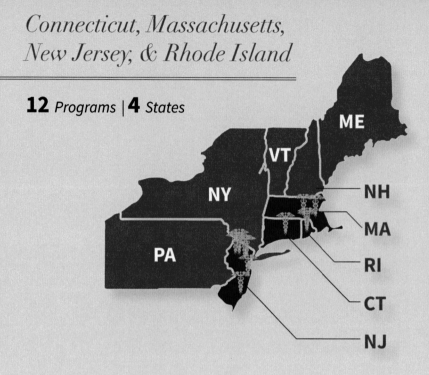

UNIVERSITY/PROGRAM	DEADLINE	MIN SAT, ACT, GPA	OTHER REQUIREMENTS
UCONN **2131 HILLSIDE RD.** **STORRS, CT 06269** **SPIM - SPECIAL PROG. IN MED**	*All app materials due by Dec. 1	Min SAT ERW+M - 1350 Min ACT - 29 Min GPA - 3.50	*Open to intl students, U.S. citizens, perm res. Special pref. to CT residents. *MCAT req.
BOSTON UNIV. **881 COMMONWEALTH AVE.** **6TH FLOOR** **BOSTON, MA 02215**	*Apply by November 15 *BS/MD only for 1st year students *3 Accel Prog. Teacher Evals. (Eng., Sci., Hist/Foreign Lang.) submitted via e-mail to *schforms@bu.edu* *Finalists will be contacted by BU to schedule a mandatory interview. All finalists must interview on campus.	Test Option, but will consider SAT, ACT and subject tests in Chem., Math II, and Foreign Language	*Comprehensive liberal education *12-week summer session req. after sophomore year *Students may not apply to another med. school & remain in the prog. *MCAT req. (80th percentile req. on each subsection

UNIVERSITY/PROGRAM	DEADLINE	MIN SAT, ACT, GPA	OTHER REQUIREMENTS
TUFTS UNIV. **145 HARRISON AVE.** **BOSTON, MA 02111** **EAP – EARLY** **ASSURANCE PROGRAM**	*App deadline - Feb. 1. *Interviews in April *In summer or fall of senior undergrad year, candidates apply via an AMCAS special prog. app.	Min SAT ERW+M - 1300 Min ACT - 30 Min GPA - 3.50	*ONLY for current Tufts undergrads. *MCAT not req. *Competitive applicants: course grades ≥ B; Bio, Chem, & Physics grades ≥ B+ *Approx. 20 students admitted into the EAP.
CALDWELL UNIV. **W/ST. GEORGE'S** **120 BLOOMFIELD AVE.** **CALDWELL, NJ 07006**	*All app materials due by Dec. 1	Min SAT ERW+M - 1270 Min ACT - 33 Min GPA - 3.50	*For Caldwell and Rutgers, GPA must be at least 3.50; SAT M+ERW must be ≥ 1450. *MCAT req.
COLLEGE OF ST. **ELIZABETH** **2 CONVENT RD,** **MORRISTOWN, NJ** **07960**	Not listed	Competitive stand. scores and GPA	*MCAT req.

MONMOUTH UNIV.
400 CEDAR AVENUE
WEST LONG BRANCH,
NJ 07764
	*Apply to Monmouth Univ.
	*Express interest in combined degree prog. in the app.
	  deadline - Dec. 1
	RD deadline - March 1
		Min SAT ERW+M - 1160
		  M, ERW ≥ 570
		ACT - 21-26
		Min GPA - 3.20
			*No limit listed on # of students accepted.
			*No binding commitment to SGU medical school
			*MCAT req.
			*AMCAS not req.

MONTCLAIR UNIV. **1 NORMAL AVE.** **MONTCLAIR, NJ 07043**	*All app materials due by Dec. 15. *Selected students invited for interview by HCP Committee; separate interview at R-NJMS.	Min SAT ERW+M - 1100 (≥ 550 in ERW & M in one sitting) ACT cannot be used in lieu of SAT	*Top 10% of graduating class *Must be a U.S. citizen or perm. res. w/NJ residency. *Must be a H.S. senior *Disadvantaged financially or educationally *MCAT req.

NORTHEAST

UNIVERSITY/PROGRAM	DEADLINE	MIN SAT, ACT, GPA	OTHER REQUIREMENTS
RUTGERS UNIV. 195 UNIVERSITY AVE. NEWARK, NJ 07102	All app materials by Nov. 1 *Apply to Rutgers. *Select Newark College of A&S *Select "Med Joint BA/MD" Interviews conducted Dec-Feb in-person or phone (not guaranteed) *Medical school in-person interviews by late March. *Notifications mailed in April.	Min SAT ERW+M - 1400 Min ACT - 32 Top 10% of grad. class. ACT may be accepted in lieu of SAT scores, however, applicant must complete Writing Section	*Only test scores through Oct. considered *Must be a H.S. senior to apply
STEVENS INST OF TECH 1 CASTLE POINT TERRACE, HOBOKEN, NJ 07030	*Interview at Stevens *All application materials due Nov 15	Min SAT ERW+M – 1400 Min ACT – competitive Top 10% of grad. Class	*SAT score must be achieved in one sitting *SAT II in Math Level 1 or 2, Bio, and Chem. req.
STOCKTON UNIVERSITY 101 VERA KING FARRIS DR., GALLOWAY, NJ 08205	*BS/DO (7-year prog.) *Apply to the dual degree program by Nov 15 *Interviews held at Stockton and Rowan SOM	Min SAT ERW+M – 1310 Min ERW – 670 Min M – 640 Min ACT M – 27 Min ACT E+R – 58 Competitive GPA	*MCAT req.
NEW JERSEY INST OF TECH W/ ST. GEORGE'S UNIVERSITY HEIGHTS NEWARK, NJ 07102	*Apply EA or rolling *Must apply by Nov. 1 *Indicate interest & complete questions pertaining to Honors College and Accelerated Prog.	SAT Min ERW+M – 1450 ACT Min - 32 GPA min - 3.50, admitted student avg. is 3.75	*Essay must be written on the topic specified by app. *Approx. 20 students are offered a spot *Only open to H.S. seniors *Must be U.S. citizen or perm resident to apply. *MCAT req.
BROWN UNIV. 91 WATERMAN STREET PROVIDENCE, RI 02912 PLME – PROGRAM IN LIBERAL MEDICAL EDUCATION	*Apply via CA for Brown and PLME *ED deadline - Nov. 1 *RD deadline - Jan. 1 *Submit video portfolio by Dec. 1 (ED) and Feb. 1 (RD) Notifications by Dec. 15 (ED) & April (RD)	SAT ERW avg. 742 SAT M avg. 770 ACT avg. 34 Rank near top of class SAT/ACT writing optional SAT II Tests in 2 areas w/ biology, chemistry, or physics	*Transfer students not eligible to apply for PLME. *Intl students considered. *Campus interviews not offered *Strongly encouraged to have alumni interview or video portfolio *MCAT not req. *AMCAS req.
ST. GEORGE'S UNIV. UNIV. CENTRE GRENADA W. INDIES, GRENADA NOTE: INCL IN NE DUE TO JOINT PROGS. W/ OTHER NE UNIV.	*Submit app to Univ. Registrar & Preclinical Program during the first term *Apply early. June 30 late deadline.	No set min SAT or ACT GPA - Website states "mostly A's and B's."	*Intl. students may apply *MCAT req. *AMCAS not req.

UNIVERSITY OF CONNECTICUT
BA/BS-MD PROGRAM (8-YEAR)

Medical School: University of Connecticut School of Medicine
200 Academic Way, Farmington, CT 06032
Undergraduate: University of Connecticut
2131 Hillside Road, Storrs, CT 06269
Program Information: *s://admissions.uconn.edu/apply/first-year/ special-programs/medicine#*
Request for Information Form:
https://connect.uconn.edu/register/join
Phone: (860) 486-3137
E-Mail: *beahusky@uconn.edu*
Additional Combined Programs: N/A
International Students: Considered

COST OF ATTENDANCE

In-State Tuition and Fees: $14,406
Additional Expenses with Room and Board: $19,894
Total: $34,300

Out-of-State Tuition and Fees: $37,074
Additional Expenses with Room and Board: $19,894
Total: $56,968

Financial Aid: Various merit-based scholarships are available. Applicants are automatically considered for most. Some require nomination from a school counselor.

ADDITIONAL INFORMATION

University of Connecticut (UConn) is a public research university founded in 1881. UConn's Special Program in Medicine is an 8-year BA/BS-MD track. Students may choose from over 110 majors for their Bachelor's degree. Although there are no state residency requirements, Connecticut residents will receive special preference. Additionally, UConn is "committed to attracting members of underrepresented populations for its programs."

To ensure matriculation into the UConn School of Medicine, as undergraduates, students must do the following:

1. Maintain a minimum 3.6 GPA
2. MCAT scores in 80th percentile with no subtest scores below 55th percentile
3. Complete relevant pre-medical coursework
4. Participate in service activities
5. Have successful interviews during senior year of undergraduate studies

BOSTON UNIVERSITY'S LIBERAL ARTS MEDICAL EDUCATION PROGRAM (7-YEAR)

Medical School: Boston University School of Medicine
2 East Concord St., Boston, MA 02118
Undergraduate: Boston University
881 Commonwealth Ave., 6th Floor, Boston, MA 02215
Program Information: *http://www.bu.edu/academics/cas/programs/seven-year-liberal-arts-medical-education-program/*
Request for Information Form:
https://onebu.tfaforms.net/forms/view/217873
Phone: (617) 353-2300
E-Mail: *admissions@bu.edu*
Additional Combined Programs: N/A
International Students: Considered

COST OF ATTENDANCE

Tuition and Fees: $58,072
Additional Expenses with Room and Board: $19,590
Total: $77,662

Financial Aid: BU meets 100% need for U.S. and permanent residents. Merit-based scholarships available, including full tuition scholarships. Applicants are automatically considered for most. BU Scholarship Assurance guarantees need-based aid for four years if you qualify as a freshman. CSS and FAFSA required.

ADDITIONAL INFORMATION

This 7-year program between the College of Arts & Sciences and Boston University School of Medicine includes a 12-week summer after the sophomore year of study. Students must be either current high school seniors or have not enrolled in any college-level, degree-granting program.

During the three years in BU's College of Arts & Sciences, the student will complete the Medical Science major, a minor, BU Hub general education program, and humanities and social science electives. Pre-med courses are completed during the first two years with the third-year for medical school-related modular medical courses to transition to the School of Medicine. Medical studies begin in year 4.

CONNECTICUT
MAINE
MASSACHUSETTS
NEW HAMPSHIRE
NEW JERSEY
NEW YORK
PENNSYLVANIA
RHODE ISLAND
VERMONT

NORTHEAST

CONNECTICUT

MAINE

MASSACHUSETTS

NEW HAMPSHIRE

NEW JERSEY

NEW YORK

PENNSYLVANIA

RHODE ISLAND

VERMONT

TUFTS UNIVERSITY EARLY ASSURANCE BS/MD PROGRAM (8-YEAR)

Medical School: Tufts School of Medicine
145 Harrison Ave, Boston, MA 02111
Undergraduate: Tufts University
419 Boston Ave, Medford, MA 02155
Program Information: *https://medicine.tufts.edu/admissions-aid/admissions-program/special-options/early-assurance*
Request for Information Form:
https://admissions.tufts.edu/connect-with-us/contact/
Phone: (617) 636-6571
E-Mail: *med-admissions@tufts.edu*
Additional Combined Programs: N/A
International Students: Considered

COST OF ATTENDANCE

Tuition and Fees: $57,324
Additional Expenses with Room and Board: $18,876
Total: $76,200

Financial Aid: All aid awarded is need-based. Tufts meets 100% of demonstrated need.

ADDITIONAL INFORMATION

Tufts University is a private university founded in 1852. Their Early Assurance Program (EAP) allows students conditional acceptance into the Tufts School of Medicine without requiring an MCAT score. In the traditional MD program, undergraduate sophomores at Tufts may apply to the EAP. Students must earn the following to be considered for the EAP:

1. Cumulative Science GPA at least 3.50
2. Cumulative GPA at least 3.50
3. All courses in Biology, Chemistry, and Physics at least a B+
4. All courses require at least a B
5. All coursework completed at Tufts University

Most applicants who were accepted into the EAP had an SAT CR/M of 1300+ or an ACT Composite score of at least 30. To ensure a seat at Tufts School of Medicine, EAP students must maintain a Science and Total GPA of 3.50 or higher. Admission to Tufts School of Medicine is guaranteed so long as all requirements are met.

CALDWELL W/ ST. GEORGE'S BA/MD PROGRAM (7-YEAR)

Medical School: St. George's University
University Centre Grenada, West Indies, Grenada
Undergraduate: Caldwell University
120 Bloomfield Ave, Caldwell, NJ 07006
Program Information: *https://www.caldwell.edu/academics/health-professions/affiliation-programs*
Request for Information Form: Press "request information" in this link: *https://www.caldwell.edu/academics/health-professions/affiliation-programs*
Pre-Medical Advisor Phone: (973) 618-3623
Admissions Phone: (973) 618-3500
E-Mail: *admissions@caldwell.edu*
Additional Combined Programs:
BA/MD with Rutgers, BA/MD with American University of Antigua, BA/DVM, BA/DMD, BA/MS OT, BA/OD, BA/DPM, BA/DC, BA/PharmD, BA/DPT, BA/MS Physician Assistant, BA/MSAT
International Students: Not listed

COST OF ATTENDANCE

Tuition and Fees: $34,900
Additional Expenses with Room and Board: $14,800
Total: $49,700

Financial Aid: Scholarships and grants available. Awards go up to full tuition.

ADDITIONAL INFORMATION

Caldwell University is a Catholic university founded in 1939. They have a BA/MD program with St. George's University (SGU). SGU is located in St. George's, Grenada in the Caribbean Islands. Caldwell also has a 3+4 BA/MD program with Rutgers University New Jersey Medical School and a 4+4 BA/MD program with American University of Antigua College of Medicine.

Applicants for the BA/MD program may only apply to one combined program on their application. Although they offer several combined programs, "only the two accelerated 7-year (3+4) BA/MD programs and BA/DVM program provisionally accept students when they enter Caldwell University". For St. George's University, applicants are required to have:

1. Minimum 3.50 GPA
2. Minimum M/CR SAT scores 1270

To ensure a seat in SGU's medical school, students must maintain a minimum 3.40 GPA as an undergraduate and receive a competitive score on the MCAT.

For Rutgers University New Jersey Medical School, applicants are required to have:

1. Minimum 3.5 GPA
2. Top 10% of high school class
3. Minimum SAT (CR&M) 1450
4. To ensure a secure seat in Rutgers University New Jersey Medical School, students must maintain a minimum 3.50 GPA as an undergraduate and receive a competitive score on the MCAT.

CONNECTICUT

MAINE

MASSACHUSETTS

NEW HAMPSHIRE

NEW JERSEY

NEW YORK

PENNSYLVANIA

RHODE ISLAND

VERMONT

ME
VT
NY
NH
MA
PA
RI
CT
NJ

NORTHEAST

CONNECTICUT

MAINE

MASSACHUSETTS

NEW HAMPSHIRE

NEW JERSEY

NEW YORK

PENNSYLVANIA

RHODE ISLAND

VERMONT

COLLEGE OF SAINT ELIZABETH
BS/MD PROGRAM (8-YEAR)

Medical School: American University of Antigua College of Medicine
University Park, Jabberwock Beach Rd., PO Box W1451, Coolidge, Antigua
Undergraduate: College of Saint Elizabeth
2 Convent Rd, Morristown, NJ 07960
Program Information: *http://cse.smartcatalogiq.com/2019-2020/ academic-catalog/academic-programs/biology/bs-in-biology-doctor-of-medicine-dual-degree-program*
Request for Information Form: *http://discover.cse.edu/inquiryform*
Phone: (973) 290-4000
E-Mail: *apply@cse.edu*
Additional Combined Programs:
BS/DPT, BS/DPM, BS/MD at St. George's University
International Students: Not listed

COST OF ATTENDANCE

Tuition and Fees: $32,250
Additional Expenses with Room and Board: $12,744
Total: $44,994

Financial Aid: Scholarships and grants available.

ADDITIONAL INFORMATION

College of St. Elizabeth is a private, Catholic liberal arts college established in 1899. They offer a BS/MD program in partnership with the American University of Antigua College of Medicine. Students must select a B.S. degree in Biology. Applicants are evaluated based on their high school record, GPA, SAT scores, and letters of recommendation from math/science teachers. To maintain eligibility to the AUA College of Medicine, students must do the following:

1. Complete prerequisite math and science courses
2. Maintain a minimum cumulative GPA of 3.25 and overall cumulative GPA of 3.5
3. Complete all general education requirements
4. Complete the B.S. in Biology requirements
5. Score a minimum 24 on the MCAT (note: this is a 498 equivalent for new MCAT)
6. Satisfactory interview conducted by AUA
7. Formal application

College of St. Elizabeth also offers a BS/MD program with St. George's University.

MONMOUTH UNIVERSITY
BS/MD PROGRAM (8-YEAR)

Medical School: St. George's University
University Centre Grenada, West Indies, Grenada
Undergraduate: Monmouth University
400 Cedar Avenue, West Long Branch, NJ 07764
Program Information:
https://www.monmouth.edu/pre-health/st-georges-program/
Request for Information Form:
https://apply.monmouth.edu/register/inquiry
Phone: (732) 571-3456
E-Mail: *admission@monmouth.edu*
Additional Combined Programs: BS/DVM
International Students: Not listed

COST OF ATTENDANCE

Tuition and Fees: $39,592
Additional Expenses with Room and Board: $19,462
Total: $59,054

Financial Aid: Some merit-based and need-based scholarships/grants available.

ADDITIONAL INFORMATION

Monmouth University (MU) is a private university founded in 1933. In partnership with St. George's University (SGU), MU offers a BS/MD 4+4 program for high school applicants. Four years are spent at MU where the student earns their Bachelor of Science degree. The next two years are at St. George's University School of Medicine. The final two years are spent in clinical rotations in hospitals in the U.S. or U.K.

While at MU, students are guided by the Pre-Health Advising (PHA) team. PHA members "provide students with information and guidance on admissions tests…and prepare them for entrance interviews". Pre-Health Advising also provides resources for students.

For students to enter SGU's School of Medicine, as undergraduates, they must maintain a minimum GPA of 3.4 and a score of 25 or higher on the MCAT (Note: this is the old MCAT scoring system, it translates to approximately the 44th percentile or 499). They must also complete a successful interview with SGU.

CONNECTICUT

MAINE

MASSACHUSETTS

NEW HAMPSHIRE

NEW JERSEY

NEW YORK

PENNSYLVANIA

RHODE ISLAND

VERMONT

NORTHEAST

CONNECTICUT

MAINE

MASSACHUSETTS

NEW HAMPSHIRE

NEW JERSEY

NEW YORK

PENNSYLVANIA

RHODE ISLAND

VERMONT

MONTCLAIR UNIVERSITY
BS/MD PROGRAM (7-YEAR, 8-YEAR)

Medical School: Rutgers-New Jersey Medical School (R-NJMS)
185 S Orange Ave, Newark, NJ 07103
Undergraduate: Montclair University
1 Normal Ave, Montclair, NJ 07043
Program Information: *https://www.montclair.edu/csam/programs-and-opportunities/health-careers-program/health-careers-program-combined-bs-md-program-eight-year/*
Request for Information Form:
https://apply.montclair.edu/register/inquire
Phone: (973) 655-4000
E-Mail: *msuadm@montclair.edu*
Additional Combined Programs: BS/MD (7-year)
International Students: Not considered

COST OF ATTENDANCE

In-State Tuition and Fees: $13,072
Additional Expenses with Room and Board: $14,140
Total: $27,212

Out-of-State Tuition and Fees: $21,032
Additional Expenses with Room and Board: $14,140
Total: $35,172

Financial Aid: Students are automatically considered for certain scholarships. Merit-based aid available.

ADDITIONAL INFORMATION

Montclair University is a public university. It is the second largest university in New Jersey. Students in the Health Careers Program spend four years at Montclair obtaining their undergraduate degree and four years at Rutgers-New Jersey Medical School (R-NJMS) to obtain their MD. Students must major in biology, chemistry, biochemistry, or molecular biology. Upon completing all program requirements, the student is automatically admitted to the medical school.

Applicants to the Health Careers Program must be a U.S. citizen or permanent resident with New Jersey residency. Students must rank in the top 10 percent and have earned at minimum a B-average. A maximum of five letters of recommendation are required, with at least one each from mathematics, science, and English teachers.

To fulfill program requirements, Health Careers Program students must maintain a minimum B grade in all science courses. They must also fulfill all requirements for the HCP Honors curriculum. Furthermore, they must maintain a semester and cumulative GPA of at least 3.20 and participate in summer studies or independent research at R-NJMS. Students are required to take the MCAT.

The accelerated BS/MD program at Montclair University is also in partnership with Rutgers University. In this program, students must have an SAT combined verbal and math score of 1400 or higher from a single test administration. Students must also be in the upper 10% of their high school class or have a GPA higher than 3.60. Required majors include biology, molecular biology, or biochemistry. This program is only open to U.S. citizens or permanent residents. However, the New Jersey residency requirement does not apply to this track. For more information about the accelerated track, visit: *https://www.montclair.edu/biology/articulation-programs/bs-md-medical-rutgers/*

RUTGERS UNIVERSITY
BA/MD PROGRAM (7-YEAR)

Medical School: Rutgers New Jersey Medical School (R-NJMS)
185 S Orange Ave, Newark, NJ 07103
Undergraduate: Rutgers University, Newark
195 University Ave, Newark, NJ 07102
Program Information: *https://sasn.rutgers.edu/student-support/
current-students/pre-professional-programs/bamd-program-njms-nwk*
Request for Information Form:
https://www.ugadmissions.rutgers.edu/forms/InfoRequest.aspx
Phone: (973) 353-5205
E-Mail: *newark@admissions.rutgers.edu*
Additional Combined Programs:
BA/MD for Rutgers University students in sophomore year; BA/MD for
Rutgers-New Brunswick students in sophomore year
International Students: Not listed

COST OF ATTENDANCE

In-State Tuition and Fees: $12,230
Additional Expenses with Room and Board: $16,525
Total: $28,755

Out-of-State Tuition and Fees: $29,012
Additional Expenses with Room and Board: $16,525
Total: $45,537

Financial Aid: Students are automatically considered for scholarships
upon applying to Rutgers.

ADDITIONAL INFORMATION

Rutgers University is a public university with three campuses:
Camden, Newark, and New Brunswick. The Newark campus offers a
7-year BA/MD program. Students in this program must choose a major
in English, Biology, Chemistry, Economics, Psychology, or History.
Students are offered guaranteed admission to the Rutgers – New
Jersey Medical School (R-NJMS) so long as they maintain certain
progress requirements. The AMCAS is not required. The MCAT is
required, although it is not used to determine admission to R-NJMS.

Rutgers University also offers a BA/MD track in conjunction with
the Rutgers Robert Wood Johnson Medical School for current
undergraduate students in their sophomore year. For more
information about this program, visit: *https://hpo.rutgers.edu/special-
programs/academic-programs/ba-md-rwj*

Additionally, a BA/MD track is available for Rutgers-New Brunswick
sophomore undergraduate students. This program is in conjunction
with the Rutgers New Jersey Medical School. For more information
about this program, visit: *https://hpo.rutgers.edu/special-programs/
academic-programs/ba-md-njms*

CONNECTICUT

MAINE

MASSACHUSETTS

NEW HAMPSHIRE

NEW JERSEY

NEW YORK

PENNSYLVANIA

RHODE ISLAND

VERMONT

NORTHEAST

CONNECTICUT

MAINE

MASSACHUSETTS

NEW HAMPSHIRE

NEW JERSEY

NEW YORK

PENNSYLVANIA

RHODE ISLAND

VERMONT

STEVENS INSTITUTE OF TECHNOLOGY BS/MD PROGRAM (7-YEAR)

Medical School: Rutgers New Jersey Medical School
185 S Orange Ave, Newark, NJ 07103
Undergraduate: Stevens Institute of Technology
1 Castle Point Terrace, Hoboken, NJ 07030
Program Information: *https://www.stevens.edu/schaefer-school-engineering-science/departments/chemistry-chemical-biology/undergraduate-programs/accelerated-chemical-biology-program*
Request for Information Form:
https://www.stevens.edu/request-information-0
Phone: (201) 216-5194
E-Mail: *admissions@stevens.edu*
Additional Combined Programs: N/A
International Students: Not listed

COST OF ATTENDANCE

Tuition and Fees: $55,952
Additional Expenses with Room and Board: $18,494
Total: $74,446

Financial Aid: Merit-based and need-based scholarships available.

ADDITIONAL INFORMATION

Stevens Institute of Technology is a private university established in 1870. The Accelerated Chemical Biology Program allows students to obtain a B.S. degree in Chemical Biology at Stevens, and an M.D. at Rutgers New Jersey Medical School in 7 years. Three years are spent at Stevens and the next four at Rutgers.

ADMISSION REQUIREMENTS:

1. Successfully complete high school coursework
   - 4 years of English
   - 4 years of Math (2 Algebra, 1 Geometry, 1 Pre-Calculus)
   - 3 years of Science (1 Biology, 1 Chemistry, 1 Physics)
   - AP Biology and AP Chemistry recommended
2. Rank in the top 10% of graduating class
3. Combined SAT score of 1400 (CR+M) in one sitting
4. Take SAT II in Math Level 1 or Level 2, Biology, and Chemistry by Oct 11
5. Write an essay on why you want to be a doctor
6. Interview with Stevens by Nov 15
7. Include a resume with outside experience (e.g., shadowing, volunteering, research)
8. Application due Nov 15

STOCKTON UNIVERSITY
BS/DO PROGRAM (7-YEAR)

Medical School: Rowan School of Osteopathic Medicine
42 E Laurel Rd, Stratford, NJ 08084
Undergraduate: Stockton University
101 Vera King Farris Dr., Galloway, NJ 08205
Program Information:
https://stockton.edu/sciences-math/health-articulation.html
Contact Link: *https://stockton.edu/admissions/contact-us.html*
Phone: (609) 652-4261
E-Mail: *admissions@stockton.edu*
Additional Combined Programs: N/A
International Students: Not listed

COST OF ATTENDANCE

In-State Tuition and Fees: $14,317
Additional Expenses with Room and Board: $12,542
Total: $26,859

Out-of-State Tuition and Fees: $21,605
Additional Expenses with Room and Board: $12,542
Total: $34,147

Financial Aid: Merit-based and need-based scholarships available.

ADDITIONAL INFORMATION

Stockton University is a public university founded in 1969. The accelerated BS/DO program is offered by Stockton in partnership with Rowan School of Osteopathic Medicine. This program is completed in 7 years. High school seniors and current Stockton University students with less than 32 credits may apply. Students must major in Biology.

To ensure entry to the Rowan SOM, accepted students must do the following:

1. Maintain a minimum GPA of 3.50 with a grade of B or better in all prerequisite coursework
2. MCAT required. The score must be at or above the 70th percentile level
3. B.S. in Biology awarded after completion of the first year at Rowan SOM

CONNECTICUT

MAINE

MASSACHUSETTS

NEW HAMPSHIRE

NEW JERSEY

NEW YORK

PENNSYLVANIA

RHODE ISLAND

VERMONT

NORTHEAST

CONNECTICUT

MAINE

MASSACHUSETTS

NEW HAMPSHIRE

NEW JERSEY

NEW YORK

PENNSYLVANIA

RHODE ISLAND

VERMONT

NEW JERSEY INSTITUTE OF TECH W/ ST. GEORGE'S BS/BA-MD PROGRAM (7-YEAR)

Medical School: St. George's University
University Centre Grenada, West Indies, Grenada
Undergraduate: New Jersey Institute of Technology
University Heights, Newark, NJ 07102
Program Information:
https://honors.njit.edu/content/pre-health-admissions
Request for Information Form:
https://www.njit.edu/apply-now
Phone: (973) 596-3000
E-Mail: *honors@njit.edu*
Additional Combined Programs:
BS/MD at New Jersey Medical School (NJMS) (3+4), BS/DMD at
Rutgers School of Dental Medicine (3+4), BS/DPT (3+3), BS/OD at
SUNY, BS/MD at American University of Antigua, BS-MBA/MD or MS/
MD at American University of Antigua (3+1+4)
International Students: Not Considered

COST OF ATTENDANCE

In-State Tuition and Fees: $17,674
Additional Expenses with Room and Board: $20,900
Total: $38,574

Out-of-State Tuition and Fees: $33,386
Additional Expenses with Room and Board: $20,900
Total: $54,286

Financial Aid: Honors scholarships available, ranging from $2500 to
full tuition and housing. Students in this program typically receive
a generous financial aid package (up to full tuition for three years at
NJIT).

ADDITIONAL INFORMATION

New Jersey Institute of Technology (NJIT) is a public university that
has partnered with St. George's University to offer students a 3+4
combined degree program. This program involves three years at
NJIT, followed by two years of studying at St. George's University in
Grenada (Caribbean Islands), and then two years of Clinical Clerkship
at St. Michael's Medical Center through NJIT in Newark. If not
admitted into the program, students may apply to NJIT's other BS/
MD programs by ranking the programs in the Common App. Students
must complete their undergraduate coursework within three years.
This program is open to high school students and current NJIT
undergraduates.

NJIT also offers another combined degree program with New Jersey
Medical School (NJMS) where students obtain their bachelor's degree
in three years at NJIT then attend NJMS for four years. Students
must fulfill all Honors College requirements while at NJIT. Students
may pursue a bachelor's degree in any department. For a full list of
accelerated paths along with the minimum SAT and ACT, visit: *https://
honors.njit.edu/accelerated-path*

BROWN UNIVERSITY PLME
BA/BS-MD PROGRAM (8-YEAR)

Medical School: Warren Alpert Medical School of Brown University
222 Richmond St, Providence, RI 02903
Undergraduate: Brown University
91 Waterman Street, Providence, RI 02912
Program Information:
https://www.brown.edu/academics/medical/plme/
Request for Information Form:
https://apply.college.brown.edu/register/joinourcontactlist
Phone: (401) 863-9790
E-Mail: *plme@brown.edu*
Additional Combined Programs: BA/BS-MD/PhD or BA/BS-MD/MPH
International Students: Considered

COST OF ATTENDANCE

Tuition and Fees: $60,696
Additional Expenses with Room and Board: $19,752
Total: $80,448

Financial Aid: Need-based and merit-based scholarships available to undergraduate and medical students.

ADDITIONAL INFORMATION

Brown University is a private, Ivy League university located in Rhode Island. The Program in Liberal Medical Education (PLME) is the only BA/MD program in the Ivy League. Approximately 50 applicants are admitted into the PLME program per year. In their medical studies, PLME students may pursue an MD/PHD or MD/MPH if they choose to. Students are also able to defer entry to medical school. The MCAT is not required. The AMCAS application is required.

Early decision applies to both the university and the PLME. If a student is admitted into Brown University but not the PLME, they are still bound to attend Brown. Students in this situation are still considered for the PLME during regular decision. Brown University also implements a need-blind admission policy, whereby the applicant's ability to pay for education is not factored into consideration when making admissions decisions.

There were 2,641 applicants for the PLME in 2019. The number of those accepted was 94 (20 ED, 74 Regular). A total of 61 students were admitted into the program. The average SAT and ACT scores for admitted students over the past three years have been 742 (SAT ERW), 770 (SAT Math), and 34 (ACT composite).

Undergraduate students of Brown University are required to live on campus for the first three years. There are a variety of enrichment activities for PLME students, including the Community Health Advocacy Program (CHAP), research opportunities, study abroad, and fellowships. For more information, visit: *https://www.brown.edu/academics/medical/plme/current-students/enrichment-activities*

CONNECTICUT

MAINE

MASSACHUSETTS

NEW HAMPSHIRE

NEW JERSEY

NEW YORK

PENNSYLVANIA

RHODE ISLAND

VERMONT

NORTHEAST

CONNECTICUT

MAINE

MASSACHUSETTS

NEW HAMPSHIRE

NEW JERSEY

NEW YORK

PENNSYLVANIA

RHODE ISLAND

VERMONT

ST. GEORGE'S UNIVERSITY
BS/MD PROGRAM (7-YEAR)

Located in the Caribbean & Affiliated w/Many Listed Programs

Medical School: St. George's University
University Centre Grenada, West Indies, Grenada
Undergraduate: St. George's University
University Centre Grenada, West Indies, Grenada
Program Information: *https://www.sgu.edu/academic-programs/school-of-medicine/md/bs-md-dual-degree/*
Request for Information Form:
https://www.sgu.edu/next-steps/request-information/
Phone: (800) 899-6337
E-Mail: *admission@sgu.edu*
Additional Combined Programs: BS/DVM (7-year)
International Students: Considered

COST OF ATTENDANCE

Tuition and Fees: $31,264
Additional Expenses with Room and Board: $3,346
Total: $34,610

Financial Aid: Merit-based scholarships available. SGU is approved for participation in the US Direct Loan Program.

ADDITIONAL INFORMATION

St. George's University is a private international university located in Grenada and established in 1976. They offer a variety of tracks for students interested in obtaining a BS and MD. The 7-year track requires a "secondary school diploma [with] strong science grades". Students complete their Bachelor's degree in three years of undergraduate studies. The next two years are spent completing the basic science coursework in Grenada. The last two years consist of clinical training in affiliated hospitals in various locations in the U.S. or the U.K. All non-residents "must live on campus for two terms."

The 6-year track is available for students who apply with the South African or Australian Matric exam qualifications, Higher School Exam, Irish Leaving Certificate, or AS Levels.

For more information on the 7-year curriculum, please visit: *https://www.sgu.edu/academic-programs/school-of-medicine/md/curriculum-preclinical-programs/*

For more information on all partnering undergraduate institutions, please visit: *https://www.sgu.edu/academic-programs/school-of-medicine/international-partnerships/*

New York

20 *Programs* | **1** *State*

UNIVERSITY/PROGRAM	DEADLINE	MIN SAT, ACT, & GPA	OTHER REQUIREMENTS
ADELPHI UNIV. W/ UPSTATE **1 SOUTH AVE.** **GARDEN CITY, NY** **11530**	*BS/MD & BS/DO (8-year) *Indicate interest in Accel Scholars Prog. (ASP) w/SUNY Upstate on Common App and SUNY's supplemental form *Must be accepted to Adelphi for ASP consideration *Strongly rec. to apply by Dec. 1 *ASP Committee evaluates & notifies on a rolling basis for Upstate's consideration *Upstate screens candidates on a rolling basis, sends invitations for interviews, & provides conditional admit letter	BS/MD w/ Upstate Min SAT ERW+M - 1360 Min ACT - 29 Min GPA - 3.50 BS/DO with PCOM, LECOM, NYIT DO w/PCOM (8-year) Min ERW – 670, M-670 Min GPA – 3.5 w/LECOM (7-year) Min ERW+M – 1360 Min ACT – 29 GPA – 3.5 w/NYIT DO (Early Interview Only)	*Up to 5 students admitted Acceptance into ASP is binding *MCAT not req. *Activities must show commitment to service, medicine, and community

UNIVERSITY/PROGRAM	DEADLINE	MIN SAT, ACT, & GPA	OTHER REQUIREMENTS
ALBANY COLLEGE OF PHARMACY AND HEALTH SCIENCES 106 NEW SCOTLAND AVE. ALBANY, NY 12208	*Indicate interest in Upstate Accel Scholars (UAS) Prog. *Must be accepted by ACPHS then rec. by ACPHS to Upstate *App to ACPHS & Statement of Interest in UAS prog due Dec 1, rec to apply by Nov. 15! *Upstate screens candidates on a rolling basis, sends invitations for interviews, & provides conditional admit letter	Min SAT ERW+M - 1360 Min ACT - 31 High GPA w/90% average	*Up to 5 students admitted per year *Activities must show experience in healthcare & commitment to service *MCAT not req.
BROOKLYN COLLEGE 2900 BEDFORD AVE. BROOKLYN, NY 11210	*App. opens Sept. 1; due Dec. 15 *Complete CUNY app. *Go to Brooklyn College online app page, complete BA-MD app. *Students may apply for the Scholars Program AND the Macaulay Honors College w/the BA-MD prog.	SAT Mid-range ERW+M - 1300-1450	Maintain a 3.50 overall AND science GPA to enter SUNY Downstate. *15 students accepted out of 250-300 who apply. *Volunteer work *Summer clinical exp. *Deferrals not allowed. *MCAT req.
CUNY/CCNY SOPHIE DAVIS 160 CONVENT AVE. NEW YORK, NY 10031	*BS/MD (7-year) *Deadline for CUNY School of Med app - Jan. 8 and CUNY general app is Feb. 1 *Notifications sent via letterhead April 1st.	No Min SAT or ACT, but competitive Competitive GPA	*Must be H.S. grad by June 30 *Transfer stud w/ ≤ 15 credits after H.S. grad may apply. *3 essays AND 5 letters of rec req.
HOFSTRA UNIV. 1000 HEMPSTEAD TURNPIKE HEMPSTEAD, NY 11549	*Apply EA by Nov 15 or Dec. 15 & be admitted to Hofstra. *In Jan, complete Supplement for Hofstra 4+4 Prog. available for eligible admitted students and must be rec. by Jan 15 *The 4+4 Suppl App submitted by Feb. 1 *Interviews conducted w/Hofstra Northwell School of Med in March. *Final dec. mailed by April 1st.	Min SAT ERW+M - 1410 Min ACT - 32 Min GPA - 3.70 Top 10% of graduating class	*CASPer™ exam rec - a 90-min online situational judgment test. *Must maintain 3.60 and 3.60 science GPA every year of undergrad study. *No course repeats *No grade lower than B in any science course nor a C in a non-science course. *Min MCAT score in the 80th percentile at first sitting.

NORTHEAST

UNIVERSITY/PROGRAM	DEADLINE	MIN SAT, ACT, & GPA	OTHER REQUIREMENTS
NEW YORK INST OF TECHNOLOGY 1855 BROADWAY (AT 61ST ST.), NEW YORK, NY 10023	*First-Year Priority Deadline: Nov 1 *Submit apps. by Dec 1	Min SAT CR+M – 1270 Min ACT – 28 Min high school avg. – 90 High class standing	*Only for U.S. citizens or permanent residents *2 Letters of Rec
PURCHASE COLLEGE 735 ANDERSON HILL RD. PURCHASE, NY 10577	*Apply to Purchase by Nov 15 *Indicate interest in Upstate Accel Scholars (UAS) Prog. on Common App and SUNY Supplemental form *Must be accepted by Purchase then rec by Purchase to Upstate *Upstate screens candidates and invites some to interview *Upstate sends decisions and provides conditional admit letter	Min SAT ERW+M - 1360 Min ACT - 29 Min GPA 90% avg.	*MCAT not req. *Acceptance into UAS is binding *Activities must show commitment to service, healthcare, and community
RPI 110 EIGHTH STREET TROY, NY USA 12180 AMC – ALBANY MEDICAL COLLEGE	*Apply by Nov 1 *Choose "Physician-Scientist Program-B.S./M.D." on app *No ED option *Students may apply to only 1 of AMC's combined programs. Applicants who apply to > 1 joint prog. will be w/d *Top applicants are interviewed by AMC from Jan - March. *Notification in April	*Most applicants invited for an interview had 1425+ (ERW+M) Accepted Students: SAT Ave. 1466 ACT Ave. 33 (MUST take optional writing) GPA avg. is A/A- SAT II Tests req. in math & science (biology, chemistry, or physics) *Tests must be taken by Nov test date	*Ave. 550 applicants *Not open to transfer students *Only U.S. citizens & perm res. *CASPer exam req. – students may take any of the 4 tests (Sept., Oct., Nov., or Dec.) *No MCAT req

UNIVERSITY/PROGRAM	DEADLINE	MIN SAT, ACT, & GPA	OTHER REQUIREMENTS
ROCHESTER INSTITUTE OF TECHNOLOGY (RIT) 1 LOMB MEMORIAL DR. ROCHESTER, NY 14623	*RIT has ED and RD. *Rec - apply by Nov 15 *Apply to RIT thru CA & select indicate interest in medicine *RIT Suppl App, sent to eligible students, must be submitted for RIT-Upstate ASP *Must be accepted to RIT, then rec by RIT to Upstate (on a rolling basis) *Upstate screens candidates & invites some to interview *Upstate sends decisions and provides conditional admit letter Intent to enroll due May 1	Min SAT ERW+M - 1360 Min ACT - 29 Min - 90% avg. GPA	*Up to 5 students admitted into RIT-Upstate ASP *MCAT not req *Acceptance into RIT-Upstate ASP is binding *Activities must show commitment to service, healthcare, and community
SIENA COLLEGE W/ALBANY MEDICAL COLLEGE 515 LOUDON ROAD LOUDONVILLE, NY 12211	*BS/MD (7-year or 8-year) *Siena App or CA w/a Biology BA and AMC suppl. essay req. *All materials except the CASPer test due Nov. 1	Min SAT ERW+M - 1360 Min ACT - 30 Min GPA - 3.50	*Top 10% of graduating class *Approx. 15 accepted *CASPer exam req. *H.S. counselor rec. and 2 teacher recs. req.
ST. BONAVENTURE UNIV. W/GWU MEDICAL SCHOOL 3261 W STATE ST. ST. BONAVENTURE, NY 14778	*Strongly rec. that students complete app. & supplemental materials be Nov. 30th due date. CA preferred. *Selected applicants interviewed at SBU in Jan. *2nd interview conducted at GW in late Feb to early March. *Dec. made in mid-late March	Min SAT ERW+M - 1390 Min ACT - 30 Min GPA - 90 SAT II Test in science required. Molecular biology pref., chemistry accepted.	*Must be a U.S. or Canadian citizen or perm res *Service & health-related experiences expected to be competitive *Min 2 letters of rec - one from a science teacher. *MCAT req

NORTHEAST

UNIVERSITY/PROGRAM	DEADLINE	MIN SAT, ACT, & GPA	OTHER REQUIREMENTS
STONY BROOK BA/MD SCHOLARS PROGRAM 100 NICOLLS RD. STONY BROOK, NY 11794	*Apply to Stony Brook U. *Send all suppl. by Jan 15 *Notified in March if admitted to the Honors prog. & rec. for review by the School of Med. *Interview offers in March *Final decs. by April 1	SAT mid-range - 1490-1590 (ERW+M) H.S. GPA - 98-99 *NEW - ACT scores now considered in place of SAT	*Must be a U.S. citizen or perm res. *2 teacher recs. and suppl essays *Complete Honors prog. of study & pre-med courses w/ 3.2 science & 3.4 min overall GPA *Earn nat. avg. MCAT score med school matriculates.
SUNY GENESEO 1 COLLEGE CIRCLE GENESEO, NY 14454	*Apply via Common App preferred *Deadline is Jan 1 *Recommend begin app. 4-6 weeks prior *Indicate on app: ¾ Osteopathic Med. Program *Decisions released Mar 1	Min SAT ERW+M – 1200 Min ACT composite – 28 High school avg. 90% or better	*MCAT req.
SUNY NEW PALTZ 1 HAWK DR. NEW PALTZ, NY 12561	*BS/DO (7-year) *App deadline is Jan 15 *Interview in-person or via Skype *Additional app. to Touro COM starting end of sophomore year	*Min SAT ERW+M- 1260 *Min ACT - 27 *Min GPA - 93	*Open to intl applicants *MCAT req.
SUNY OLD WESTBURY 223 STORE HILL RD. CAMPUS CENTER H-310 OLD WESTBURY, NY 11568	*BS/DO Program (7-year) *App. deadline: Mar 15 *Supplemental App. given if the applicant meets criteria *Interviews offered *Decisions: 2 weeks after the interview	Min SAT ERW+M – 1270 Min ACT - 27 Min GPA avg. - 92	*10 students admitted *MCAT req. *Intl. students may apply *AACOMAS not req.
SUNY POLYTECHNIC INST. 100 SEYMOUR AVE. UTICA, NY 13502	*Apply by Dec 15 to SUNY Poly, indicate interest in ASP w/ Upstate on CA & SUNY suppl form. *Must be accepted by SUNY Poly then rec by SUNY Poly to Upstate *Upstate screens candidates & invites some to interview *Upstate sends decs. & conditional admit letter	Min SAT ERW+M - 1360 Min ACT - 29 Min GPA - 3.50	*MCAT not req. *Acceptance into ASP is binding *Activities must show commitment to service, healthcare, and community

UNIVERSITY/PROGRAM	DEADLINE	MIN SAT, ACT, & GPA	OTHER REQUIREMENTS
THE UNION COLLEGE LEADERSHIP IN MEDICINE 807 UNION ST. SCHENECTADY, NY 12308 AMC – ALBANY MEDICAL COLLEGE	*Apply by Nov. 15 on CA or Coalition app; submit F.A. docs by Nov. 15 *Complete CASPer by Nov. 19 *Union notifies select candidates to complete AMC suppl. app. *AMC interviews bet. Jan - March *Applicants forwarded to AMC will receive admission to Union and F.A. pkg for undergrad prog *Leadership in Medicine (LIM) prog. have until May 1 to enroll	Min ERW+M - 1410 Min ACT - 30 SAT II above 650 in math and science (Physics pref but not req.) SAT I & II, ACT req. by Nov. of senior year Rank near top of the class	*Must be U.S. Citizen or perm res *Approx. 270 apply, 15 enroll *CASPer exam *No MCAT req. *Clinical/volunteer exp. in the medical field *Must apply to ONLY one of the 3 AMC combined progs
UNIV. AT ALBANY SUNY 1400 WASHINGTON AVE. ALBANY, NY 12222	*Apply by EA deadline Nov 1 *Indicate interest in UAS prog. w/SUNY Upstate on CA and SUNY Suppl Form *Must be accepted by Univ. at Albany who recs candidates to Upstate; they screen apps and invite students to interview *In-person interviews in Feb. or early March *Upstate sends decs. & sends conditional admit letter	Min ERW+M - 1360 Min ACT - 29 GPA min - 90% avg.	*Approximately 10 students accepted *MCAT not req. *Acceptance into UAS is binding *Activities must show commitment to service, healthcare, and community

NORTHEAST

UNIVERSITY/PROGRAM	DEADLINE	MIN SAT, ACT, & GPA	OTHER REQUIREMENTS
ROCHESTER UNIV. 500 JOSEPH C. WILSON BLVD. ROCHESTER, NY 14627 REMS - ROCHESTER EARLY MEDICAL SCHOLARS	*Apply through CA or Coalition by Nov 15. Indicate interest in REMS on app. *Notification of finalist status in Jan. *Interview with School of Med req. of finalists in Feb. *Final REMS dec. in April.	SAT ERW+M - 1450 admit avg. 3.95 uwt GPA Though now test optional, past SAT II score req.: Bio or Chem, and Math I or II (700+ admit avg.)	They are now test-optional *Strong REMS applicants rank in the top 3% of H.S. class. *No MCAT req. *Approx. 1000 apply; 10-12 admitted *50 invited to interview
YESHIVA UNIV. 500 W 185TH ST. NEW YORK, NY 10033	*Apply by Nov. 1 *Indicate interest in UAS prog. on Yeshiva app *Must be accepted by Yeshiva *Yeshiva recs. candidates to Upstate *Upstate screens candidates and invites some to interview *Upstate sends decs. & sends conditional admit letter	Min ERW+M - 1360 Min ACT - 29 GPA min - 90% avg.	*Up to 5 students admitted *MCAT not req *Acceptance into UAS is binding *Activities must show commitment to service, healthcare, and community

ADELPHI UNIVERSITY W/ UPSTATE BA/BS/BFA-MD PROGRAM (8-YEAR)

Medical School: SUNY Upstate Medical University
750 E Adams St, Syracuse, NY 13210
Undergraduate: Adelphi University
1 South Ave, Garden City, NY 11530
Program Information:
https://www.upstate.edu/com/admissions/options/bs-md.php
Request for Information Form:
https://admissions.adelphi.edu/contact-us/request-info/
Phone: (516) 877-3140
Contact Bob Schwartz, E-Mail: *rschwartz@adelphi.ed*
Additional Combined Programs: BA/BS-DO at PCOM, BA/BS-DO at LECOM, BA/BS-DDS at NYU, BS/OD at SUNY,
International Students: Not listed

COST OF ATTENDANCE

Tuition and Fees: $38,470
Additional Expenses with Room and Board: $12,260
Total: $50,730

Financial Aid: Merit-based and need-based scholarships and grants are available. Some require an application.

ADDITIONAL INFORMATION

Adelphi University is a private university established in 1896. Upstate Medical University was originally founded in 1834, known as Geneva Medical College. After disbanding in 1871, it became a part of Syracuse University. In 1950, Adelphi sold the medical school to SUNY.

In partnership with SUNY Upstate, Adelphi offers an 8-year combined BA/BS/BFA and MD Accelerated Scholars Program (ASP), open for high school seniors to apply. Only 5 students are admitted into this program each year. The MCAT is not required.

Students interested in applying to the ASP must meet the following requirements:

1. Minimum 90% average or 3.50 GPA
2. SAT minimum of 1360 (CR&M) or
3. ACT minimum of 29
4. Extra-curricular activities indicating demonstrated commitment to service in the healthcare setting
5. Meet all requirements for Adelphi's BA, BS or BFA program

Continuing Requirements for admission to SUNY Upstate:

1. Unofficial transcripts sent by the student to Upstate at the end of each semester
2. Complete all Adelphi graduation major requirements
3. Complete certain medical school prerequisite courses
4. No grade lower than a "B" in the medical school prerequisites
5. Minimum 3.50 cumulative GPA and 3.50 science GPA each semester
6. 40 hours of volunteer service, preferably in direct contact with patients or physicians

Adelphi University offers several combined degree programs, open to high school senior applicants and current Adelphi undergraduates. For more information, visit: *https://prepare.adelphi.edu/professional/*

CONNECTICUT

MAINE

MASSACHUSETTS

NEW HAMPSHIRE

NEW JERSEY

NEW YORK

PENNSYLVANIA

RHODE ISLAND

VERMONT

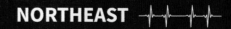

NORTHEAST

CONNECTICUT

MAINE

MASSACHUSETTS

NEW HAMPSHIRE

NEW JERSEY

NEW YORK

PENNSYLVANIA

RHODE ISLAND

VERMONT

ALBANY COLLEGE OF PHARMACY AND HEALTH SCIENCES BS/MD PROGRAM (8-YEAR)

Medical School: SUNY Upstate Medical University
750 E Adams St, Syracuse, NY 13210
Undergraduate: Albany College of Pharmacy and Health Sciences
106 New Scotland Ave, Albany, NY 12208
Program Information:
https://www.upstate.edu/com/admissions/options/bs-md.php
Request for Information Form: *https://www.acphs.edu/requestinfo*
Phone: (518) 694-7200
Director of Pre-Professional Pathways, Elizabeth Brookins E-Mail:
Elizabeth.Brookins@acphs.edu
Additional Combined Programs: BS/DO at LECOM (3+4 and 4+4), BS/DO at NYIT (3+4 and 4+4), BS/DMD at LECOM (4+4)
International Students: Not listed

COST OF ATTENDANCE

Tuition and Fees: $36,120
Additional Expenses with Room and Board: $11,711
Total: $47,831

Financial Aid: Recommended to apply to outside scholarships and for federal financial aid.

ADDITIONAL INFORMATION

Albany College of Pharmacy and Health Sciences (ACPHS) is a private college established in 1881. The Upstate Accelerated Scholars (UAS) program is for high school students interested in obtaining guaranteed acceptance into SUNY Upstate's MD Program. Students are encouraged to select any major. The MCAT is not required.

Students interested in applying to the UAS program must meet the following requirements:

1. minimum 90% average
2. SAT minimum of 1360 (CR&M) or
3. ACT minimum of 31
4. Extra-curricular activities indicating demonstrated commitment to community service in a healthcare setting

Continuing Requirements for admission to SUNY Upstate:

1. Unofficial transcripts sent by the student to Upstate at the end of each semester
2. Complete all ACPHS graduation major requirements
3. Complete certain medical school prerequisite courses
4. No grade lower than a "B" in the medical school prerequisites
5. Minimum 3.50 cumulative GPA and 3.50 science GPA each semester
6. 40 hours of volunteer service, preferably in direct contact with patients or physicians

BROOKLYN COLLEGE
BA-MD PROGRAM (8-YEAR)

Medical School: SUNY Downstate College of Medicine
450 Clarkson Ave, Brooklyn, NY 11203
Undergraduate: Brooklyn College
2900 Bedford Avenue, Brooklyn, NY 11210
Program Information: *http://www.brooklyn.cuny.edu/web/academics/ honors-academy/programs/ba-md.php*
Request for Information Form: *https://cunybrooklyn.askadmissions. net/emtinterestpage.aspx?ip=freshman*
Phone: (718) 951-5000
E-Mail: *adminqry@brooklyn.cuny.edu*
Additional Combined Programs: N/A
International Students: Not considered
Note: For more information, contact the Director: Dr. Steven B. Silbering

COST OF ATTENDANCE

In-State Tuition and Fees: $6,930
Additional Expenses with Room and Board: $9,870
Total: $16,800

Out-of-State Tuition and Fees: $14,012
Additional Expenses with Room and Board: $21,662 Total: $35,674

Financial Aid: BA-MD students will receive the Brooklyn College Foundation Presidential Scholarship, which provides up to $4,000 annually for four years during undergraduate study. Students may apply for financial aid as well.

ADDITIONAL INFORMATION

This program allows students to choose any major for their undergraduate degree. Out-of-state students are welcome to apply. Brooklyn College does not provide housing for students. However, they have recommended living areas near campus. The estimated cost of room and board for students not living at home is $13,591. Additionally, BA/MD students do not take specialized courses for their program. Instead, they instead take classes with the general population of the college.

BA/MD students are required to complete a minimum of 320 hours of clinical experience in the summer following freshman, sophomore, or junior year of their undergraduate study. The work must be completed within the U.S. Additionally, the student must complete 60 hours of non-medical community service each semester after completing their freshman year.

Students are not allowed to complete the BA degree in 3 years and move into Downstate early, even if all requirements have been completed. Additionally, the AMCAS application must be completed and received no later than November 1 of the student's senior year.

The minimum MCAT score requirement is communicated to the BA/MD student who sits for the exam during that cycle. The current minimum MCAT scores required for the graduating class of 2020 are as follows:

1. Chemical and Physical Foundations of Biological Systems: 127
2. Critical Analysis and Reasoning Skills: 126
3. Biological and Biochemical Foundations of Living Systems: 128
4. Psychological, Social, and Biological Foundations of Behavior: 127
5. Minimum total score requirement: 509

CONNECTICUT

MAINE

MASSACHUSETTS

NEW HAMPSHIRE

NEW JERSEY

NEW YORK

PENNSYLVANIA

RHODE ISLAND

VERMONT

NORTHEAST

CONNECTICUT

MAINE

MASSACHUSETTS

NEW HAMPSHIRE

NEW JERSEY

NEW YORK

PENNSYLVANIA

RHODE ISLAND

VERMONT

CUNY/CCNY SOPHIE DAVIS SCHOOL OF BIOMEDICAL EDUCATION BS/MD PROGRAM (7-YEAR)

Medical School: CUNY School of Medicine
Harris Hall, 160 Convent Avenue, New York, NY 10031
Undergraduate: The City College of New York
160 Convent Ave, New York, NY 10031
Program Information: *https://www.ccny.cuny.edu/csom/sophie-davis-biomedical-education-program*
Request for Information Form: *https://www.ccny.cuny.edu/cps/request-information*
Phone: (212) 650-7718
E-Mail: *sdadmissions@med.cuny.edu*
Additional Combined Programs: N/A
International Students: Not listed

COST OF ATTENDANCE

In-State Undergrad Tuition and Fees: $6,930
Medical School Tuition and Fees: $40,710

Out-of-State Undergrad Tuition and Fees: $14,012
Estimated Housing costs: $19,500

Financial Aid: Federal finance options are available.

ADDITIONAL INFORMATION

Established in 1973, the CUNY School of Medicine was created to provide healthcare to underserved communities. The university is ranked within the top 5 for recruitment of African American students. The student to faculty ratio is 12:1.

A significant factor that is considered is the applicant's interest in becoming a primary care doctor in an underserved area. This program contains a specially designed curriculum and courses for the students.

All applicants are required to create a Sophie Davis VIP Interest Page to become a VIP member. There are two, separate applications to submit:

1. The online application to the Sophie Davis Biomedical Education Program/CUNY School of Medicine and
2. The general CUNY online application or the CUNY Macaulay Honors College application.

This university also offers the Health Professions Mentorship Program to allow high school students to learn more about the field of medicine and conduct a community-based project. This is a two-year program that is conducted in two, 3-week summer sessions to follow the student's sophomore and junior years of high school.

HOFSTRA UNIVERSITY
BS-BA/MD PROGRAM (8-YEAR)

Medical School: Zucker School of Medicine at Hofstra/Northwell
500 Hofstra University, Hempstead, NY 11549
Undergraduate: Hofstra University
1000 Hempstead Turnpike, Hempstead, NY 11549
Program Information:
https://www.hofstra.edu/admission/adm_4plus4.html
Request for Information Form:
https://www.hofstra.edu/graduate/inquiry.html
Phone: (516) 463-6700
E-Mail: *BSMD@hofstra.edu*
Additional Combined Programs:
BS/MS for Physician Assistant Studies
International Students: Considered

COST OF ATTENDANCE

Tuition and Fees: $46,450
Additional Expenses with Room and Board: $17,504
Total: $63,954

Financial Aid: Recommended to apply for scholarships and federal financial aid.

ADDITIONAL INFORMATION

Hofstra University is a private institution established in 1935. Their 4+4 BS-BA/MD program allows students to enjoy a typical college experience during their undergraduate study. Students are in classes with the general population. BS-BA/MD students are encouraged to choose any of the undergraduate majors if pre-med requirements are fulfilled.

Students must apply during one of Hofstra University's two Early Action deadlines: November 15 or December 15. Expect to see the Hofstra 4+4 Program: BS-BA/MD Application Supplement in your student portal in January. This will only be available for students who have met the eligibility criteria to apply for the program.

Students are admitted into the Donald and Barbara Zucker School of Medicine at Hofstra/Northwell if they fulfill a minimum GPA requirement, course grade requirement, and receive an MCAT score at least in the 80th percentile.

On-campus housing is available for undergraduate and graduate students.

129

CONNECTICUT

MAINE

MASSACHUSETTS

NEW HAMPSHIRE

NEW JERSEY

NEW YORK

PENNSYLVANIA

RHODE ISLAND

VERMONT

NORTHEAST

CONNECTICUT

MAINE

MASSACHUSETTS

NEW HAMPSHIRE

NEW JERSEY

NEW YORK

PENNSYLVANIA

RHODE ISLAND

VERMONT

NEW YORK INSTITUTE OF TECHNOLOGY BS/ DO PROGRAM (7-YEAR)

Medical School: New York Institute of Technology College of Osteopathic Medicine
101 Northern Blvd, Glen Head, NY 11545
Undergraduate: New York Institute of Technology
1855 Broadway (at 61st St.), New York, NY 10023
Program Information: *https://www.nyit.edu/arts_and_sciences/ osteopathic_medicine_bsdo_admissions*
Request for Information Form:
https://www.nyit.edu/admissions/inquire/
Program Director, Prof. Halina Diener Phone: (516) 686-3887
Program Director, Prof. Halina Diener E-Mail: *hdiener@nyit.edu*
Admissions E-Mail: *admissions@nyit.edu*
Additional Combined Programs:
BS/MS for Physician Assistant Studies
International Students: Not considered

COST OF ATTENDANCE

Tuition and Fees: $39,900
Additional Expenses with Room and Board: $12,220
Total: $52,120

Financial Aid: Scholarships available, no separate application required. Require completion of FAFSA.

ADDITIONAL INFORMATION

New York Institute of Technology is a private research school established in 1955. The accelerated BS/DO program is available to first-year applicants. This program is not open to international students. Students earn their BS degree after successful completion of the first year of medical school. NYIT has two campuses, one in Manhattan and one in Old Westbury (Long Island).

First-year applicant requirements are as follow:

1. Minimum combined (CR + M) SAT score of 1270 or
2. Minimum ACT score of 28
3. High class standing
4. 2 Letters of Recommendation
5. 300 to 350-word essay on their desire to work in osteopathic medicine

After three years in the program, students are admitted to the DO program at the College of Osteopathic Medicine so long as they meet the following criteria:

1. Maintain a cumulative and semester GPA of 3.5
2. MCAT score within median range of previous entering class
3. Letters of recommendation from NYIT's departmental BS/DO committee
4. Application package submitted by Feb 1 (must include MCAT)
5. Successful interview from NYIT COM

PURCHASE COLLEGE
BA/BS/BM/BFA-MD PROGRAM (8-YEAR)

Medical School: SUNY Upstate Medical University
750 E Adams St, Syracuse, NY 13210
Undergraduate: Purchase College
735 Anderson Hill Rd, Purchase, NY 10577
Program Information:
https://www.purchase.edu/academics/school-of-natural-social-sciences/premedical-studies/suny-upstate-partnerships/
Request for Information Form:
https://admission.purchase.edu/register/inquiryform
Phone: (914) 251-6300
E-Mail: *admissions@purchase.edu*
Additional Combined Programs: Post-Bacc
International Students: Not listed

COST OF ATTENDANCE

In-State Tuition and Fees: $8,953
Additional Expenses with Room and Board: $19,362
Total: $28,315

Out-of-State Tuition and Fees: $18,863
Additional Expenses with Room and Board: $19,362
Total: $38,225

Financial Aid: Scholarships are available. Applicants are automatically considered for some scholarships.

ADDITIONAL INFORMATION

State University of New York at Purchase is a public college established in 1967. In partnership with SUNY Upstate, high school seniors may apply to the Upstate Accelerated Scholars Program (UAS). A goal of this program is to encourage diversity and allow students of various academic backgrounds a pathway to medical school. Students are encouraged to select a major outside of the sciences. Students who choose to major in science will still be considered.

This program is binding. Additionally, the MCAT is not required and no further interviewing is required.

Students interested in applying to the UAS program must meet the following requirements:

1. Minimum 90% average
2. SAT minimum of 1360 (CR&M) or
3. ACT minimum of 29
4. Extra-curricular activities indicating demonstrated commitment to community service in healthcare setting

Continuing Requirements for admission to SUNY Upstate:

1. Complete all Purchase major requirements
2. Complete certain medical school prerequisite courses
3. No grade lower than a "B" in the medical school prerequisites
4. Minimum 3.50 cumulative GPA and 3.50 science GPA each semester
5. 40 hours of volunteer service, preferably in direct contact with patients or physicians

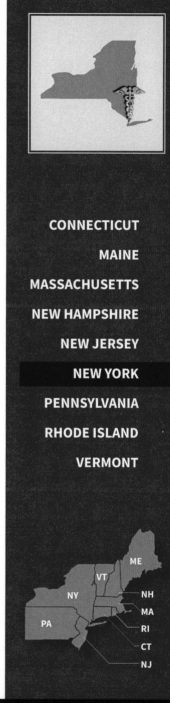

CONNECTICUT

MAINE

MASSACHUSETTS

NEW HAMPSHIRE

NEW JERSEY

NEW YORK

PENNSYLVANIA

RHODE ISLAND

VERMONT

NORTHEAST

CONNECTICUT

MAINE

MASSACHUSETTS

NEW HAMPSHIRE

NEW JERSEY

NEW YORK

PENNSYLVANIA

RHODE ISLAND

VERMONT

RENSSELAER POLYTECHNIC INSTITUTE BS/MD PROGRAM (7-YEAR)

Medical School: Albany Medical College
43 New Scotland Ave, Albany, NY 12208
Undergraduate: Rensselaer Polytechnic Institute
110 Eighth Street, Troy, NY 12180
Program Information: *https://admissions.rpi.edu/undergraduate-admissions/accelerated-combined-programs*
Request for Information Form:
https://apply-undergrad.rpi.edu/register/information_request
Phone: (518) 276-6000
E-Mail: *admissions@rpi.edu*
Additional Combined Programs: N/A
International Students: Not considered

COST OF ATTENDANCE

Tuition and Fees: $54,000
Additional Expenses with Room and Board: $19,816
Total: $73,816

Financial Aid: Rensselaer merit-based scholarships are available.

ADDITIONAL INFORMATION

Rensselaer Polytechnic Institute's Physician-Scientist Program allows students to earn their B.S. and M.D. in seven years. This accelerated degree program has been established for over 50 years. This science-based program intensively trains graduate physicians in practice and medical research. Three years are spent at Rensselaer and four years at Albany Medical College (AMC). Students enrolled are not allowed to dual or double major, given the accelerated track. A laptop is required to complete coursework. There is no MCAT requirement.

This program utilizes an integrated approach using organ systems to understand the relationship between knowledge and problem-solving. Case presentations and patients are seen throughout all years of medical school. Clinical experience occurs during the third and fourth years. A patient-centered professional career is emphasized as well, with courses in the ethical and legal aspects of care, the health care system, and patient interviewing skills.

ROCHESTER INSTITUTE OF TECHNOLOGY BS/MD PROGRAM (8-YEAR)

Medical School: SUNY Upstate Medical University
750 E Adams St, Syracuse, NY 13210
Undergraduate: Rochester Institute of Technology
1 Lomb Memorial Dr., Rochester, NY 14623
Program Information:
https://www.upstate.edu/com/admissions/options/bs-md.php
Request for Information Form: *https://join.rit.edu/register/ugrd_info*
Phone: (585) 475-6012
Dr. Douglas Merrill, Director of Premedical and Health Professions Advisory Program, E-Mail: *douglas.merrill@rit.edu*
Additional Combined Programs: yes, through LECOM
International Students: Not listed

COST OF ATTENDANCE

Tuition and Fees: $50,564
Additional Expenses with Room and Board: $16,740
Total: $67,304

Financial Aid: Merit-based scholarships and grants available.

ADDITIONAL INFORMATION

Rochester Institute of Technology (RIT) is a private research university founded in 1829. In partnership with SUNY Upstate, high school seniors may apply to their RIT-Upstate Accelerated Scholars Program (RIT-Upstate ASP). A goal of this program is to encourage diversity and allow students of various academic backgrounds a pathway to medical school. The RIT-Upstate ASP does not require students to enter into a specific academic program, although the "program chosen should contain enough flexibility in the curriculum to incorporate the required science courses within four years."

This program is binding. Additionally, the MCAT is not required.

Students interested in applying to the RIT-Upstate ASP must meet the following requirements:

1. High GPA with minimum 90% average
2. SAT minimum of 1360 (CR&M) or
3. ACT minimum of 29
4. Extra-curricular activities indicating demonstrated commitment to community service in healthcare setting

Continuing Requirements for admission to SUNY Upstate:

1. Complete all RIT major requirements
2. Complete certain medical school prerequisite courses
3. No grade lower than a "B" in the medical school prerequisites
4. Minimum 3.50 cumulative GPA and 3.50 science GPA each semester
5. 40 hours of volunteer service, preferably in direct contact with patients or physicians

CONNECTICUT

MAINE

MASSACHUSETTS

NEW HAMPSHIRE

NEW JERSEY

NEW YORK

PENNSYLVANIA

RHODE ISLAND

VERMONT

NORTHEAST

CONNECTICUT

MAINE

MASSACHUSETTS

NEW HAMPSHIRE

NEW JERSEY

NEW YORK

PENNSYLVANIA

RHODE ISLAND

VERMONT

SIENA COLLEGE WITH ALBANY MEDICAL COLLEGE
BA/MD PROGRAM (8-YEAR)

Medical School: Albany Medical College
43 New Scotland Ave, Albany, NY 12208
Undergraduate: Siena College
515 Loudon Road, Loudonville, NY 12211
Program Information:
https://www.siena.edu/programs/albany-medical-college-program/ or
*https://www.amc.edu/academic/Undergraduate_Admissions/special_
programs.cfm*
Request for Information Form: *https://www.siena.edu/offices/
admissions/request-info/*
Phone: (518) 783-2300
E-Mail: *admissions@siena.edu*
Additional Combined Programs: N/A
International Students: Not considered
Note: For additional information, contact Marie Nocella at
mnocella@siena.edu

COST OF ATTENDANCE

Tuition and Fees: $39,200
Additional Expenses with Room and Board: $20,699
Total: $59,899

Financial Aid: Scholarships and federal financial aid recommended.

ADDITIONAL INFORMATION

Siena College is a private Franciscan liberal arts college. The Albany
Medical College (AMC) BA/MD program emphasizes demonstrated
service to the community. Each summer, Siena-AMC students embark
on the Summer of Service, where they volunteer in a part of the world
with demonstrated need. Students may stay in the U.S. or go abroad
to assist in orphanages/homes, medical clinics, youth programs, and
more. Grants are provided for travel expenses.

Only U.S. citizens or permanent residents may apply. High school
seniors are eligible to apply for this program. Submit an application
to Siena College. Applicants who are eligible will be forwarded to
Albany Medical College and then sent a supplemental application to
complete. Invitations for an interview are extended to semi-finalists.

Siena College has several partnerships with various medical schools.
For more information on these programs, visit: *https://www.siena.edu/
programs/health-professions/affiliation/*

ST. BONAVENTURE UNIVERSITY W/ GWU BS/ BA-MD PROGRAM (8-YEAR)

Medical School: George Washington University Medical School
2300 Eye Street, NW Washington, D.C., 20037
Undergraduate: St. Bonaventure University
3261 W State St, St Bonaventure, NY 14778
Program Information:
https://www.sbu.edu/academics/pre-medicine/franciscan-health-care-professions-program/sbu-gw-dual-admit-program-in-medicine-(m-d-)
Request for Information Form:
https://www.sbu.edu/admission-aid/request-information
Phone: (716) 375-2000
E-Mail: *fhcp@sbu.edu*
Additional Combined Programs: BS/BA-DO (4+4 and 3+4), BS/DMD (4+4), BS/PharmD (3+4 and 3+3), BS/DPT (3+3), BS/DPT (4+3)
International Students: Considered

COST OF ATTENDANCE

Tuition and Fees: $35,450
Additional Expenses with Room and Board: $19,082
Total: $54,532

Financial Aid: More than 95% of students receive financial assistance. Applying for scholarships and federal aid is recommended.

ADDITIONAL INFORMATION

St. Bonaventure University (SBU) is a private, Franciscan university that was established in 1858. Upon successful completion of the SBU bachelor's degree, students attend George Washington University Medical School. Requirements to transition into the MD program are as follow: minimum 3.60 overall GPA, no C grade or lower in any science courses, MCAT scores, and participation in medically-related experiences.

SBU has an active campus. 75% of students (96% of freshman) live on campus. Housing is available for students in all years. Meal plans are required for students living in freshman housing.

At George Washington University Medical School, students have the opportunity to learn in the GW Hospital in Washington, D.C. Students are paired with primary care physicians for an apprenticeship where they learn clinical skills. The curriculum engages students in early Clinical Clerkships to promote active learning. Additionally, the Office of Student Professional Enrichment (OSPE) allows students to engage in a variety of experiences, such as interning on Capitol Hill or researching at the National Institutes of Health (NIH).

CONNECTICUT

MAINE

MASSACHUSETTS

NEW HAMPSHIRE

NEW JERSEY

NEW YORK

PENNSYLVANIA

RHODE ISLAND

VERMONT

NORTHEAST

CONNECTICUT

MAINE

MASSACHUSETTS

NEW HAMPSHIRE

NEW JERSEY

NEW YORK

PENNSYLVANIA

RHODE ISLAND

VERMONT

STONY BROOK
BA/MD SCHOLARS PROGRAM (8-YEAR)

Medical School: Stony Brook University School of Medicine
101 Nicolls Road, Stony Brook, NY 11794
Undergraduate: SUNY Stony Brook University
100 Nicolls Road, Stony Brook, NY 11794
Program Information:
https://www.stonybrook.edu/commcms/wise/college/scholars.php
Request for Information Form: *https://www.stonybrook.edu/
undergraduate-admissions/contact/request-information/*
Phone: (631) 632-6868
E-Mail: *enroll@stonybrook.edu*
Additional Combined Programs: BA/DDS
International Students: Not considered

COST OF ATTENDANCE

In-State Tuition and Fees: $7,221
Additional Expenses with Room and Board: $9,082
Total: $16,303

Out-of-State Tuition and Fees: $16,056
Additional Expenses with Room and Board: $9,082
Total: $25,138

Financial Aid: Federal financial assistance and scholarships
recommended.

ADDITIONAL INFORMATION

Stony Brook's Scholars for Medicine is a 4+4 BA/MD program offered to
high school students. Students participate in medical school classes
and activities during their undergraduate studies. Admission into
the medical school requires a minimum 3.40 GPA and above average
MCAT scores.

At Stony Brook, only select students from the Honors College, WISE
Program, or University Scholars Program are given an opportunity to
complete the 4+4 track. To attend Stony Brook University's School of
Medicine, students must complete the Honors program of study, all
pre-medical coursework, maintain a minimum 3.2 science GPA and
3.4 cumulative GPA, and complete the MCAT with an acceptable score.
The MCAT score is determined by the School of Medicine. Stony Brook
also offers a Scholars for Dental Medicine program. Students are not
allowed to apply to both Scholars programs.

SUNY GENESEO BS/DO PROGRAM (7-YEAR)

Medical School: New York Institute of Technology College of Osteopathic Medicine (NYITCOM)
101 Northern Blvd, Glen Head, NY 11545
Undergraduate: SUNY Geneseo
1 College Cir, Geneseo, NY 14454
Program Information:
https://www.geneseo.edu/premed/3-4-osteopathic-medicine-program
Request for Information Form: *https://connect.geneseo.edu/ register/?id=1533ec14-09ac-4d1d-a0be-676baabf786a*
Program Advisor, Jennifer Haines Phone: (585) 245-6467
Admissions: (866) 245-5211
Program Advisor, Jennifer Haines E-Mail: *premed@geneseo.edu*
Additional Combined Programs: N/A
International Students: Not listed

COST OF ATTENDANCE

In-State Tuition and Fees: $8,877
Additional Expenses with Room and Board: $16,415
Total: $25,292

Out-of-State Tuition and Fees: $18,787
Additional Expenses with Room and Board: $16,415
Total: $35,202

Financial Aid: New students are automatically considered for scholarships. Current students are able to apply for scholarships through Academic Works.

ADDITIONAL INFORMATION

SUNY Geneseo is a public university established in 1871. In partnership with the New York Institute of Technology College of Osteopathic Medicine (NYITCOM), SUNY Geneseo offers a 7-year BS/DO program for high school applicants. Students applying for this program must declare themselves as Biology majors. After successful completion of the first year at NYCOM, students receive their B.S. or B.A. degree. Eligible applicants must have the following:

1. Combination SAT score of 1200+ or
2. ACT composite of 28+
3. High school average of 90% or better

Students are accepted to NYITCOM when the following requirements are met:

1. Maintain a 3.5 GPA each semester with one semester grace period
2. Complete all Biology degree coursework requirements
3. MCAT score at or higher than average MCAT of previous year's entering class
4. Recommendation by SUNY Geneseo PreMed Committee
5. Interview with NYITCOM

CONNECTICUT

MAINE

MASSACHUSETTS

NEW HAMPSHIRE

NEW JERSEY

NEW YORK

PENNSYLVANIA

RHODE ISLAND

VERMONT

NORTHEAST

CONNECTICUT

MAINE

MASSACHUSETTS

NEW HAMPSHIRE

NEW JERSEY

NEW YORK

PENNSYLVANIA

RHODE ISLAND

VERMONT

SUNY NEW PALTZ
BA/DO PROGRAM (7-YEAR)

Medical School: Touro College of Osteopathic Medicine
60 Prospect Ave., Middletown, NY 10940
Undergraduate: SUNY New Paltz
1 Hawk Dr., New Paltz, NY 12561
Program Information:
https://www.newpaltz.edu/pre-health/opto.html
Request for Information Form:
https://admissions.newpaltz.edu/register/inquiry
Phone: (845) 257-3200
E-Mail: *admissions@newpaltz.edu*
Additional Combined Programs:
BS/OD (7-year), BS/DO with NYITCOM (7-year)
International Students: Not listed

COST OF ATTENDANCE

In-State Tuition and Fees: $8,720
Additional Expenses with Room and Board: $18,350
Total: $27,070

Out-of-State Tuition and Fees: $18,267
Additional Expenses with Room and Board: $18,350
Total: $36,617

Financial Aid: Apply for scholarships through SUNY New Paltz and externally. Federal financial assistance recommended.

ADDITIONAL INFORMATION

SUNY New Paltz is a public university founded in 1828. In partnership with Touro College of Osteopathic Medicine, SUNY New Paltz offers high school applicants the opportunity to apply for a 7-year BS/DO program. Typically, students major in one of the sciences. However, there is a degree of flexibility when it comes to the choice of a major. Three years are spent at SUNY New Paltz, where students participate in clinical mentoring with local physicians and they attend the Pre-Osteopathic Seminar.

Continuing requirements to enter Touro College of Osteopathic Medicine are as follow:

1. MCAT is taken at the end of the second year with minimum score determined by prior entering class
2. Maintain GPA (3.50 every semester)
3. Positive recommendation from the Program Director

If students meet these criteria, they are given an interview. Upon successful completion of this interview, they are guaranteed a streamlined process to TouroCOM. Students receive their bachelor's degree at the end of the first year at TouroCOM.

SUNY OLD WESTBURY
BS/DO PROGRAM (7-YEAR)

Medical School: New York Institute of Technology College of Osteopathic Medicine (NYITCOM)
101 Northern Blvd, Glen Head, NY 11545
Undergraduate: SUNY Old Westbury
223 Store Hill Road Campus Center H-310, Old Westbury, NY 11568
Program Information: *https://www.oldwestbury.edu/academics/ offerings/bsdo-osteopathic-medicine*
Request for Information Form:
https://www.oldwestbury.edu/admissions/info-request
Phone: (516) 876-3073
E-Mail: *enroll@oldwestbury.edu*
Additional Combined Programs: N/A
International Students: Considered

COST OF ATTENDANCE

In-State Tuition and Fees: $7,070
Additional Expenses with Room and Board: $12,708
Total: $19,778

Out-of-State Tuition and Fees: $16,980 Additional Expenses with Room and Board: $12,708
Total: $29,688

Financial Aid: Merit-based and need-based scholarships available. Students must submit a separate application to be considered.

ADDITIONAL INFORMATION

SUNY College at Old Westbury is a public college established in 1965. In partnership with New York Institute of Technology College of Osteopathic Medicine (NYITCOM), SUNY College at Old Westbury offers a 7-year BS/DO program for high school applicants. Students in this program receive their bachelor's degree upon successful completion of their first year at NYITCOM. Students are not required to submit an AACOMAS application.

Students are assured admission to NYITCOM so long as they meet the following criteria:

1. Maintain a minimum 3.50 GPA
2. Provide adequate scores on MCAT
3. Successful interview with NYITCOM
4. Complete pre-medical science coursework within first three years.

CONNECTICUT

MAINE

MASSACHUSETTS

NEW HAMPSHIRE

NEW JERSEY

NEW YORK

PENNSYLVANIA

RHODE ISLAND

VERMONT

NORTHEAST

CONNECTICUT

MAINE

MASSACHUSETTS

NEW HAMPSHIRE

NEW JERSEY

NEW YORK

PENNSYLVANIA

RHODE ISLAND

VERMONT

SUNY POLYTECHNIC INSTITUTE
BS/BA-MD PROGRAM (8-YEAR)

Medical School: SUNY Upstate Medical University
750 E Adams St, Syracuse, NY 13210
Undergraduate: SUNY Polytechnic Institute
100 Seymour Ave, Utica, NY 13502
Program Information:
https://www.upstate.edu/com/admissions/options/bs-md.php
Request for Information Form:
https://sunypoly.edu/admissions/request-more-information.html
Phone: (315) 792-7500
Gina Liscio, Director of Admissions, E-Mail:
gina.liscio@sunypoly.edu
Additional Combined Programs: N/A
International Students: Not listed

COST OF ATTENDANCE

In-State Tuition and Fees: $8,533
Additional Expenses with Room and Board: $8,278
Total: $16,811

Out-of-State Tuition and Fees: $18,443
Additional Expenses with Room and Board: $8,278
Total: $26,721

Financial Aid: Scholarships available. It is recommended that students apply for federal financial aid.

ADDITIONAL INFORMATION

SUNY Polytechnic Institute is a public university established in 1966. In partnership with SUNY Upstate, high school seniors may apply to their Accelerated Scholars Program (ASP). A goal of this program is to encourage diversity and allow students of various academic backgrounds a pathway to medical school. The ASP encourages students to apply to any academic program, although the "program chosen should contain enough flexibility in the curriculum to incorporate the required science courses within four years."

This program is binding. Additionally, the MCAT is not required.

Students interested in applying to the ASP must meet the following requirements:

1. Minimum 90% average or 3.50 GPA
2. SAT minimum of 1360 (CR&M) or
3. ACT minimum of 29
4. Extra-curricular activities indicating demonstrated commitment to community service in healthcare setting

Continuing Requirements for admission to SUNY Upstate:

1. Complete all SUNY Poly major requirements
2. Complete certain medical school prerequisite courses
3. No grade lower than a "B" in the medical school prerequisites
4. Minimum 3.50 cumulative GPA and 3.50 science GPA each semester
5. 40 hours of volunteer service, preferably in direct contact with patients or physicians

UNION COLLEGE LEADERSHIP IN MEDICINE BS/MS-MBA/MD PROGRAM (8-YEAR)

Medical School: Albany Medical School (AMC)
47 New Scotland Avenue, Albany, NY 12208
Graduate: Clarkson University-Capital Region Campus
80 Nott Terrace, Schenectady, NY 12308
Undergraduate: Union College – 807 Union St, Schenectady, NY 12308
Program Information: *https://www.union.edu/leadership-medicine*
Request for Information Form:
https://www.union.edu/admissions/contact
Phone: (518) 388-6112
E-Mail: *admissions@union.edu*
Additional Combined Programs: N/A
International Students: Not considered

COST OF ATTENDANCE

Tuition and Fees: $55,290 Additional Expenses with Room and Board: $16,095 Total: $71,385

Financial Aid: Union College merit-based and need-based scholarships available

ADDITIONAL INFORMATION

Union College offers a Leadership in Medicine (LIM) Health Management program. This program offers a combined bachelor's, master's, and doctoral degree. Students receive a B.S. from Union College, an M.S. or M.B.A. in Health Care Management from Clarkson University-Capital Region Campus, and an M.D. from Albany Medical College (AMC). Three degrees are obtained in eight years. Additionally, as undergraduates, students are required to pursue an Interdisciplinary (ID) Bachelor's degree: both a science/math major and social science/humanities major, which allows them to learn about areas outside of the sciences. LIM students must maintain a minimum cumulative GPA of 3.5 since they are dually enrolled as undergraduates at Union College and graduates at Clarkson University. There is no MCAT required.

This program offers students an understanding of the business of healthcare. Matriculated students are equipped to be leaders in transforming healthcare delivery. Students who opt for the M.S. in Healthcare Management do not need to pay any additional costs beyond undergraduate tuition. Students who choose the 16-course M.B.A. in Healthcare Management program need to pay for four classes beyond undergraduate tuition (approximately $14,000).

Additionally, LIM students have a term abroad/international experience requirement. Students may fulfill this in the following ways:

1. Complete a full term abroad
2. Complete the National Health Systems summer program
3. Complete a 3-week mini-term over the school break
4. Complete an Independent Study Abroad experience
5. Complete a foreign experience that does not fit into these categories

141

CONNECTICUT

MAINE

MASSACHUSETTS

NEW HAMPSHIRE

NEW JERSEY

NEW YORK

PENNSYLVANIA

RHODE ISLAND

VERMONT

NORTHEAST

CONNECTICUT

MAINE

MASSACHUSETTS

NEW HAMPSHIRE

NEW JERSEY

NEW YORK

PENNSYLVANIA

RHODE ISLAND

VERMONT

UNIVERSITY AT ALBANY
SUNY BS/MD PROGRAM (8-YEAR)

Medical School: SUNY Upstate Medical University
750 E Adams St, Syracuse, NY 13210
Undergraduate: University at Albany - SUNY
1400 Washington Ave, Albany, NY 12222
Program Information: *https://www.albany.edu/advisement/*
guaranteed-entrance-to-upstate-college-of-medicine.shtml
Request for Information Form:
https://admissions.albany.edu/register/info
Phone: (518) 442-5435
Contact Matthew Narode, E-Mail: *mnarode@albany.edu*
Additional Combined Programs: N/A
International Students: Not listed

COST OF ATTENDANCE

In-State Tuition and Fees: $10,236
Additional Expenses with Room and Board: $14,010
Total: $24,246

Out-of-State Tuition and Fees: $27,616
Additional Expenses with Room and Board: $14,010
Total: $41,626

Financial Aid: Merit-based scholarships available for first-year students. Presidential Scholarship is available.

ADDITIONAL INFORMATION

The State University of New York at Albany is a public research university established in 1844. In partnership with SUNY Upstate, high school seniors may apply to their Guaranteed Entrance Program (GEP). A goal of this program is to encourage diversity and allow students of various academic backgrounds a pathway to medical school. The GEP encourages students to apply to any academic program, although the "program chosen should contain enough flexibility in the curriculum to incorporate the required science courses within four year." Approximately 10 students will be accepted.

This program is binding. Additionally, the MCAT is not required.

Students interested in applying to the ASP must meet the following requirements:
1. Minimum 90% average
2. SAT minimum of 1360 (CR&M) or
3. ACT minimum of 29
4. Extra-curricular activities indicating demonstrated commitment to community service in healthcare setting

Continuing Requirements for admission to SUNY Upstate:
1. Complete all University at Albany major requirements
2. Complete certain medical school prerequisite courses
3. No grade lower than a "B" in the medical school prerequisites
4. Minimum 3.50 cumulative GPA and 3.50 science GPA each semester
5. 40 hours of volunteer service, preferably in direct contact with patients or physicians

ROCHESTER UNIVERSITY REMS
BA/BS + MD PROGRAM (8-YEAR)

Medical School: Rochester University School of Medicine and Dentistry
601 Elmwood Ave, Rochester, NY 14642
Undergraduate: Rochester University
500 Joseph C. Wilson Blvd., Rochester, NY 14627
Program Information:
https://enrollment.rochester.edu/combined-degree-programs/rems/
Request for Information Form:
https://admissions.enrollment.rochester.edu/register/request
Phone: (585) 275-3221
E-Mail: *admit@admissions.rochester.edu*
Additional Combined Programs: N/A
International Students: Not listed

COST OF ATTENDANCE

Tuition and Fees: $57,188
Additional Expenses with Room and Board: $20,854
Total: $78,042

Financial Aid: Scholarships and federal aid assistance available.

ADDITIONAL INFORMATION

The Rochester Early Medical Scholars (REMS) program was established in 1991. It allows students admission to the University's School of Medicine and Dentistry upon successful completion of the student's bachelor's degree, pre-med courses, and minimum GPA requirement. This program allows exemption from the MCAT.

Although the University of Rochester has an optional testing policy, it is highly recommended to submit test scores for the REMS program. Students can obtain a diverse undergraduate experience by being able to choose his or her major. There is also a first-year on-campus housing requirement. On-campus housing is available during all years.

As with any BS/MD program, REMS suggests that students take challenging courses, a rigorous science/math course load, perform exceptionally well in high school (strong applicants have 3.95 unweighted GPA and rank in top 3%), submit their standardized tests, have substantial medical experience, and be involved in non-medical activities.

CONNECTICUT

MAINE

MASSACHUSETTS

NEW HAMPSHIRE

NEW JERSEY

NEW YORK

PENNSYLVANIA

RHODE ISLAND

VERMONT

NORTHEAST

CONNECTICUT

MAINE

MASSACHUSETTS

NEW HAMPSHIRE

NEW JERSEY

NEW YORK

PENNSYLVANIA

RHODE ISLAND

VERMONT

YESHIVA UNIVERSITY
BS/BA-MD PROGRAM (8-YEAR)

Medical School: SUNY Upstate Medical University
750 E Adams St, Syracuse, NY 13210
Undergraduate: Yeshiva University
500 W 185th St, New York, NY 10033
Program Information:
https://www.upstate.edu/com/admissions/options/bs-md.php
Contact Information: *https://www.yu.edu/admissions/contact*
Phone: (212) 960-5400
Lolita Wood-Hill, Executive Director of Pre-Professional Advising Programs, E-Mail: *woodhill@yu.edu*
Additional Combined Programs: for current Yeshiva undergraduates only, visit: *https://www.yu.edu/gradpath*
International Students: Not listed

COST OF ATTENDANCE

Tuition and Fees: $46,475
Additional Expenses with Room and Board: $12,750
Total: $59,225

Financial Aid: Students in the Honors Programs receive scholarships. Additional scholarships are available.

ADDITIONAL INFORMATION

Yeshiva University is a private research university established in 1886. Its religious affiliation is Modern Orthodox Judaism. In partnership with SUNY Upstate, high school seniors may apply to their Upstate Accelerated Scholars (UAS) Program. A goal of this program is to encourage diversity and allow students of various academic backgrounds a pathway to medical school. The UAS encourages students to apply to any academic program, although the "program chosen should contain enough flexibility in the curriculum to incorporate the required science courses within four year."

This program is binding. Additionally, the MCAT is not required.

Students interested in applying to the UAS must meet the following requirements:

1. Minimum 90% average
2. SAT minimum of 1360 (CR&M) or
3. ACT minimum of 29
4. Extra-curricular activities indicating demonstrated commitment to community service in healthcare setting

Continuing Requirements for admission to SUNY Upstate:

1. Complete all Yeshiva University major requirements
2. Complete certain medical school prerequisite courses
3. No grade lower than a "B" in the medical school prerequisites
4. Minimum 3.50 cumulative GPA and 3.50 science GPA each semester
5. 40 hours of volunteer service, preferably in direct contact with patients or physicians

Pennsylvania

10 *Programs* | **1** *State*

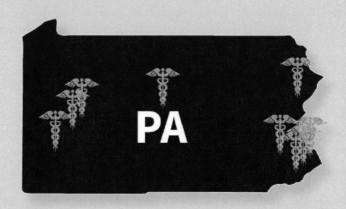

UNIVERSITY/PROGRAM	DEADLINE	MIN SAT, ACT, & GPA	OTHER REQUIREMENTS
DREXEL UNIV. **3141 CHESTNUT ST.** **PHILADELPHIA, PA** **19104**	*Apply by Nov. 1 via CA or Coalition *College of Med Suppl App also due Nov. 1 *Interview notification - late Jan and conducted in-person Feb./March. Interviews *College of Med notifies applicant of dec. via mail in late March	Min ERW+M - 1420 Min ACT - 31 SAT II strongly rec., pref. in science GPA min - 3.50	*Must be a U.S. citizen or perm. *Freshman admission only *2 letters of rec req. - H.S. counselor one from a science teacher *MCAT req.

UNIVERSITY/PROGRAM	DEADLINE	MIN SAT, ACT, & GPA	OTHER REQUIREMENTS
DUQUESNE UNIV. 600 FORBES AVE. PITTSBURGH, PA 15282 PMHPP – PRE-MEDICAL AND HEALTH PROFESSIONS PROGRAM	*Must apply to Duquesne and LECOM by April 1 *When applying, select academic major and check both PMHPP and LECOM Linkage boxes *For osteopathic medicine only *LECOM contacts applicants for interview, generally the summer before matriculation to Duquesne *Provisional acceptance decisions after interviews	Min ERW+M - 1240 Min ACT - 26 (one sitting) GPA min - 3.50	LECOM does not "Superscore" *MCAT may not be req. *LECOM uses an Academic Index Score (AIS) that considers ACT or SAT along with GPA to determine MCAT exemption. *Must be U.S. Citizen
LEHIGH UNIV. 27 MEMORIAL DR. WEST BETHLEHEM, PA 18015 *THE BS/MD PROGRAM HAS BEEN DISCONTINUED, HOWEVER THEY OFFER A BA/DMD AND BA/OD	*2 programs: BA/DMD and BA/OD *Apply directly through Lehigh's Office of Adm. *App due Jan. 1 *Decision date in early April	Min -1350 (BA/MD) 1300 (BA/OD) GPA - Top 10% for both programs	*Applicants for BA/OD prog. may apply as H.S. senior or while attending Lehigh *BA/OD program students must attain score of 320 or above on Optometry Admission Test (OAT) to interview
PENN STATE UNIV, 201 SHIELDS BUILDING, UNIVERSITY PARK, PA 16802	*Apply by Nov. 1 via CA, Coalition App, or MyPennState App *Candidates interview at SKMC at Thomas Jefferson Univ. in Jan. *Admission offers in early Feb. *Accepted applicants may spend a day at Penn State in April alongside prog. students	Min ERW+M - 1470 Min ACT - 32 - Writing score no longer required All scores must be earned on a single test date no later than Sept. of senior year. GPA - Must be in the top 10%	*Must be H.S. senior. *25 students enter each year *No waiting list or transfer students *MCAT req.
ROSEMONT COLLEGE DUAL DEGREE 1400 MONTGOMERY AVE. ROSEMONT, PA 19010	*Apply for the 3+4 BA/DO program during jr yr of undergrad studies *Apply for the 4+4 BA/DO program during sr yr of undergrad studies	Min ERW+M - 1110 Min ACT - 31 Min GPA - 3.40	*For the 3+4 prog., overall and science GPA must be 3.75+. Min MCAT score of 500+ w/125 in each subsection. For the 4+4 prog., overall and science GPA must be 3.25+. MCAT score of 504+ w/126 in each subsection.

NORTHEAST

DIRECT MED PROGRAMS
Pennsylvania

UNIVERSITY/PROGRAM	DEADLINE	MIN SAT, ACT, & GPA	OTHER REQUIREMENTS
TEMPLE UNIV. HEALTH SCHOLARS 1801 N BROAD ST. PHILADELPHIA, PA 19122	*Apply preferably EA to Temple and Pre-Med Health Scholar Program app. after Sept 14 & bef. Nov 1 *Suppl materials for Pre-Med Health Scholar Program must be rec. by mid-Dec. *To be considered for an interview in Feb., you must have already been accepted to Temple and the Honors Program by Jan. (No separate Honors Prog. app) *Interview invitations in mid-Jan. *Interview day in mid-Feb. *Offers extended mid-March to early April	Test-optional Min - 3.80 unwt	*Applicants must apply as a senior in H.S. *Only U.S. citizens and perm. res. may apply *Must have volunteer exp. *2 letters of rec. req. – one from a science teacher and one from health-related shadowing or volunteering *MCAT req.
UNIV. OF PITTSBURGH, GUARANTEED ADMISSIONS 4200 FIFTH AVE PITTSBURGH, PA 15260	*Apply on or before Nov. 15 *Indicate interest in pre-medicine or bioengineering on app *Students will be notified by the School of Med for eligibility to apply for the GAP (guaranteed admissions program) *If selected, then submit supplemental info *Selected students are invited to interview in March *Selection notification - April 15	Min ERW+M - 1490 Min ACT - 34 GPA - highest possible	*Only U.S. citizens and perm. res may apply *Must be first-year applicant *8-12 students are chosen *MCAT not req.
UNIV. OF THE SCIENCES WITH LECOM 600 SOUTH 43RD STREET PHILADELPHIA, PA 19104	*BS.MD (8-year) *BS/DO (7-year & 8-year prog.) *Apply directly to the Early Acceptance Program (EAP) via LECOM by March 1 *May reapply if not initially selected	Min ERW+M - 1200 Min ACT - 25 GPA min - 3.50	*Only U.S. Citizens and perm. res. may apply *H.S. seniors, plus 3 seats for 1st or 2nd-year current students *No grades lower than a C *MCAT req. *No AMCAS req.

UNIVERSITY/PROGRAM	DEADLINE	MIN SAT, ACT, & GPA	OTHER REQUIREMENTS
WASHINGTON AND JEFFERSON COLLEGE 60 S LINCOLN ST. WASHINGTON, PA 15301	*Send W&J College Application early in the Fall. *Info. about the Medical Scholars prog. is sent to eligible candidates until late Nov. *Medical Scholars App due Dec. 10 *Interviews are offered to eligible candidates - 2 interviews - one w/ Pre-Health Professions Committee at W&J, the other at LKSOM	Min ERW+M - 1350 (no score below 600) Min ACT - 31 SAT/ACT req. for this prog., even though W&J is generally test optional. Top 5% of graduating class.	*U.S. Citizens and perm res only. *MCAT req. *AMCAS req.
WEST CHESTER UNIV. 700 S HIGH ST. WEST CHESTER, PA 19383	*Req differ based on prog. *For PA State College of Med, students apply as WCU undergrad w/ ≥ 60 credits *For Philadelphia College of Osteopathic Medicine, WCU undergrads w/≥ 60 credits can apply *For LECOM, students may apply as H.S. seniors or beginning soph year at WCU. Students must indicate his or her intent to apply for LECOM Early Acceptance Program *Interview with LECOM occurs before starting as a WCU student	Min ERW+M - 1240 Min ACT - 26 GPA min - 3.50 Must be in the top 10%	MCAT req.

CONNECTICUT

MAINE

MASSACHUSETTS

NEW HAMPSHIRE

NEW JERSEY

NEW YORK

PENNSYLVANIA

RHODE ISLAND

VERMONT

DREXEL UNIVERSITY
BA/BS-MD PROGRAM (8-YEAR)

Medical School: Drexel College of Medicine
2900 W Queen Ln, Philadelphia, PA 19129
Undergraduate: Drexel University
3141 Chestnut Street, Philadelphia, PA 19104
Program Information:
https://drexel.edu/undergrad/apply/freshmen-instructions/accelerated/
Request for Information Form:
https://drexel.edu/undergrad/contact/request-info/
Phone: (215) 895-2000
E-Mail: *enroll@drexel.edu*
Additional Combined Programs: N/A
International Students: Not considered

COST OF ATTENDANCE

Tuition and Fees: $53,868
Additional Expenses with Room and Board: $18,413
Total: $72,281

Financial Aid: Scholarships available

ADDITIONAL INFORMATION

Drexel University is a private research university that offers a 4+4 BA/BS +MD program. High school students who are on track to graduate and are U.S. citizens may apply. This program is only open to biological sciences, chemistry, psychology, or biomedical engineering majors. First-year students admitted to the program had an average GPA of 4.42 and an average combined SAT of 1542 or ACT 35 composite.

While in the program, students must fulfill the following requirements to ensure their spot at the medical school:

1. Maintain a 3.60 GPA in all coursework without repeating courses and with no grades lower than a C
2. Complete a minimum of 100 hours of service
3. Complete a six-month co-op
4. Complete 12 quarters of study
5. Receive a minimum MCAT score of 513:
   - chemical and physical foundations: 128+
   - critical analysis and reasoning skills: 127+
   - biological and biochemical foundations: 128+
   - psychological, social, and biological foundations: 128+

DUQUESNE UNIVERSITY
BS/DO PROGRAM (8-YEAR)

Medical School: Lake Erie College of Osteopathic Medicine
1858 W Grandview Blvd, Erie, PA 16509
Undergraduate: Duquesne University
600 Forbes Avenue, Pittsburgh, PA 15282
Program Information: *https://www.duq.edu/academics/degrees-and-programs/pre-medical-and-health-professions/undergraduate-post-secondary-certificate-program/linkage-agreements*
Request for Information Form:
https://www.duq.edu/admissions-and-aid/request-information
Phone: (412) 396-6000
E-Mail: *admissions@duq.edu*
Additional Combined Programs: 2 Early Assurance Programs for current undergraduates only (LECOM and RUSVM) and Preferred Admissions Review Program (PCOM)
International Students: Not considered

COST OF ATTENDANCE

Tuition and Fees: $41,892
Additional Expenses with Room and Board: $7,253
Total: $49,145

Financial Aid: 80% of Duquesne students receive financial aid. Scholarships are available.

ADDITIONAL INFORMATION

Duquesne University is a private Catholic university. The 4+4 BS/MD program is a linkage program run through Duquesne University and Lake Erie College of Osteopathic Medicine (LECOM) and is known as the LECOM Linkage Program. High school students may apply. When students apply for this linkage program, they must apply to Duquesne University and check off both the academic program and the PMHPP and LECOM Linkage boxes in the application. If accepted into the LECOM Linkage program, students have their choice of four campuses: Erie (PA), Greensburg (PA), Elmira (NY), or Bradenton (FL). Students are exempt from the MCAT so long as their Academic Index Score qualifies them an exemption. LECOM determines the Academic Index Score by considering the SAT or ACT score and cumulative GPA.

For current undergraduates:

Duquesne University has an Undergraduate Pre-Medical and Health Professions Program (UG-PMHPP) prepares undergraduate students for pre-medical coursework and the application and interview process. The UG-PMHPP is not a 4+4 degree program or an academic major, but instead a post-secondary certificate program. In this program, students take 7 specialized pre-health courses.

Duquesne also offers programs for current PMHPP students. There are two Early Assurance Programs and one Preferred Admissions Review Program

The two Early Assurance Programs are through LECOM and Ross University School of Veterinary Medicine (RUSVM). The Preferred Admission Review is through the Philadelphia College of Osteopathic Medicine (PCOM). There is currently no linkage or early assurance program with the PMHPP for the Duquesne University College of Osteopathic Medicine (DUCOM). These programs are for current undergraduates.

CONNECTICUT

MAINE

MASSACHUSETTS

NEW HAMPSHIRE

NEW JERSEY

NEW YORK

PENNSYLVANIA

RHODE ISLAND

VERMONT

ME
VT
NY
NH
MA
PA
RI
CT
NJ

NORTHEAST

CONNECTICUT

MAINE

MASSACHUSETTS

NEW HAMPSHIRE

NEW JERSEY

NEW YORK

PENNSYLVANIA

RHODE ISLAND

VERMONT

LEHIGH UNIVERSITY
BA/DMD OR BA/OD PROGRAM (7-YEAR)

Dental Medical School: School of Dental Medicine at the University of Pennsylvania
240 S 40th St, Philadelphia, PA 19104
Optometry School: SUNY College of Optometry
33 W 42nd St, New York, NY 10036
Undergraduate: Lehigh University
27 Memorial Dr. W., Bethlehem, PA 18015
Program Information: *https://careercenter.lehigh.edu/node/86*
Request for Information Form:
https://www1.lehigh.edu/admissions/request-info
Admissions Phone: (610) 758-3100
Curriculum Questions: (610)758-3710
E-Mail: *admissions@lehigh.edu*
Additional Combined Programs: two offered – BA/DMD and BA/OD
International Students: Not listed

COST OF ATTENDANCE

Tuition and Fees: $54,790
Additional Expenses with Room and Board: $9,470
Total: $64,260

Financial Aid: Merit-based and need-based scholarships are offered.

ADDITIONAL INFORMATION

*This school used to have a BS/MD program. However, it has been discontinued as of Fall 2017.

Lehigh University is a private research university established in 1865. They offer two accelerated programs. The first one is a BA/DMD 3+4 program. The DMD degree is awarded by the School of Dental Medicine at the University of Pennsylvania. Applicants should apply directly to this program through the Office of Admissions. Students must maintain a minimum cumulative and science GPA of 3.5 throughout undergraduate studies. The Dental Admission Test (DAT) must be taken as well. Admission to this program is based on SAT scores, ranking in the top 10%, and demonstrated motivation for dental school.

The second program offered by Lehigh University is the BA/OD 3+4 program. Students in this program are admitted simultaneously into a behavioral neuroscience major at Lehigh and to candidacy in SUNY College of Optometry. High school seniors and current Lehigh undergraduate students may apply to this program. Requirements for high school students include maturity, interest, a minimum combined SAT score of 1300, and ranking in the top 10% of the graduating class. For second-year undergraduate students, the requirement is a minimum overall and math/science GPA of 3.3 with no grades below a C. Students are required to take the Optometry Admission Test (OAT) and score 320 or higher to receive an interview.

PENN STATE UNIVERSITY
ACCELERATED MEDICAL BS/MD PROGRAM
(7-YEAR)

Medical School: Sidney Kimmel Medical College at Thomas Jefferson University
1025 Walnut St #100, Philadelphia, PA 19107
Undergraduate: Pennsylvania State University
201 Shields Building, University Park, PA 16802
Program Information:
https://science.psu.edu/interdisciplinary-programs/premed-med-bsmd
Contact Information: *https://admissions.psu.edu/contact/*
Phone: (814) 865-5471
E-Mail: *admissions@psu.edu*
Additional Combined Programs: BS/MBA
International Students: Not listed

COST OF ATTENDANCE

In-State Tuition and Fees: $17,416
Additional Expenses with Room and Board: $12,760
Total: $30,716

Out-of-State Tuition and Fees: $33,820
Additional Expenses with Room and Board: $12,760
Total: $46,580

Financial Aid: Not eligible for tuition scholarships from Schreyer Honors College or Braddock scholarships.

ADDITIONAL INFORMATION

The Penn State Pre-Medical/Medical (PMM) Program is a BS/MD program established in 1963 and in partnership with Sidney Kimmel Medical College (SKMC) at Thomas Jefferson University. Students earn their BS after their first year in medical school (year four). The MD is earned after the student's last year of medical school (year seven). Although students earn their BS in year four, they only study at Penn State for three years. Since students are at Penn State for three years, they are not eligible for tuition scholarships from the Schreyer Honors College or Braddock.

PMM students take the same courses and have similar schedules as pre-medical students who are in the traditional four-year program. MCAT scores are required for matriculation to SKMC. The current requirement is an MCAT composite score of 504 with no less than 126 on any subsection. Students must also maintain a 3.5 GPA, especially in the sciences.

Students may also apply to the Schreyer Honors College. However, if both offer admission, only one can be accepted. PMM students are also able to study abroad and conduct research abroad. Currently, AP credits cannot shorten a PMM student's time at Pennsylvania State. Students begin studies at the University Park campus in the fall.

CONNECTICUT

MAINE

MASSACHUSETTS

NEW HAMPSHIRE

NEW JERSEY

NEW YORK

PENNSYLVANIA

RHODE ISLAND

VERMONT

NORTHEAST

CONNECTICUT

MAINE

MASSACHUSETTS

NEW HAMPSHIRE

NEW JERSEY

NEW YORK

PENNSYLVANIA

RHODE ISLAND

VERMONT

ROSEMONT COLLEGE
DUAL DEGREE BA/DO PROGRAM
(7-YEAR, 8-YEAR)

Medical School: Philadelphia College of Osteopathic Medicine
4170 City Ave, Philadelphia, PA 19131
Undergraduate: Rosemont College
1400 Montgomery Ave, Rosemont, PA 19010
Program Information:
https://www.rosemont.edu/academics/academic-partnerships/
Request for Information Form:
https://www.rosemont.edu/admissions/request-information.php
Phone: (610) 526-2966
E-Mail: *admissions@rosemont.edu*
Additional Combined Programs: For current undergraduates only:
BA/DPT (3+3), BA/PharmD (3+4), BSN (4+1), BA/*M.Ed* in TVI, BA/MS in
LVR, BA/MS in O&M, BA/MS in VRT, BA/MMS, BA/AuD, and BA/OD (3+4)
International Students: Not listed

COST OF ATTENDANCE

Tuition and Fees: $19,500
Additional Expenses with Room and Board: $15,805
Total: $35,305

Financial Aid: Accepted students are automatically considered for
merit-based scholarships. Additional scholarships available, including
the full tuition Cornelian Scholarship.

ADDITIONAL INFORMATION

Rosemont College is a private Catholic liberal arts college. It was
founded in 1921 as a women's college. The college opened to male
students in 2009. They offer a variety of dual degree programs for current
undergraduate students. There are no current combined programs that
high school seniors can apply to. Rosemont is in partnership with the
Philadelphia College of Osteopathic Medicine in offering a 3+4 and 4+4 BA/
DO program. Applicants for the 3+4 program are considered during their
junior year at Rosemont. The applicant's overall and science GPA must
be at least a 3.75. Additionally, an MCAT composite score of 500 and a
minimum of 125 in each subsection is required. Students in this program
are awarded their undergraduate degree upon completion of their first
year of medical school.

Applicants are considered for the 4+4 program during their last year at
Rosemont. The overall and science GPA must be at least 3.25. A minimum
MCAT composite score is 504, with at least 126 in each subsection.

Rosemont College is also in partnership with the University of the
Sciences to offer a 3+4 Doctor of Pharmacy program and a 3+3 Doctor
of Physical Therapy program. Additionally, they are in partnership with
Salus University and offer multiple BA/Master's programs and BA/Doctoral
degree programs. The programs are as follow:

1. M.Ed in Blindness and Visual Impairment (TVI)
2. M.S., Low Vision Rehabilitation (LVR)
3. M.S., Occupational Therapy (MSOT)
4. M.S., Orientation and Mobility (O&M)
5. M.S., Vision Rehabilitation Therapy (VRT)
6. Physician Assistant (MMS)
7. Doctor of Audiology (AuD) On-Campus
8. Doctor of Optometry 3+4 (OD)
9. Doctor of Optometry (OD) Traditional Program

TEMPLE UNIVERSITY HEALTH SCHOLARS BS/MD PROGRAM (7-YEAR, 8-YEAR)

Medical School: Lewis Katz School of Medicine at Temple University
3500 N Broad St, Philadelphia, PA 19140
Undergraduate: Temple University
1801 N Broad St, Philadelphia, PA 19122
Program Information:
http://www.temple.edu/healthadvising/healthscholars.html
Request for Information Form:
https://education.temple.edu/admissions/contact/requestinfo
Phone: (215) 204-2513
E-Mail: *healthadvising@temple.edu*
Additional Combined Programs: N/A
International Students: Not considered

COST OF ATTENDANCE

In-State Tuition and Fees: $9,972
Additional Expenses with Room and Board: $9,400
Total: $19,372

Out-of-State Tuition and Fees: $16,404
Additional Expenses with Room and Board: $9,400
Total: $25,804

Financial Aid: Merit-based scholarships available for first-year students, ranging from $2,000 to full tuition. Other merit-based and need-based scholarships available as well

ADDITIONAL INFORMATION

Temple University is a public research university founded in 1885. Scholar students are automatically put in the 4+4 track. They may choose to show their interest in the 3+4 track during their freshman year at Temple University. These are the requirements for the 3+4 program:

1. Accepted as a Pre-Med Health Scholar
2. 3+4 Application submitted during first semester at Temple
3. Decision made after a review of first semester grades

Health Scholar students may choose any major if they can complete the pre-med requirements and major requirements. Students who choose to do the 3+4 track must select Biology or Chemistry as their major. Provisional acceptance is given to Health Scholars if they fulfill the following requirements by January of their Junior year in college:

1. Course credits
2. Cumulative GPA of 3.60
3. Cumulative science GPA of 3.60
4. MCAT minimum composite of 509 with subsections 126+
5. Volunteer experience

CONNECTICUT

MAINE

MASSACHUSETTS

NEW HAMPSHIRE

NEW JERSEY

NEW YORK

PENNSYLVANIA

RHODE ISLAND

VERMONT

NORTHEAST

CONNECTICUT

MAINE

MASSACHUSETTS

NEW HAMPSHIRE

NEW JERSEY

NEW YORK

PENNSYLVANIA

RHODE ISLAND

VERMONT

UNIVERSITY OF PITTSBURGH
BS/MD PROGRAM (8-YEAR)

Medical School: University of Pittsburgh School of Medicine
3550 Terrace St, Pittsburgh, PA 15213
Undergraduate: University of Pittsburgh
4200 Fifth Ave, Pittsburgh, PA 15260
Program Information: *https://www.medadmissions.pitt.edu/ programs/guaranteed-admissions-program*
Request for Information Form: *https://oafa.pitt.edu/request-info/*
Phone: (412) 624-7488
E-Mail: *pitt.admissions@pitt.edu*
Additional Combined Programs: BA/DMD, BA/MA or DNP or PhD nursing, BA/OTD, BA/PharmD, BA/DPT, BA/M.S. for PA, BA/MPH, BA/ MPH-MIC, MPH-PEL, or, MS, and BA/MS, MS-HDS, or MS-SCG
International Students: Not considered

COST OF ATTENDANCE

In-State Tuition and Fees: $18,628
Additional Expenses with Room and Board: $11,814
Total: $30,442

Out-of-State Tuition and Fees: $32,656
Additional Expenses with Room and Board: $11,814
Total: $44,470

Financial Aid: No separate application for University of Pittsburgh scholarships, but students must complete the short answer questions to be considered. Scholarships range from $2,000 to full tuition and room & board.

ADDITIONAL INFORMATION

The University of Pittsburgh is a research university founded in 1787. There are several Guaranteed Admissions Programs (GAP) for students. The GAP is available to high school students.

For matriculation to the School of Medicine, GAP students must do the following:

1. Maintain an overall GPA and math/science GPA of 3.75
2. Complete the degree within four years
3. Gain medically-related experiences during undergraduate years
4. Seek research opportunities
5. Seek community service opportunities
6. Meet with the director every semester to discuss progress
7. Meet with the pre-medical advisor each semester
8. Provide an official transcript at the end of the junior year.

GAP students who meet these requirements then should apply to AMCAS to obtain an AMCAS ID. This should be submitted to the School of Medicine's Office of Admissions as well.

For a detailed school cohort profile: *https://oafa.pitt.edu/explore/ guaranteed-admissions-programs/medicine-gap/*

They also offer a linkage program for current undergraduates. For more information on those programs, visit: *https://www.medadmissions.pitt. edu/programs/linkage-program*

Other healthcare-related Guaranteed Admissions Programs offered:

9. BA/DMD
10. BA/MA or DNP or PhD in Nursing
11. BA/Occupational Therapist Doctorate
12. BA/PharmD
13. BA/Doctor of Physical Therapy
14. BA/M.S. for Physician's Assistant
15. BA/MPH for Behavioral and Community Health Sciences
16. BA/MS, MS-HDS, or MS-SCG in Biostatistics
17. BA/MPH or MS in Environmental and Occupational Health
18. BA/MPH or MS in Epidemiology
19. BA/MPH in Health Policy and Management
20. BA/MPH or MS in Human Genetics or Genome Bioinformatics
21. BA/MPH-MIC, MPH-PEL, or MS in Infectious Diseases and Microbiology

CONNECTICUT

MAINE

MASSACHUSETTS

NEW HAMPSHIRE

NEW JERSEY

NEW YORK

PENNSYLVANIA

RHODE ISLAND

VERMONT

NORTHEAST

CONNECTICUT

MAINE

MASSACHUSETTS

NEW HAMPSHIRE

NEW JERSEY

NEW YORK

PENNSYLVANIA

RHODE ISLAND

VERMONT

UNIVERSITY OF THE SCIENCES
BS/MD (8-YEAR WITH CMSRU)
BS/DO PROGRAM W/LECOM (7-YEAR, 8-YEAR)

Medical School: Lake Erie College of Osteopathic Medicine
1858 W Grandview Blvd, Erie, PA 16509
Undergraduate: University of the Sciences
600 South 43rd Street, Philadelphia, PA 19104
Program Information: *https://www.usciences.edu/misher-college-of-arts-and-sciences/pre-med-program/medical-partnerships.html*
Request for Information Form:
https://www.usciences.edu/admission/request-information/index.html
Phone: (215) 596-8800
E-Mail: *prehealth@usciences.edu*
Additional Combined Programs: 4+4 BA/DMD via LECOM
International Students: Not considered

COST OF ATTENDANCE

Tuition and Fees: $27,500
Additional Expenses: $11,050
Total: $38,550

Financial Aid: USciences offers merit-based scholarships

ADDITIONAL INFORMATION

The University of the Sciences in Philadelphia is a private university offering a combined BS/DO program with Lake Erie College of Medicine (LECOM). The Early Acceptance Program (EAP) is open to high school students who are interested in earning their DO in 7- or 8-years. Only U.S. citizens or permanent residents may apply. Only Biology or Biomedical Sciences Majors are eligible. Additionally, the MCAT and an AMCAS application are not required.

The requirements for high school applicants are as follows:

1. High school GPA of 3.70 on a 4.00 scale
2. Minimum SAT score of 1340 or higher on a single exam
3. Minimum ACT Composite score of 28 in a single exam
4. A provisional letter of acceptance in EAP before starting a second year at USciences

Official acceptance into LECOM occurs when the student:

1. Completes at least 75% of credits for major
2. Maintains an overall GPA of 3.5 and science GPA of 3.2
3. No grade lower than a "C"

USciences offers several combined degree programs for both high school students and current USciences undergraduates. For more information on these programs, visit the link in "Program Information".

WASHINGTON AND JEFFERSON COLLEGE BA/MD PROGRAM (8-YEAR)

Medical School: Lewis Katz School of Medicine (LKSOM) at Temple University
3500 N Broad St, Philadelphia, PA 19140
Undergraduate: Washington and Jefferson College
60 S Lincoln St., Washington, PA 15301
Program Information: *https://www.washjeff.edu/academics/majors-and-minors/partnerships/pre-health-professions-school-affiliations/wj-medical-scholars-program-with-the-lewis-katz-school-of-medicine-at-temple-university/*
Request for Information Form: *https://connect.washjeff.edu/register/inquiry?*
Phone: (888) 926-3529
E-Mail: *prehealth@washjeff.edu*
Additional Combined Programs: BA/MD through Sidney Kimmel Medical College, Early Acceptance Program through LECOM
International Students: Not considered

COST OF ATTENDANCE

Tuition and Fees: $48,758
Additional Expenses with Room and Board: $13,628
Total: $62,386

Financial Aid: Various merit-based scholarships are available. Some may cover the total cost of tuition.

ADDITIONAL INFORMATION

Washington and Jefferson College is a private college established in the 1780s. In partnership with Lewis Katz School of Medicine (LKSOM) at Temple University Medical Scholars Program, students may engage in an 8-year BA/MD program. U.S. Citizens and permanent residents may apply.

High school seniors must meet the following requirements to be considered in the Medical Scholars Program:

1. Accepted into W&J
2. Submit Medical Scholars Program application by December 10
3. Combined SAT CR+M score greater than 1350, no single section in verbal, math, or writing below 600
4. OR have ACT Composite score at least a 31
5. Be in the top 5% of graduating class
6. Interview at W&J
7. Interview at LKSOM

To receive an assured seat at LKSOM, as undergraduates, students must meet the following requirements:

1. Overall undergraduate GPA and science GPA at least 3.50 average over the first 3 years
2. No grade less than B- and without course repetitions
3. All pre-medical courses taken at W&J
4. Minimum acceptable MCAT score is 509, with no individual subsection lower than 126.
5. 50 completed hours of medically-related experiences
6. 50 hours of community service

There are also programs at W&J for current W&J undergraduates. Some of these programs are to obtain an M.D. Others are for a DMD, OD, DPT and more. For more information on the various partnership programs, visit: *https://www.washjeff.edu/academics/majors-and-minors/partnerships/pre-health-professions-school-affiliations/*

CONNECTICUT

MAINE

MASSACHUSETTS

NEW HAMPSHIRE

NEW JERSEY

NEW YORK

PENNSYLVANIA

RHODE ISLAND

VERMONT

NORTHEAST

CONNECTICUT

MAINE

MASSACHUSETTS

NEW HAMPSHIRE

NEW JERSEY

NEW YORK

PENNSYLVANIA

RHODE ISLAND

VERMONT

WEST CHESTER UNIVERSITY
BS/DO PROGRAM (8-YEAR)

Medical School: Lake Erie College of Osteopathic Medicine
1858 W Grandview Blvd, Erie, PA 16509
Undergraduate: West Chester University of Pennsylvania
700 S High St, West Chester, PA 19383
Program Information: *https://www.wcupa.edu/sciences-mathematics/preMed/earlyAssuranceUndergrad/default.aspx*
Request for Information Form:
https://www.wcupa.edu/veteransCenter/requestInfo.aspx
Phone: (610) 436-1000
E-Mail: *PMED@wcupa.edu*
Additional Combined Programs:
BA/MS in Physician Assistant Studies
International Students: Not listed

COST OF ATTENDANCE

In-State Tuition and Fees: $10,421
Additional Expenses with Room and Board: $11,336
Total: $21,757

Out-of-State Tuition and Fees: $22,244
Additional Expenses with Room and Board: $11,336
Total: $33,580

Financial Aid: Merit-based scholarships and federal financial aid assistance available.

ADDITIONAL INFORMATION

West Chester University (WCU) of Pennsylvania is a public university established in 1871. They offer three BS/Doctorate programs. Only one is open to high school students. Current WCU undergraduates may apply to any of the three programs

For High School Seniors and current WCU undergraduates:

The first partnership is with Lake Erie College of Osteopathic Medicine (LECOM). Applicants may apply either as a high school senior or at the beginning of sophomore year at WCU. High school students must obtain:

1. A minimum 1250 SAT score
2. A GPA of 3.50 or better
3. Admission to the WCU Pre-Medical Program.

Note: Students notify the program of intent to apply for LECOM. The interview takes place "prior to matriculation at WCU."

Students at WCU may apply to LECOM given they have:

1. An overall GPA of at least 3.40
2. An overall science GPA of at least 3.20.

For current WCU undergraduates only:

Another partnership is with the Philadelphia College of Osteopathic Medicine (PCOM). Applicants must have at least 60 completed credits at WCU. Furthermore, they must have:

1. Completed the undergraduate course requirements
2. Maintain a GPA of at least 3.25
3. Earn a minimum 50th percentile score in each section of the MCAT
4. Interview and gain nomination from the WCU Pre-Medical Committee
5. Have a successful interview at PCOM.

The MCAT must be taken no later than the fall of senior year. Students "must submit an application to PCOM through AACOMAS no later than October 31st of the senior year and must submit an application to PCOM Supplemental Application (with application fee) no later than November 30th of the senior year." A letter of recommendation from an Osteopathic Physician is required as well.

The third partnership is with Pennsylvania State College of Medicine (PSU COM). Apply after 60 credits have been completed at WCU. Requirements for this program include:

1. Minimum total SAT of 1300
2. Minimum 3.50 GPA
3. Completion of 8/10 of the required pre-requisite courses
4. Interview and nomination from WCU Pre-Medical Committee
5. Successful interview at PSU Hershey Medical Center

The first interview will take place at the end of the applicant's sophomore year at WCU. The last interview takes place during the summer between sophomore and junior year. The AMCAS is sent from PSU. The student must return it to PSU COM.

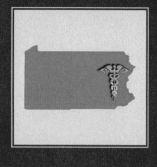

CONNECTICUT

MAINE

MASSACHUSETTS

NEW HAMPSHIRE

NEW JERSEY

NEW YORK

PENNSYLVANIA

RHODE ISLAND

VERMONT

NORTHEAST

ILLINOIS

INDIANA

IOWA

KANSAS

MICHIGAN

MINNESOTA

MISSOURI

NEBRASKA

NORTH DAKOTA

OHIO

SOUTH DAKOTA

WISCONSIN

REGION TWO
MIDWEST

17 *Programs* | **12** *States*

1. *IL – Illinois Institute of Technology BS/DO (8-year)*
2. *IL – Loyola University DAP (6-year)*
3. *IL – Northwestern University HPME (7-year, 8-year)*
4. *IL – University of Illinois Chicago GPPA (8-year)*
5. *IN – Indiana State University (8-year)*
6. *IN – University of Evansville B/MD (8-year)*
7. *MI – Wayne State Med-Direct Program (8-year)*
8. *MN – University of Minnesota (7-year)*
9. *MO – St. Louis U. Medical Scholar Program (8-year)*
10. *MO – University of Missouri Kansas City BA/MD (6-year)*
11. *MO – Washington Univ. in St. Louis Med Scholars (8-year)*
12. *NE – Chadron State College (RHOP) (8-year)*
13. *OH – Kent State University BS/MD (6-year)*
14. *OH – Case Western Reserve University (8-year)*
15. *OH - Cleveland State University BS/MD (8-year)*
16. *OH – University of Cincinnati BS/MD (8-year)*
17. *OH – University of Toledo (8-year)*

DIRECT MED PROGRAMS

UNIVERSITY/PROGRAM	DEADLINE	MIN SAT, ACT, GPA	OTHER REQUIREMENTS
ILLINOIS INST. OF TECH 1032 W SHERIDAN RD, CHICAGO, IL 60660	*BS/DO (8-year) *Application due Dec 1 *Invitation to interview in early Jan *On-campus interview: early Feb *Final decisions: early Mar	Min ACT Composite – 32 Min SAT (V+M) – 1400 Min GPA – 3.5 Top 10% of class	*MCAT req. *AACOMAS not req. *Must be U.S. citizen/ perm. res.
LOYOLA UNIV. CHICAGO 1032 W SHERIDAN RD CHICAGO, IL 60660	*App. deadline around Sep *App. materials due around Sep	Undergrad science GPA of 3.6 Undergrad cum. GPA of 3.6 No "C" grades	*Up to 10 students *Undergrads only *MCAT req. *AMCAS req. *Interview req. *3 Letters of Rec from LUC fac.
NORTHWESTERN UNIV. 303 E. CHICAGO AVENUE WARD BUILDING 1-003 CHICAGO, IL 60611 HPME – HONORS PROGRAM IN MEDICAL EDUCATION	*HPME Applicants must submit a separate app in addition to CA. *Material must be sent through the online app link to be considered. *HPME App Request: Oct.–Dec. 1 *Standardized tests must be taken no later than Nov. *Invite to interview in Chicago Feb. or March *Students notified of HPME decisions electronically by April.	SAT I avg. ERW – 762, M – 792 SAT may be Superscored ACT avg. – 35 (writing – 12) ACT or SAT. Although writing is optional, it is req. for ACT. Must take SAT II Math 2 & Chem SAT II avg. Chem – 777, Math 2 - 790 Ranking near the top of class	*HPME only open to H.S. seniors. *MCAT not req. *There is no ED for HPME. However, a select few who apply ED may be invited to apply for the HPME in Jan.
UNIV. OF ILLINOIS CHICAGO 1200 W HARRISON ST. CHICAGO, IL 60607 GPPA – GUARANTEED PROFESSIONAL PROGRAM ADMISSIONS	*Students must submit CA, UIC first-year suppl. (incl both GPPA & Honors College apps); submit 2 letters of rec *Deadline for GPPA Prog is Nov 1 *Interviews conducted: Jan.-Feb. *Applicants informed of dec: March Note: Students may only apply to one GPPA prog.	Min SAT ERW+M - 1300 Avg. ACT – 35 (range 29-36) Min GPA - 3.85 (range unwt 3.59-4.00) Honors College Entrance Reqs: min ACT of 28; 3.5 GPA	*Must be U.S. citizen or perm. res. & Il resident *700 apps, 93 interviews, 32 members in each class *Female – 59% *Must show medical volunteer work in H.S. *For eligibility: (1) maintain cum GPA of 3.6, (2) science GPA of 3.6, (3) senior thesis, (4) MCAT score of 512

UNIVERSITY/PROGRAM	DEADLINE	MIN SAT, ACT, GPA	OTHER REQUIREMENTS
INDIANA STATE UNIV. 200 N 7TH ST, TERRE HAUTE, IN 47809	*Applications open in Oct *Apply and be accepted to ISU *Once accepted, complete separate application through The Branch by Dec 15	Min SAT ERW+M – 1270 Min ACT – 27 Min GPA – 3.5	*Superscoring not allowed *Must be IN resident *MCAT req.
U. OF EVANSVILLE 1800 LINCOLN AVE, EVANSVILLE, IN 47722	*B/MD App due Nov 2 *Notification of interview mid-Nov *Interviews late Nov *Notification of decision mid-Dec *Acceptance letter – Mar *Intent to enroll – May 1	Admitted SAT ERW+M – 1350 Admitted ACT – 29 Admitted GPA – 4.0	*Up to 8 students admitted. *Must be IN residents *Must interview
WAYNE STATE UNIV. MED-DIRECT PROGRAM 42 W WARREN AVE DETROIT, MI 48202 RHOP - RURAL HEALTH OPPORTUNITIES PROGRAM	*WSU undergrad app available August 1 (may use CA) *App deadline for Wayne Med-Direct is Dec. 1 (only available thru WSU app portal) *Semifinalist's notified by Mid-Jan. *Interviews late Jan.-early Feb. *Finalists notified one week after interviews *Students must decide to accept or not by mid-to-late Feb.	Min SAT ERW+M - 1310 Min Act - 28 Min GPA - 3.50	*Must be a U.S. Citizen or perm. resident *Must be an incoming freshman *Healthcare and comm. service exp. considered *25 semifinalists called for an interview *10 finalists accepted *Wayne Med-Direct is a Binding ED prog. *Pref. given to students from disadvantaged SES interested in studying health disparities *MCAT req.
UNIV. OF MINNESOTA 231 PILLSBURY DR., S.E. MINNEAPOLIS, MN 55455	*Students must be invited to apply *Indicate interest in medical school *Apply by Nov 1 deadline *Interview req.	Competitive scores and GPA	*Up to 10 students *MCAT req. *AMCAS req.

MIDWEST

DIRECT MED PROGRAMS

UNIVERSITY/PROGRAM	DEADLINE	MIN SAT, ACT, GPA	OTHER REQUIREMENTS
ST. LOUIS UNIV. **1 N GRAND BLVD** **ST. LOUIS, MO 63103** **MSP - MEDICAL** **SCHOLAR PROGRAM**	*Medical Scholars Prog. app due Dec. 1 *Decisions mailed in March *Commitment due May 1	Min SAT ERW+M - 1360 Min Act - 30 Min GPA – 4.0 unwt (admitted std)	*Students with a C or lower in a science not considered *Latest date to take ACT or SAT is Dec. *MCAT req.
UMKC **1 N GRAND BLVD** **ST. LOUIS, MO 63103**	*App available in Aug. *2 apps: (1) Admission's app to UMKC, (2) School of Med Suppl App *Both apps due Nov. 1 *Suppl materials due Dec. 15 *Interview offers given in Jan. *College transcript deadline: Jan. 20 (for current college students only) *Interviews in Feb.; offers by Apr 1	Min SAT ERW+M – 1160 (avg. score 1420) Min Act – 24 (avg. 32 of admitted students) Min GPA – 3.0 unwt, 3.9 (avg. admitted) Must take ACT and/or SAT by Nov. 1 Latest test score accepted is Oct. test date SAT II not considered	*Must be U.S. citizen or perm res *H.S. students or college students w/less than 24 college credits may apply *ACT preferred *MCAT not req. *AMCAS not req.
WASH. U. IN ST. LOUIS **MED SCHOLARS** **1 BROOKINGS DR.** **ST. LOUIS, MO 63130**	*Submit the CA by Jan. 2 *Submit a separate app for the Univ. Scholars Prog. in Med. In the WashU Pathway *Finalists' weekend (interviews) at the end of March. WashU pays for finalists' round-trip expenses to St. Louis from w/i US to attend. *Notification shortly after finalists' weekend	ACT - 34 (avg. admitted)	*3 letters of rec req. One must be a research or service advisor or support your interest in med. (Use CA 'other' rec area) *Intl students welcome to apply. *5-10 admitted students *MCAT req.
CHADRON STATE **COLLEGE** **1000 MAIN ST,** **CHADRON, NE 69337**	*Apply to Chadron State *Submit RHOP app. *All materials due Dec 1	Min ACT – 24	*Must be rural NE resident
CWRU **10900 EUCLID AVE.** **CLEVELAND, OH 44106** **PPSP - PRE-** **PROFESSIONAL** **SCHOLARS PROGRAM**	*Apply for RD or ED I *Students who apply ED I are bound to commit to CWRU regardless of finalist status for Pre-Professional Scholars Program	SAT ERW+M – 1370-1490 ACT – 31-34 Top 10% of graduating class	*15-20 H.S. seniors admitted *MCAT not req. unless applying for Dean's Merit Scholarship *AMCAS req. *BS/DDS also

UNIVERSITY/PROGRAM	DEADLINE	MIN SAT, ACT, GPA	OTHER REQUIREMENTS
CLEVELAND STATE UNIV. **2121 EUCLID AVE,** **CLEVELAND, OH 44115**	*App. available through NEOMED in Oct *App. deadline in Jan *Invited to interview Feb and Mar *Offered admission in Apr *Admit. Stud. enroll late-May/June *Phase 1 of program Mid-Aug	Min ACT – 26 (or SAT equivalent) College GPA – 3.4 20 sem. hrs of coursework grades "C-"or higher	*For current undergrad. only *U.S. citizen/perm. res. only *Apply during soph. or junior *CASPer test req. *Interview req.
KENT STATE UNIVERSITY **800 E SUMMIT ST,** **KENT, OH 44240**	*This program has been temporarily suspended since Fall 2019		
UNIV. OF CINCINNATI **2600 CLIFTON AVE.** **CINCINNATI, OH 45221**	*2 apps to be submitted: CA and the Connections app *Connections app opens mid-Sept. *Must select a major or minor in Medical Sciences *Interviews invites sent in Feb. *Interviews in Feb. and March *Decisions sent via email in April *Students must respond by May	Min SAT ERW+M - 1300 Min Act - 29 Min GPA - 3.94 unwt Composite scores only. They do not Superscore multiple attempts	*Must be a U.S. citizen or perm. res. *Must be part of the University Honors Program *Students must either major or minor in Medical Science *Must take MCAT in one sitting
UNIV. OF TOLEDO **2801 W. BANCROFT ST.** **TOLEDO, OH 43606**	*Submit online UT undergrad app or the CA *Apply to major in: (1) College of Natural Sciences & Mathematics, (2) College of Arts & Letters, or (3) College of Engineering's Dept of Bioengineering *Must select PMED conc code *Select "Yes" to be considered for Bacc2MD Pathway	Min SAT ERW+M - 1310 Min Act - 28 Min GPA - 3.50 unwt	*Must be U.S. Citizen or perm. res. *Must be a H.S. student to apply. No transfer students. *MCAT not req. *Admission into the Bacc2MD Program guarantees an interview

MIDWEST

168

ILLINOIS

INDIANA

IOWA

KANSAS

MICHIGAN

MINNESOTA

MISSOURI

NEBRASKA

NORTH DAKOTA

OHIO

SOUTH DAKOTA

WISCONSIN

ILLINOIS INSTITUTE OF TECHNOLOGY
BS/DO PROGRAM (8-YEAR)

Medical School: Midwestern University Chicago College of Osteopathic Medicine
Midwestern University, Downers Grove, IL 60515
Undergraduate: Illinois Institute of Technology
1032 W Sheridan Rd, Chicago, IL 60660
Program Information:
https://www.iit.edu/academics/pre-health-pre-med/dual-admission
Request for Information Form:
https://www.iit.edu/admissions-aid/request-information
Director of Pre-Health Programs, Kathryn Spink Phone:
(312) 567-3441
Director of Pre-Health Programs, Kathryn Spink E-Mail:
spink@iit.edu
Admissions E-Mail: *admission@iit.edu*
Additional Combined Programs:
BS/OD, BS/PharmD, LECOM: BS/DO, BS/PharmD, BS/DMD
International Students: Not considered

COST OF ATTENDANCE

Tuition and Fees: $48,670
Additional Expenses with Room and Board: $22,498
Total: $71,168

Financial Aid: Merit-based scholarships available.

ADDITIONAL INFORMATION

Illinois Institute of Technology is a private research university established in 1890. The BS/DO program is in partnership with Midwestern University Chicago College of Osteopathic Medicine. This 4+4 program is very competitive, with 20 finalists invited to interview and 5-10 accepted students. This program is only open to first-year applicants.

Materials required (in addition to the application to Illinois Tech):

1. BS/DO Supplemental App
2. Essays
3. Letters of recommendation
   - 1 math/science teacher
   - 1 humanities/social science teacher
   - 1 medically-related

Minimum requirements to be considered are as follow:

1. Minimum 3.5/4.0 GPA
2. Minimum 32 ACT composite
3. Minimum 1400 SAT (verbal + math) composite
4. Top 10% of class

To maintain a place in this program, students must meet the following criteria:

1. Maintain a 3.50 GPA
2. MCAT score above the national average

Illinois Institute of Technology also offers a BS/DO, BS/PharmD, or BS/DMD with Lake Erie College of Osteopathic Medicine (LECOM).

LOYOLA UNIVERSITY CHICAGO
BS/MD PROGRAM (6-YEAR)

Medical School: Loyola's Stritch School of Medicine (SSOM)
2160 S 1st Ave, Maywood, IL 60153
Undergraduate: Loyola University Chicago (LUC)
1032 W Sheridan Rd, Chicago, IL 60660
Program Information:
https://www.luc.edu/prehealth/services/dualacceptanceprogramdap/
Request for Information Form: *https://www.luc.edu/requestinformation/*
Phone: (773) 274-3000
E-Mail: *admission@luc.edu*
Additional Combined Programs: Post-baccalaureate pre-health, (DAP)
BS/PharmD for high school students and current first-year LUC students
International Students: Not listed

COST OF ATTENDANCE

Tuition and Fees: $45,500
Additional Expenses with Room and Board: $16,218
Total: $61,718

Financial Aid: According to LUC, the average financial aid award is
$27,700. LUC offers merit-based and need-based scholarships.

ADDITIONAL INFORMATION

Loyola University Chicago (LUC) is a private Catholic research university
founded in 1870. LUC offers an Early Assurance Program (EAP) that allows
current Loyola undergraduates to receive conditional acceptance to the
Loyola Stritch School of Medicine (SSOM).

Applicants are required to:
1. Be enrolled full time at LUC
2. Complete all science courses at LUC
3. Earn at least 60 credits over past four consecutive semesters at LUC
4. Minimum science GPA of 3.6
5. Minimum cumulative GPA of 3.6
6. No grade lower than "C"
7. Strong preference for students who have an academic record
   without incompletes, withdrawals, or repeated coursework
8. Complete certain pre-medical requirements
9. Submit an application

Students who are considered for admission will be offered an interview. Up
to ten candidates are guaranteed acceptance.

Ongoing requirements that must be met:
1. Completion of all SSOM prerequisites
2. Participation in activities sponsored by SSOM
3. Endorsement by Director of the Pre-Health Professions Program
4. Submit AMCAS no later than July 1
5. Minimum science GPA of 3.6 and cumulative GPA of 3.6 with no "C" grade
6. MCAT with minimum 509 composite score

LUC also offers a dual acceptance program (DAP) for high school students
and current LUC undergraduates in their first year. This program consists
of two years at LUC and four years in the Chicago
College of Pharmacy (CCP) of Midwestern University
to obtain a PharmD. Students are not required to
take the Pharmacy College Admission Test (PCAT).
The PharmCAS is required, but it is free, and it is an
abbreviated version.

ILLINOIS

INDIANA

IOWA

KANSAS

MICHIGAN

MINNESOTA

MISSOURI

NEBRASKA

NORTH DAKOTA

OHIO

SOUTH DAKOTA

WISCONSIN

MIDWEST

ILLINOIS

INDIANA

IOWA

KANSAS

MICHIGAN

MINNESOTA

MISSOURI

NEBRASKA

NORTH DAKOTA

OHIO

SOUTH DAKOTA

WISCONSIN

NORTHWESTERN UNIVERSITY
BS/MD PROGRAM (7-YEAR, 8-YEAR)

Medical School: Northwestern University Feinberg School of Medicine
420 E Superior St, Chicago, IL 60611
Undergraduate: Northwestern University (Evanston)
303 E. Chicago Avenue, Ward Building 1-003, Chicago, IL 60611
Program Information: *https://www.feinberg.northwestern.edu/sites/hpme/program-overview/index.html*
Request for Information Form:
https://ugadmission.northwestern.edu/register/request
Phone: (312) 503-8915
E-Mail: *hpme@northwestern.edu*
Additional Combined Programs: MD/PHD
International Students: Not listed

COST OF ATTENDANCE

Tuition and Fees: $56,232
Additional Expenses with Room and Board: $22,422
Total: $78,654

Financial Aid: Need-based aid available for students. 60% of Northwestern students receive some form of financial aid.

ADDITIONAL INFORMATION

The Honors Program in Medical Education (HPME) is a program where students enter undergraduate studies at Northwestern University and are given conditional admission to Feinberg School of Medicine in Chicago. HPME students are encouraged to take a gap year after obtaining their undergraduate degree and before starting at medical school. They emphasize pursuing research, traveling abroad for international opportunities, and engaging in fellowship experiences. Students who engage in the gap year must get it approved from the HPME director and may not apply to other medical schools. Only students on a gap year are prohibited to apply to other medical schools. The HPME program is otherwise non-binding. Additionally, the MCAT is not required for this program.

HPME students are not required to major in a science. They may select Human Communication Sciences, Biomedical Engineering, or any major within the College of Arts and Sciences. Students also have opportunities to be involved in research while obtaining their undergraduate degree. Many students participate in the HPME Summer Research Program (HPME SRP).

Students who graduate from Northwestern University and intend to matriculate into Feinberg School of Medicine must maintain a 3.55 GPA or higher in their science courses and an overall minimum GPA of 3.7.

UNIVERSITY OF ILLINOIS - CHICAGO BA/BS-MD PROGRAM (8-YEAR)

Medical School: University of Illinois – Chicago School of Medicine
1853 W Polk St, Chicago, IL 60612
Undergraduate: University of Illinois - Chicago
1200 W Harrison St, Chicago, IL 60607
Program Information: *https://medicine.uic.edu/gppa/*
Request for Information Form:
https://admissions.uic.edu/undergraduate/request-information
Phone: (312) 413-2263
E-Mail: *gppauic@uic.edu*
Additional Combined Programs:
BA/BS-PharmD, BA/BS-DPT, BA/BS-DMD
International Students: Not listed

COST OF ATTENDANCE

In-State Tuition and Fees: $10,584
Additional Expenses with Room and Board: $15,978
Total: $26,562

Out-of-State Tuition and Fees: $24,276
Additional Expenses with Room and Board: $15,978
Total: $40,254

Financial Aid: Students are automatically considered for scholarships and awards when they apply.

ADDITIONAL INFORMATION

In the Guaranteed Professional Programs Admissions (GPPA) program, students are allowed to major in whatever they choose. It is only available to U.S. citizens or permanent residents who are also Illinois residents. The GPPA is non-binding, in that students admitted to the program are not required to attend the University of Illinois College of Medicine. However they are offered conditional admission. According to UIC, "over 80% of our graduates continue training at the University of Illinois College of Medicine." Students in the GPPA program can partake in the College of Medicine (COM) activities, seminars, and research. For more information about the curriculum, visit: *https://medicine.uic.edu/gppa/about/curriculum/*

The 2019 Class Profile consisted of 700 applications, 93 interviews, and 32 admitted students. The admitted students' academics ranged from 29-36 (ACT) and an average of 3.85 GPA. 59% admitted were female, while 41% were male.

The College of Medicine has campuses in Chicago, Peoria, and Rockford. They review applications and decide on the site placement for the student. For more information on the application guide, visit: *https://gppa.uic.edu/prospective-students/prospective-students-application-guide/*

171

ILLINOIS

INDIANA

IOWA

KANSAS

MICHIGAN

MINNESOTA

MISSOURI

NEBRASKA

NORTH DAKOTA

OHIO

SOUTH DAKOTA

WISCONSIN

MIDWEST

ILLINOIS

INDIANA

IOWA

KANSAS

MICHIGAN

MINNESOTA

MISSOURI

NEBRASKA

NORTH DAKOTA

OHIO

SOUTH DAKOTA

WISCONSIN

INDIANA STATE UNIVERSITY
BS/MD PROGRAM (8-YEAR)

Medical School: Indiana University School of Medicine
620 Chestnut St, Terre Haute, IN 47809
Undergraduate: Indiana State Universit
200 N 7th St, Terre Haute, IN 47809
Program Information: *https://www.indstate.edu/cas/pre-professional-programs/bmd-rural-health-program/overview*
Request for Information Form:
https://www.indstate.edu/academics/online/requestinfo
Phone: (812) 237-2121
E-Mail: *admissions@indstate.edu*
Additional Combined Programs: N/A
International Students: Not considered

COST OF ATTENDANCE

Tuition and Fees: $0
Room & Board (Living On Campus): $3,962
Total (Living On Campus): $3,962

Financial Aid: Full tuition waiver at the undergraduate level.

ADDITIONAL INFORMATION

Indiana State University is a public school founded in 1865. Their Rural Health Program, open to only IN residents, allows high school seniors the opportunity to go into their BS/MD program. Admitted students may choose any major from a list of 125 degree programs. This program is designed for students who have a desire to provide care in rural Indiana as a primary care physician. This program also offers full tuition waivers during undergraduate studies.

Other unique aspects of this program include summer internship experiences in rural clinics, undergraduate research, specialized academic advising, attendance to the Indiana Rural Health Association Conference, attendance at Mini-Medical School, and full participation in ISU's Honors Program.

Matriculation to Indiana University School of Medicine requires the following:

1. Completion of the undergraduate degree with a minimum GPA of 3.50
2. Score on the MCAT equal to the mean score of previous year's entering class

UNIVERSITY OF EVANSVILLE
B/MD PROGRAM (8-YEAR)

Medical School: IU School of Medicine-Evansville
515 Walnut St, Evansville, IN 47708
Undergraduate: University of Evansville
1800 Lincoln Ave, Evansville, IN 47722
Program Information:
https://www.evansville.edu/majors/BtoMD/program.cfm
Request for Information Form:
https://www.evansville.edu/admission/requestmore.cfm
Phone: (812) 488-3250
E-Mail: *fr25@evansville.edu*
Additional Combined Programs: N/A
International Students: Not considered

COST OF ATTENDANCE

(After scholarship) Tuition and Fees: $7,500
Additional Expenses with Room and Board: $14,076
Total: $21,576

Financial Aid: Students receive $30,000/year scholarship. Must live in on-campus housing for first two years.

ADDITIONAL INFORMATION

The University of Evansville is a private liberal arts school founded in 1854. The purpose of the B/MD program is to "increase the number of physicians in southwestern and southern Indiana and increase the opportunities for Indiana residents to obtain training at the Indiana University School of Medicine." Only IN residents may apply.

B/MD Scholars are given a $30,000/year scholarship to fund their UE bachelor's degree and these students receive provisional admission to the Indiana University School of Medicine in Evansville. However, students must live on-campus for the first two years.

Majoring in science is not required. However many B/MD Scholars choose a science-based major because of pre-medical coursework requirements. B/MD Scholars must meet the following requirements to ensure their spot at IU School of Medicine:

1. Cumulative GPA of 3.0 for the first 31 undergraduate hours
2. Cumulative GPA of 3.5 from 62 hours until Bachelors degree completion
3. Complete all U of Evansville undergraduate degree requirements
4. Complete all prerequisite courses
5. Take MCAT and obtain a score equal to avg. of last year's entering class
6. Complete AAMC application

ILLINOIS

INDIANA

IOWA

KANSAS

MICHIGAN

MINNESOTA

MISSOURI

NEBRASKA

NORTH DAKOTA

OHIO

SOUTH DAKOTA

WISCONSIN

MIDWEST

ILLINOIS

INDIANA

IOWA

KANSAS

MICHIGAN

MINNESOTA

MISSOURI

NEBRASKA

NORTH DAKOTA

OHIO

SOUTH DAKOTA

WISCONSIN

WAYNE STATE MED-DIRECT PROGRAM
BS/BA-MD PROGRAM (8-YEAR)

Medical School: Wayne State University School of Medicine
540 E Canfield St, Detroit, MI 48201
Undergraduate: Wayne State University
42 W Warren Ave, Detroit, MI 48202
Program Information: *https://provost.wayne.edu/wayne-med-direct*
Request for Information Form: *https://slate.wayne.edu/register/info*
Phone: (313) 557-2200
E-Mail: *med-direct@wayne.edu*
Additional Combined Programs: N/A
International Students: Not considered

COST OF ATTENDANCE

Tuition and Fees: $0
Additional Expenses with Room and Board: $0
Total: $0

Financial Aid: Wayne Med-Direct Scholarship (covers both undergraduate and medical school)

ADDITIONAL INFORMATION

Wayne State University (WSU) is a public research university. The Med-Direct Program is an early-decision binding program. Therefore, students may not apply to other early-decision binding programs. If the applicant does not get accepted into the Med-Direct program, they are not bound to attending WSU under general admissions. Students are not required to wait until they are accepted to WSU to submit the supplemental WSU Med-Direct application.

Three letters of recommendation are required. Two must come from teachers. One must come from a community member. Volunteer work and community service are emphasized. Students from a disadvantaged SES background are given preference, especially if they are interested in studying health disparities.

The interviews will take place on campus. Students who come from out-of-state and are flying are reimbursed for the student and one guest/guardian attending. Lodging and transportation are provided as well. Those planning to drive are also reimbursed for mileage.

Med-Direct students may choose their major from a selection of 40 offered by the College of Liberal Arts and Sciences. These students must pursue a minor from any department at WSU. Med-Direct students are not typically in the same classes. All students take classes with the general undergraduate population. Students are required to take the MCAT.

WSU offers a generous scholarship package for Med-Direct scholars. The Undergraduate scholarships covers (1) full-time tuition and fees for fall and winter terms, (2) tuition and fees for spring and summer terms, and (3) undergraduate room and board for fall, winter, spring, and summer terms. Eligibility for this scholarship include:
1. File FAFSA
2. Major in College of Liberal Arts and Sciences following pre-medical coursework
3. Enroll as full-time student
4. Complete requirements of Med-Direct curriculum

Eligibility for this scholarship for four consecutive years:
1. Cumulative GPA of at least 3.50 at the end of each semester
2. Maintain a cumulative GPA of at least 3.0 as an undergraduate

WSU School of Medicine also offers a full scholarship for four years. For more information, visit: *https://provost.wayne.edu/wayne-med-direct/scholarship*

UNIVERSITY OF MINNESOTA
BA/MD PROGRAM (7-YEAR)

Medical School: University of Minnesota Medical School
420 Delaware St SE, Minneapolis, MN 55455
Undergraduate: University of Minnesota
231 Pillsbury Dr., S.E. Minneapolis, MN 55455
Program Information:
https://admissions.tc.umn.edu/admissioninfo/bamd.html
Request for Information Form:
http://umn.force.com/admissions/KnowledgeTCAdmissionsAskaQuestion
Phone: (612) 625-2008
Contact Link: *https://twin-cities.umn.edu/contact-us*
Additional Combined Programs: N/A
International Students: Not considered

COST OF ATTENDANCE

In-State Tuition and Fees: $15,542
Additional Expenses with Room and Board: $16,082
Total: $31,624

Out-of-State Tuition and Fees: $35,978
Additional Expenses with Room and Board: $16,082
Total: $53,560

Financial Aid: Scholarships available ranging from $1,000 to $60,000 over four years. No separate application required.

ADDITIONAL INFORMATION

The University of Minnesota is a public university established in 1851. The BA/MD Joint Admissions Scholars (JAS) Program is available for eligible Minnesota residents. The goal of this program is to help diverse Minnesota students become physicians to meet the healthcare needs of Minnesota's communities. The JAS program is 7 years, with the first three spent at University of Minnesota and the last four at the Medical School. Only 10 students will enroll in this program per year.

Students who are interested in the JAS program should indicate an interest in medical school in their application. Those who are eligible will be selected and invited to apply. Expect the following in the JAS application:

1. Letters of recommendation
2. Personal statement
3. Diversity statement
4. Resume
5. Interview required

Students are encouraged to apply by Nov 1 for consideration. JAS students must pursue a BA in either Biology, Society, and Environment or Physiology. Continuing eligibility requirements to enter the Medical School are as follow:

1. Participation in the Summer Enrichment Program
2. Medical Education Seminar series completion
3. Completion of a research project with poster, publication, or presentation
4. Complete community service with a presentation
5. MCAT
6. Submit AMCAS
7. Meet all undergraduate program requirements
8. Successfully complete year one of medical school
9. Bachelor degree conferred after this requirement is met

ILLINOIS

INDIANA

IOWA

KANSAS

MICHIGAN

MINNESOTA

MISSOURI

NEBRASKA

NORTH DAKOTA

OHIO

SOUTH DAKOTA

WISCONSIN

MIDWEST

ILLINOIS

INDIANA

IOWA

KANSAS

MICHIGAN

MINNESOTA

MISSOURI

NEBRASKA

NORTH DAKOTA

OHIO

SOUTH DAKOTA

WISCONSIN

ST. LOUIS UNIVERSITY
MEDICAL SCHOLAR PROGRAM
BS/MD (8-YEAR)

Medical School: Saint Louis University School of Medicine
1402 S Grand Blvd, St. Louis, MO 63104
Undergraduate: Saint Louis University
1 N Grand Blvd, St. Louis, MO 63103
Program Information:
https://www.slu.edu/scholars/medical-scholars/index.php
Request for Information Form:
https://www.slu.edu/request-information/request-info.php
Phone: (314) 977-2500
E-Mail: *admission@slu.edu*
Additional Combined Programs: BA/PharmD
International Students: Not listed

COST OF ATTENDANCE

Tuition and Fees: $46,400
Additional Expenses with Room and Board: $12,184
Total: $58,584

Financial Aid: Scholarships available. Students encourage to apply.
97% of SLU students receive financial aid.

ADDITIONAL INFORMATION

Saint Louis University (SLU) is a private Catholic university founded in 1818. They have a campus in Missouri, as well as Madrid, Spain. The Medical Scholar Program is for high school students who are interested in conditional acceptance into the SLU School of Medicine. The MCAT is required. Program scholars must fulfill certain requirements to be completely accepted. In addition, Medical Scholar students may choose from a selection of approved majors. For more information about these specific requirements and majors, visit: *https://www.slu.edu/scholars/medical-scholars/overview.php*

UNIVERSITY OF MISSOURI - KANSAS CITY BA/MD PROGRAM (6-YEAR)

Medical School: University of Missouri - Kansas City School of Medicine
2411 Holmes Street, Kansas City, MO 64108
Undergraduate: University of Missouri - Kansas City
5000 Holmes St, Kansas City, MO 64110
Program Information: *https://med.umkc.edu/bamd/*
Request for Information Form: *https://futureroo.umkc.edu/register/?id=f6fe097a-7582-499d-a7cf-0bfe867183b0*
Phone: (816) 235-1870
E-Mail: *medicine@umkc.edu*
Additional Combined Programs: N/A
International Students: Not considered

COST OF ATTENDANCE

In-State Tuition and Fees: $21,876
Additional Expenses with Room and Board: $14,466
Total: $36,342

Out-of-State Tuition and Fees: $42,248
Additional Expenses with Room and Board: $14,466
Total: $56,714

Financial Aid: Merit-based and need-based scholarships available.

ADDITIONAL INFORMATION

University of Missouri - Kansas City (UMKC) is a public research university. In the first two years of this six-year program, students spend 75% of their time completing their bachelor's degree requirements. The remaining 25% of their time is spent engaging in medical school coursework. During the last four years of this program, most of the student's time is completing medical school coursework while still spending a small amount of time fulfilling their baccalaureate degree requirements.

Students in the BA/MD program start clinical experiences in the third week of this six-year program. A teaching physician, a docent, mentors the student in groups. During the first two years, students are placed in docent teams of 10-15 students. In the remaining four years, students are assigned to docent teams of 12-15. During this time, students spend of half of a day/week in outpatient care. Research opportunities are also available for BA/MD students. Additionally, UMKC School of Medicine students are encouraged to delve into community service and participate in community partnerships.

Although the minimum ACT and SAT are 24 and 1160 respectively, the average student admitted to the BA/MD Program has a 32 ACT and 1420 SAT. Furthermore, the average unweighted GPA of admitted BA/MD students is 3.90. In regards to standardized scores, Missouri residents must submit an ACT score. Regional and out-of-state students may submit either an ACT or an SAT score. However, the ACT score is preferred.

Tuition, fees, and housing vary by the year the student is in as well as residency/regional/out-of-state costs. For a more detailed analysis of the cost of attendance and financial aid, visit: *https://med.umkc.edu/bamd/finance/*

ILLINOIS
INDIANA
IOWA
KANSAS
MICHIGAN
MINNESOTA
MISSOURI
NEBRASKA
NORTH DAKOTA
OHIO
SOUTH DAKOTA
WISCONSIN

MIDWEST

ILLINOIS

INDIANA

IOWA

KANSAS

MICHIGAN

MINNESOTA

MISSOURI

NEBRASKA

NORTH DAKOTA

OHIO

SOUTH DAKOTA

WISCONSIN

WASHINGTON UNIVERSITY IN ST. LOUIS MED SCHOLARS BS/MD PROGRAM (8-YEAR)

Medical School: Washington University School of Medicine in St. Louis
660 S. Euclid Ave., St. Louis, MO 63110
Undergraduate: Washington University in St. Louis
1 Brookings Dr., St. Louis, MO 63130
Program Information: https://admissions.wustl.edu/academics/special-programs/university-scholars-program-in-medicine/
Request for Information Form:
https://pathway.wustl.edu/register/request-information
Phone: (314) 935-6000
E-Mail: admissions@wustl.edu
Additional Combined Programs: N/A
International Students: Considered

COST OF ATTENDANCE

Tuition and Fees: $56,300
Additional Expenses with Room and Board: $18,488
Total: $74,788

Financial Aid: Applicants automatically considered for academic scholarships. Students are encouraged to apply for scholarships and financial aid as well.

ADDITIONAL INFORMATION

Washington University in St. Louis is a private research university. Students accepted into the University Scholars program may defer enrollment for up to two years in undergraduate or graduate studies. There are summer programs available for all high school students, not only those interested in the University Scholars in Medicine Program.

Applicants who are selected for an interview will attend the finalists' weekend towards the end of March. Washington University covers the cost of finalists' round-trip expenses within the U.S. and while in St. Louis. Notification of admissions decisions will be given soon after the interview weekend. Students who are not selected as finalists may still be admitted to another undergraduate program.

University Scholars in Medicine have a mentor in the School of Medicine starting from their first year. They are also able to engage in research and obtain pre-professional advising. There are various shadowing opportunities and invitations to events and lectures in the School of Medicine as well.

Acceptance to the School of Medicine is given to students so long as they (1) maintain a 3.80 GPA and (2) achieve a minimum MCAT score equal to the 97th percentile or above and (3) fulfill all prerequisite coursework for medical school. According to the website, if students do not meet these requirements, "...eligibility for graduate study will be up to the School of Medicine's discretion." As a medical student at the Washington University School of Medicine in St. Louis, students receive patient contact within the first month of their studies.

CHADRON STATE COLLEGE RHOP
BS/MD PROGRAM (8-YEAR)

Medical School: University of Nebraska Medical Center
42nd and, Emile St, Omaha, NE 68198
Undergraduate: Chadron State College
1000 Main St, Chadron, NE 69337
Program Information: *https://www.csc.edu/sci/rhop/*
Request for Information Form: *http://future.csc.edu/inquiryform*
Phone: (308) 432-6000
E-Mail: *start@csc.edu*
Additional Combined Programs: BS/DDS, BS/PharmD, BS/DPT
International Students: Not considered

COST OF ATTENDANCE

Tuition and Fees: $0
Additional Expenses with Room and Board: $6,496
Total: $6,496

Financial Aid: Tuition waiver for RHOP students. Students may also receive up to $5700 in renewable scholarships.

ADDITIONAL INFORMATION

Chadron State is a public college established in 1911. Through the Rural Health Opportunities Program (RHOP), Chadron State and the University of Nebraska Medical Center offer high school students from Nebraska the opportunity to apply for to the BS/MD program. Along with the BS/MD program, they offer programs in Medical Lab Science, Dental Hygiene, Dentistry, Nursing, Pharmacy, Physical Therapy, Physician Assistants, and Radiography.

To be eligible for this program, students must meet the following criteria:

1. Be a rural Nebraska resident
2. Apply and be accepted to Chadron State College
3. Preferred minimum ACT score of 24
4. Apply for one professional field only
5. Apply by Dec 1

Chadron State is seeking students who are dedicated to healthcare and show demonstrated commitment to the rural areas of Nebraska.

Benefits of being an RHOP Scholar:

1. All RHOP scholars receive a tuition waiver at Chadron State
2. All participants receive early acceptance into UNMC
3. Early registration privileges
4. Visiting privileges to UNMC
5. Receive up to $5700 in renewable scholarships
6. Alternates with an ACT of 23+ receive up to $2500 in renewable scholarships

ILLINOIS

INDIANA

IOWA

KANSAS

MICHIGAN

MINNESOTA

MISSOURI

NEBRASKA

NORTH DAKOTA

OHIO

SOUTH DAKOTA

WISCONSIN

MIDWEST

ILLINOIS

INDIANA

IOWA

KANSAS

MICHIGAN

MINNESOTA

MISSOURI

NEBRASKA

NORTH DAKOTA

OHIO

SOUTH DAKOTA

WISCONSIN

CASE WESTERN RESERVE UNIVERSITY BA/BS-MD PROGRAM (8-YEAR)

Medical School: Case Western Reserve University School of Medicine
9501 Euclid Ave, Cleveland, OH 44106
Undergraduate: Case Western Reserve University
10900 Euclid Ave, Cleveland, OH 44106
Program Information: *https://case.edu/medicine/admissions-programs/md-programs/pre-professional-scholars-programs*
Request for Information Form:
https://go.case.edu/register/requestinformation
Phone: (216) 368-4450
E-Mail: *admission@case.edu*
Additional Combined Programs: BA/DDS (3+4)
International Students: Not listed

COST OF ATTENDANCE

Tuition and Fees: $50,450
Additional Expenses with Room and Board: $19,213
Total: $69,663

Financial Aid: Merit-based and need-based aid available. Applicants are automatically considered for some scholarships. Some scholarships require separate applications.

ADDITIONAL INFORMATION

Case Western Reserve University is a private university established in 1967. Students in the Pre-Professional Scholars Program may choose any major so long as they complete certain pre-medical courses. 15-20 high school seniors are accepted into the Pre-Professional Scholars Program. Students who complete their undergraduate degree in less than four years are not allowed to enter the School of Medicine early. Case Western Reserve University recommends students in this situation pursue other experiences such as research or study abroad.

Continuing requirements for Pre-Professional Scholars include the following:

1. Cumulative GPA of at least 3.63
2. Cumulative AMCAS GPA and AMCAS Biology, Chemistry, Physics, and Math GPA of 3.63 at time of application
3. MCAT not required, but if taken, must be above 94th percentile
4. AMCAS required
5. Interview required

CLEVELAND STATE UNIVERSITY

Medical School: Northeast Ohio Medical University College of Medicine
4209 St. Rt. 44, Rootstown, OH 44272
Undergraduate: Cleveland State University
2121 Euclid Ave, Cleveland, OH 44115
Program Information: *https://sciences.csuohio.edu/neomed/neomed-csu-early-assurance-undergraduate-pathway*
Request for Information Form:
https://go.case.edu/register/requestinformation
Phone: (216) 687-2000
E-Mail: *admissions@csuohio.edu*
Additional Combined Programs: N/A
International Students: Not considered

COST OF ATTENDANCE

In-State Tuition and Fees: $10,460
Additional Expenses with Room and Board: $17,018
Total: $27,478

Out-of-State Tuition and Fees: $13,926
Additional Expenses with Room and Board: $17,018
Total: $30,944

Financial Aid: Honors Program scholarship available (full tuition for up to 8 semesters). Other scholarships are available.

ADDITIONAL INFORMATION

Cleveland State University is a public school established in 1964. The NEOMED program is offered only to current CSU undergraduates. Students must apply through the online application to the Undergraduate Early Assurance Program. Students may apply during their sophomore or junior years. Applicants should meet the following criteria to be considered for admission:

1. Minimum ACT score of 26 or SAT equivalent or be enrolled in good standing in CSU's honor's college
2. Minimum college GPA of 3.4
3. Be a sophomore/junior when submitting the application
4. Successfully complete at least 20 hours of coursework in Biology, Chemistry, Physics, and/or Math with at least "C-" grades or higher
5. Complete certain prerequisite coursework
6. Complete CASPer
7. Be U.S. citizen or permanent resident
8. Successfully complete interview

ILLINOIS

INDIANA

IOWA

KANSAS

MICHIGAN

MINNESOTA

MISSOURI

NEBRASKA

NORTH DAKOTA

OHIO

SOUTH DAKOTA

WISCONSIN

MIDWEST

ILLINOIS

INDIANA

IOWA

KANSAS

MICHIGAN

MINNESOTA

MISSOURI

NEBRASKA

NORTH DAKOTA

OHIO

SOUTH DAKOTA

WISCONSIN

KENT STATE UNIVERSITY
BS/MD PROGRAM (6-YEAR)

*This program has been temporarily suspended since Fall 2019

Undergraduate: Kent State University
800 E Summit St, Kent, OH 44240
Program Information:
http://catalog.kent.edu/colleges/as/integrated-life-sciences-bs-md/

*This program has been temporarily suspended since Fall 2019

UNIVERSITY OF CINCINNATI
BS/MD PROGRAM (8-YEAR)

Medical School: University of Cincinnati College of Medicine
3230 Eden Ave, Cincinnati, OH 45267
Undergraduate: University of Cincinnati
2600 Clifton Ave, Cincinnati, OH 45221
Program Information: *https://med.uc.edu/connections/eligibility*
Request for Information Form:
https://admissions.uc.edu/contact/request-info.html
Phone: (513) 558-5581
E-Mail: hs2md@uc.edu
Additional Combined Programs: N/A
International Students: Not considered

COST OF ATTENDANCE

In-State Tuition and Fees: $11,660
Additional Expenses with Room and Board: $11,668
Total: $23,328

Out-of-State Tuition and Fees: $26,994
Additional Expenses with Room and Board: $11,668
Total: $38,662

Financial Aid: May apply for the University of Cincinnati's Darwin T. Turner Scholarship among other merit-based scholarships

ADDITIONAL INFORMATION

The Connections Program utilizes the Multiple Mini Interview (MMI) Process, whereby "approximately six to eight interview 'stations' or encounters that last eight to 10 minutes are centered on a scenario." This interviewing process was developed around 10 years ago and has been implemented in other schools over the years. The University of Cincinnati College of Medicine is the first U.S. medical school to solely use this technique.

The University of Cincinnati holds information sessions in Summer/Fall for students interested in making an appointment to learn more about the program. They recommend attending the Preview UC and College Close-Up events before going to an information session.

For information on the statistics for the entering class of 2019, visit: *http://med.uc.edu/connections/connections/eligibility-requirements-to-apply*

Students in the Connections Program cannot begin medical school early (i.e., they must complete four years). If they have completed requirements early, they are encouraged to participate in multiple majors or study abroad. Furthermore, Connections Program students must meet the following requirements to ensure their reserved seat at the UC College of Medicine:

1. Minimum AMCAS-calculated 3.50 overall GPA and 3.50 Biology, Chemistry, Physics, and Math GPA
2. Graduate from University Honors Program
3. Complete either (a) minor in Medical Sciences or (b) major in Medical Sciences
4. Obtain at least minimum score requirement for MCAT in one sitting
5. Satisfy baccalaureate graduation requirements

ILLINOIS

INDIANA

IOWA

KANSAS

MICHIGAN

MINNESOTA

MISSOURI

NEBRASKA

NORTH DAKOTA

OHIO

SOUTH DAKOTA

WISCONSIN

MIDWEST

ILLINOIS

INDIANA

IOWA

KANSAS

MICHIGAN

MINNESOTA

MISSOURI

NEBRASKA

NORTH DAKOTA

OHIO

SOUTH DAKOTA

WISCONSIN

UNIVERSITY OF TOLEDO
BS/MD PROGRAM (8-YEAR)

Medical School: University of Toledo College of Medicine
3000 Arlington Ave, Toledo, OH 43614
Undergraduate: University of Toledo
2801 W. Bancroft St., Toledo, OH 43606
Program Information:
https://www.utoledo.edu/success/pre-health-advising/bacc2md.html
Request for Information Form:
https://www.utoledo.edu/admission/transfer/request.html
Phone: (800) 586-5336
E-Mail: *prehealthadvising@utoledo.edu*
Additional Combined Programs: N/A
International Students: Not considered

COST OF ATTENDANCE

In-State Tuition and Fees: $10,514
Additional Expenses with Room and Board: $15,404
Total: $25,918

Out-of-State Tuition and Fees: $19,874
Additional Expenses with Room and Board: $15,404
Total: $35,278

Financial Aid: Encourage eligible Bacc2MD Pathway applicants to apply for Presidential Scholarship, which covers full tuition and housing.

ADDITIONAL INFORMATION

University of Toledo is a public research university. The Bacc2MD Program is an 8-year program that offers students a guaranteed interview to the University of Toledo College of Medicine. According to their website, "All applicants are admitted to the undergraduate portion of the Bacc2MD program if they meet the requirements." These requirements are as follow:

1. U.S. citizenship or permanent residency
2. Cumulative high school GPA of at least 3.50
3. Minimum composite ACT score of 28 or combined math and critical reading SAT score of at least 1310

Students interested in the Bacc2MD Program must select a major in one the following colleges:

1. College of Natural Sciences and Mathematics
2. College of Arts and Letters
3. College of Engineering's Department of Bioengineering

Admission to the University of Toledo College of Medicine is not guaranteed. Students must maintain a 3.5 GPA to receive a guaranteed interview. The Bacc2MD program is designed as a 4+4 program. Students are not allowed to begin medical school early. The university strongly encourages students to take up study abroad or internship opportunities. Additionally, students are not required to take the MCAT. However, they must submit an early admission application at the end of their sophomore year of college and the AMCAS application at the end of their junior year.

According to data on the college website, 32 freshman applied to the Bacc2MD Program, 17 interviewed with the College of Medicine, 10 were offered a seat, and 10 accepted the offer. For more information, visit: *https://www.utoledo.edu/success/pre-health-advising/bacc2md-frequently-asked-questions.html*

REGION THREE
SOUTH

ALABAMA

ARKANSAS

DELAWARE

DISTRICT OF COLUMBIA

FLORIDA

GEORGIA

KENTUCKY

LOUISIANA

MARYLAND

MISSISSIPPI

NORTH CAROLINA

OKLAHOMA

SOUTH CAROLINA

TENNESSEE

TEXAS

VIRGINIA

WEST VIRGINIA

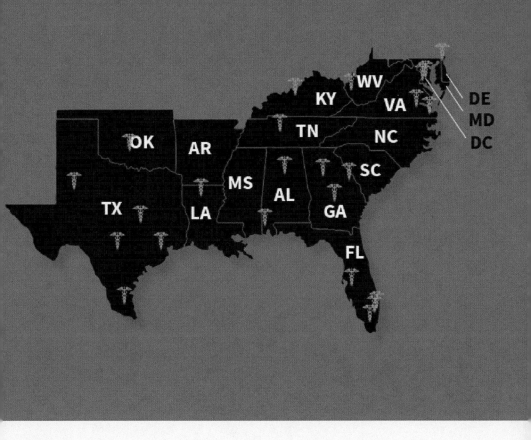

25 *Programs* | **17** *States*

1. *AL – University of Alabama – Birmingham EMSAP (8-year)*
2. *AL – University of South Alabama (8-year)*
3. *DE – University of Delaware (8-year)*
4. *DC – The George Washington University (7-year)*
5. *DC - Howard University (6-year)*
6. *FL – Florida Atlantic University Med Scholars (7-year, 8-year)*
7. *FL – Nova Southeastern BS/DO (7-year, 8-year)*
8. *FL – University of Miami Medical Scholars (7-year, 8-year)*
9. *FL – University of South Florida (7-year)*
10. *GA – Mercer University SCP (8-year)*
11. *GA – Augusta University BS/MD (7-year)*
12. *GA – Spelman College (8-year)*
13. *KY – University of Louisville (8-year)*
14. *LA – Grambling State University (7-year, 8-year)*
15. *OK – University of Oklahoma (8-year)*
16. *TN – Fisk University (7-year, 8-year)*
17. *TX – Baylor University BS/MD (8-year)*
18. *TX – Rice Baylor BS/MD (8-year)*
19. *TX – Texas JAMP (6-year, 7-year, 8-year)*
20. *TX – Texas Tech University (8-year)*
21. *TX – The University of Texas – Rio Grande Valley (8-year)*
22. *TX – The University of Texas Health San Antonio (7-year)*
23. *VA – Hampton University (8-year)*
24. *VA – Virginia Commonwealth University – Guaranteed Admissions GMED (8-year)*
25. *WV – Marshall University (7-year)*

DIRECT MED PROGRAMS

UNIVERSITY/PROGRAM	DEADLINE	MIN SAT, ACT, GPA	OTHER REQUIREMENTS
UNIV. OF ALABAMA AT BIRMINGHAM 1720 UNIV. BLVD, BIRMINGHAM, AL 35294 EMSAP - EARLY MEDICAL SCHOOL ACCEPTANCE PROGRAM	*Submit EMSAP app & U. of AL's undergrad app *EMSAP app opens mid-Sept. *EMSAP app w/all suppl materials due Dec. 1 *Submit UAB's undergrad app ASAP *In-person interviews	Min SAT ERW+M – 1400 Min Act – 30 Min GPA - 3.50	*Must be a U.S. citizen or perm. res. *14 accepted *Approx. 36 offered an interview *Must be first-time freshman *2 letters of rec. req. *Superscores are not accepted *MCAT and AMCAS req.
UNIV. OF SOUTH AL 307 N UNIV. BLVD. MOBILE, AL 36688 EAP – EARLY ACCEPTANCE PROGRAM JAGSPOT – JAGUAR SCHOLARSHIP PROG. OPPORTUNITY TRACKER	*Apply for Early Acceptance Program in JagSPOT *Apply to Honors College in JagSPOT *App deadlines in mid-Dec. *Invitation to interview in early-Feb. *Interviews in March *Applicants simultaneously interviewed for Honors College acceptance.	Min SAT ERW+M – 1260 (AL resident); 1360 (out-of-state) Min Act – 27 (AL resident); 30 (out-of-state) Min GPA - 3.50	*Must be a U.S. citizen or perm. res. *Req. differ for AL residents & out-of-state applicants *Must apply to Honors College. *Letters of rec. not req. & not incl. *Pref for AL applicants or certain areas in MS and FL. *MCAT & AMCAS req.
UNIV. OF DELAWARE 4 KENT WAY NEWARK, DE 19716	*2nd semester fr stud. invited to orientation mtg to join interest gp *15 students from this gp selected at the end of soph yr	Min SAT ERW+M – 1200 Act – 30-33 for Honors Prog. Min GPA - 3.50	*Current UD undergrads *MCAT req., min. score 504 w/no subsection less than 126.
THE GEORGE WASHINGTON UNIVERSITY (GWU) 2121 I ST. NW WASH., D.C. 20037	*7-year BA/MD *Apply RD for GWU Columbian College of A&S by Nov. 15 *Selected applicants invited to submit additional essay *Apps reviewed by the committee for MD admissions *Interviews are conducted in early Feb. *Decisions are made in late March	Near-perfect avg. scores and GPA admitted SAT/ACT test scores are req. SAT II tests req. in science & math **Please do not send scores to the GWU MD Program.**	*U.S. citizens, perm res, and Canadian citizens considered *Must be H.S. senior *If you apply for BS/MD, you cannot apply to other GWU special progs.

UNIVERSITY/PROGRAM	DEADLINE	MIN SAT, ACT, GPA	OTHER REQUIREMENTS
HOWARD UNIV. 2400 6TH ST. NW WASH., D.C. 20059	*Apply to A&S as a Bio or Chem major *Apply by Nov 1 EA deadline *Decision by Dec. 15 *Early spring, invites sent to select appl to apply to the prog. *Submit 2 hard copies of essay demonstrating interest, 3 rec. letters, and updated transcript & resume by March 15	Min SAT ERW+M – 1300 Min Act – 28 Min GPA - 3.50	*Apply as a H.S. senior *2+ years of foreign lang. req. in H.S. *H.S. classes must incl. bio, chem, physics, and math thru pre-calc *MCAT req., min. score of 504.
FLORIDA ATLANTIC UNIV. 777 GLADES RD BOCA RATON, FL 33431	*Must be accepted to FAU and Wilkes Honors College *Medical Pipeline Suppl App open in Aug. *Deadline to submit Medical Pipeline App in Jan. *Must be admitted to FAU & Wilkes Honors College bef. Jan. 10	Min SAT ERW+M – 1490 Min Act – 33 Min GPA – 4.30 wt	*Must be U.S. citizen or perm. residents *Exp. w/patients highly rec. *MCAT req., min score of 510 *AMCAS req.
NOVA SOUTHEASTERN 3301 COLLEGE AVE, FORT LAUDERDALE, FL 33314	*BS/DO (7-year & 8-year) *Dual admission deadline Mar 1	7-year Min SAT – 1360 Min ACT – 30 Min GPA – 3.50 8-year Min SAT – 1270 Min ACT – 27 Min GPA – 3.5	*MCAT req. *Interview req. *Bio, Chem, Pre-Calc, or Trig req. 7-year *4 yrs. of Math, Science, and Eng 8-year *4 yrs. of Math, 3 of Science, 4 of Eng.
UNIV. OF MIAMI 1320 S DIXIE HWY CORAL GABLES, FL 33146 MSP – MEDICAL SCHOLARS PROGRAM HPM – HEALTH PROFESSIONS MENTORING	*Must be in 4th consecutive sem. FT at UM to apply *Selected applicants are offered an interview *Interviews held before end of spring term *Decisions in early June	Min SAT ERW+M – 1300 Min Act – 31 Min GPA - 3.70 undergrad GPA by end of soph year	*Must be U.S. citizen or perm. res. *Only for U. of Miami students *MCAT and AMCAS req. Note: UM's HPME direct med program has been discontinued but not the early assurance program

SOUTH

DIRECT MED PROGRAMS

UNIVERSITY/PROGRAM	DEADLINE	MIN SAT, ACT, GPA	OTHER REQUIREMENTS
U. OF S. FL **4202 E FOWLER AVE.** **TAMPA, FL 33620**	*Apply to USF *Students w/4.0 wt GPA get auto-admit to Judy Genshaft Honors College *Once admitted to USF & Honors College, no addl. appl. req. for BS/MD program	Min SAT ERW+M – 1500 Min Act – 34 Min GPA - 4.00 wt SAT/ACT superscored	*Must be U.S. citizen or perm res. *MCAT and AMCAS req.
MERCER UNIV. **1501 MERCER UNIV.** **DR. MACON, GA 31207**	*3-part app in Mercer app portal *App deadline in Jan. *Interview notification by the end of Jan. *Interviews held mid-Feb. *Accepted students notified by the end of Feb.	Min SAT ERW+M – 1390 Min Act – 30 Min GPA - 3.70	*Must be U.S. citizen or perm res. *Must have GA residency for at least 4 yrs. bef. starting at Mercer *MCAT and AMCAS req. *Up to 40 applicants invited for interviews *Up to 18 students accepted
AUGUSTA UNIV. **2500 WALTON WAY** **AUGUSTA, GA 30912**	*Apply to Augusta *Select Biology or Cell & Molecular Bio major *If req. met, Augusta will contact w/suppl. app. *EA deadline is Nov. 15. *EA applicants will be notified by Dec. of secondary app.	Min SAT ERW+M – 1400 Min Act – 32 Min GPA - 3.70 Students may superscore SAT	*1 letter of rec. req. for supplemental app. *No essay qs in general app *MCAT req.
SPELMAN COLLEGE **350 SPELMAN LN SW** **ATLANTA, GA 30314**	*Indicate ASP prog. interest on app. *Must be accepted by Spelman *Strongly rec to apply during early in app process: ED due Nov. 1, EA due Nov. 15 *App pkg (Spelman app & statement of interest in ASP) *Spelman recs candidates to Upstate; Upstate screens candidates & invites some to interview *Upstate sends decs w/ conditional admit letter	Min SAT ERW+M – 1360 Min Act – 29 Min GPA - 3.50 wt	*Up to 5 students admitted *MCAT not req. *Acceptance into UAS is binding *Activities show commitment to service, healthcare, and community

UNIVERSITY/PROGRAM	DEADLINE	MIN SAT, ACT, GPA	OTHER REQUIREMENTS
UNIV. OF LOUISVILLE **2301 S 3RD ST,** **LOUISVILLE, KY 40292**	*Apply to Univ. of Louisville *Then complete GEMS application online *All materials due Dec 15	Min SAT – 1420 Min ACT – 31 Min GPA – 3.75	*Only open to KY residents *MCAT req.
GRAMBLING STATE UNIV. **403 MAIN ST.** **GRAMBLING, LA 71245**	*GSU freshman apply after 1st term on campus	Min SAT ERW+M – 900 Min Act – 20 Min GPA - 3.25	*Students apply after they enroll at Grambling State *Must be Black/African American *Economically/ Educationally disadvantaged *6-week summer programs
HAMPTON UNIV. **100 E QUEEN ST.** **HAMPTON, VA 23669**	*Indicate UAS prog. interest on Hampton app *Must be accepted by Hampton *App package (Hampton app & statement of interest in medicine & UAS prog.) due Nov. 1 *Hampton recs candidates to Upstate; Upstate screens candidates & invites some to interview *Upstate sends decs w/ conditional admit letter	Min SAT ERW+M – 1360 Min Act – 31 Min GPA - 90% average	*Up to 5 students admitted *MCAT not req. *Acceptance into UAS is binding *Activities show commitment to service, healthcare, and community
UNIV. OF OK **660 PARRINGTON OVAL, NORMAN, OK 73019** **MHSP - MEDICAL HUMANITIES SCHOLARS PROGRAM**	*Must be accepted to U. of OK before applying to MHSP *Once accepted, apply to Honors College *MHSP app due mid-Jan. *Submit OU & Honors College apps ≥ two weeks bef. submitting MHSP app *Finalists invited for on-campus interviews at the end of March *Notification in early April	Min SAT ERW+M – 1390 Min Act – 30 Min GPA - 3.75 Top 10% of grad. class	*125-150 apply, 5 admitted *Interested in the humanities *Familiarity w/clinical med. (e.g., shadowing a physician) *Suppl mat. not req. nor accepted *MCAT req.

SOUTH

DIRECT MED PROGRAMS

UNIVERSITY/PROGRAM	DEADLINE	MIN SAT, ACT, GPA	OTHER REQUIREMENTS
FISK UNIV. **1000 17TH AVE. N.** **NASHVILLE, TN 37208**	*Apply during 2nd sem at Fisk *Two-stage app. process -Stage 1: Personal statement & transcript from Fisk due by early Jan. If accepted, move on to Stage 2. -Stage 2: 3 letters of rec from Fisk faculty. *Interviews in Feb. after 2nd stage	Min GPA - 3.20 (undergrad)	*Only for current Fisk students. *Strong ACT scores req *MCAT req.
BAYLOR UNIV. **1311 S 5TH ST.** **WACO, TX 76706**	*Submit Baylor app by Nov. 1; select "pre-med" *2 events: Nov. 1 and Jan. 24 *For Nov. 1 event, submit Baylor Medical Track Program app by mid-Sept. *For Jan. 24 event, submit Baylor Medical Track Program app by mid-Nov. *Addl. info. on deadlines and dates, please see school profile below.	Min SAT ERW+M – 1430 Min Act – 32 Min GPA - 3.70 Top 5% of grad class	*Must be U.S. citizen or perm. res. *6 admitted *MCAT req., must score in range of 501-507 w/no section < 125 *Scholarship consideration based on the essay in response to Baylor event
RICE/BAYLOR **6100 MAIN ST.** **HOUSTON, TX 77005** **MSP - MEDICAL SCHOLARS PROGRAM**	*Apply to Rice & Rice/Baylor app by Dec. 1 *MSP applicants may apply ED or RD *ED applicants must commit to Rice by Jan. 1, though Baylor's dec is made in the spring. *ED applicants must submit app. mat. by Nov. 1. Rice/Baylor app. not due until Dec. 1 *MSP finalists notified of interview by late Jan. *Interviews conducted in Feb. *Rice/Baylor Scholars notified Apr 1	Highly competitive; high grades and scores req.	*Intl & U.S. students welcome to apply. *6 admitted *MCAT req.

UNIVERSITY/PROGRAM	DEADLINE	MIN SAT, ACT, GPA	OTHER REQUIREMENTS
TEXAS JAMP **P.O. BOX 2175** **AUSTIN, TX 78768** **JAMP - JOINT** **ADMISSIONS MEDICAL** **PROGRAM** **JAMP PARTNERS W/68** **COLLEGES & UNI. IN** **TEXAS**	*Apply to Texas college/univ. *JAMP app deadline is Oct. 1 *Apply for financial aid. *Early admission track for those w/27+ college credits (may obtain B.S. degree in 3 yrs). *Regular admit track – applicants must complete 27 college credits during 1st year of college	Min SAT ERW+M – 1022 (2019 mean for TX res.) Min Act – 20.5 (2019 mean for TX res.) Min GPA - 3.25	*Must be a senior at a Texas H.S. w/U.S. citizen or perm. res. *Scores must not be lower than the mean SAT/ACT score for Texas *Must have Expected Family Contribution (EFC) ≤ 8000 *MCAT is req.
TEXAS TECH UNIV. **2500 BROADWAY** **LUBBOCK, TX 79409**	*Use ApplyTexas & apply separately for Texas Tech's Honors College *Then apply for UMSI; opens Oct. 1 *UMSI app & suppl. mat. due Dec. 6 *Semifinalists are offered an in-person interview	Min SAT ERW+M – 1360 Min Act – 30 Min GPA - 3.70 Single seating only; Superscore not accepted	*Prefer top 10% of grad class *CASPer test req. bef. Oct. 1 of H.S. senior year *MCAT not req..
UT – RIO GRANDE VALLEY **1201 W UNIVERSITY DR., EDINBURG, TX 78539**	Discontinued	Min SAT ERW+M – 1100 Min Act – 21 Min GPA - 3.25	*Must be a senior at a Texas H.S. w/U.S. citizen or perm. resident *Economically and educationally disadvantaged, EFC < 8000
UTSA HEALTH - FAME **1 UTSA CIRCLE** **SAN ANTONIO, TX 78249**	Discontinued		
VCU **907 FLOYD AVE.** **RICHMOND, VA 23284** **GAPM (GUARANTEED ADMISSIONS PROGRAM FOR MEDICINE)**	*2 apps req.: (1) VCU Undergrad & (2) Honors College GAMP *Both available online in early August and due by mid- Nov.	Min SAT ERW+M – 1330 (one sitting) Min Act – 29 Min GPA - 3.50 Nov. SAT/ACT taken year of app not considered.	*15 accepted *2-4 letters of rec. *MCAT req.
MARSHALL UNIV. **1 JOHN MARSHALL DR.** **HUNTINGTON, WV 25755**	*App deadline in Jan. *On-campus interview	Min SAT ERW+M – 1390 (one sitting; M ≥ 630) Min Act – 30 Min GPA - 3.75	*Only for WV H.S. students *3 letters of rec, ≥ 2 H.S. teachers *Must choose biology major. *MCAT not req.

SOUTH

UNIVERSITY OF ALABAMA AT BIRMINGHAM BS/MD PROGRAM (8-YEAR)

Medical School: University of Alabama at Birmingham School of Medicine
1670 University Blvd, Birmingham, AL 35233
Undergraduate: University of Alabama at Birmingham
1720 University Blvd, Birmingham, AL 35294
Program Information: *https://www.uab.edu/students/academics/emsap/application-process*
Request for Information Form:
https://www.uab.edu/online/request-information
Phone: (205) 934-8221
E-Mail: *chooseuab@uab.edu*
Additional Combined Programs: BS/DPT, BS/DDS, BS/OD
International Students: Not considered

COST OF ATTENDANCE

In-State Tuition and Fees: $10,710
Additional Expenses with Room and Board: $17,665
Total: $28,375

Out-of-State Tuition and Fees: $25,500
Additional Expenses with Room and Board: $18,354
Total: $43,854

Financial Aid: There are no special scholarships for EMSAP students. However, most EMSAP students receive ACT and GPA-BASED scholarships.

ADDITIONAL INFORMATION

The University of Alabama at Birmingham is a public university established in 1936. The Early Medical School Acceptance Program (EMSAP) is available to U.S. citizens and permanent residents. There are three EMSAP programs available: Early Medical, Early Dental, or Early Optometry. EMSAP students may defer entry into the School of Medicine up to one year. The MCAT is required. Admitted EMSAP students must also submit the AMCAS.

The average admitted EMSAP student had an ACT score of 34 and high school GPA of 4.5. Requirements for applicants include:

1. Minimum high school GPA of 3.50
2. Minimum ACT score of 30
3. Minimum SAT score of 1400
4. 4 years of English, 4 years of math, 1 year of chemistry or physics, and 1 year of biology
5. Super-scoring not allowed

UNIVERSITY OF SOUTH ALABAMA
BS/MD PROGRAM (8-YEAR)

Medical School: University of South Alabama College of Medicine
390 Student Center Circle, Mobile, AL 36688
Undergraduate: University of South Alabama
307 N University Blvd, Mobile, AL 36688
Program Information: *https://www.southalabama.edu/
departments/admissions/earlyacceptance/*
Request for Information Form: *https://www.southalabama.edu/
departments/admissions/requestinfo.html*
Phone: (251) 460-7834
E-Mail: *recruitment@southalabama.edu*
Additional Combined Programs: BS/DPT, BS/PharmD
International Students: Not considered

COST OF ATTENDANCE

In-State Tuition and Fees: $6,930
Additional Expenses with Room and Board: $9,870
Total: $16,800

Out-of-State Tuition and Fees: $14,012
Additional Expenses with Room and Board: $21,662
Total: $35,674

Financial Aid: *https://www.southalabama.edu/departments/
financialaffairs/studentaccounting/tuition.html*

ADDITIONAL INFORMATION

The University of South Alabama is a public university founded in
1963. The College of Medicine Early Acceptance Program (COMEAP)
is open to U.S. citizens or permanent residents who are current high
school seniors. Applicants must apply to the Honors College and
the Early Acceptance Program in their application system, JagSPOT.
Letters of recommendation are not required nor considered for the
EAP program.

Continuing requirements to ensure acceptance into the College of
Medicine are as follow:

1. All prerequisite courses must be taken at University of South
   Alabama unless approved by an advisor in advance
2. Must maintain a minimum overall GPA of 3.50 on 4.0 scale
3. Must maintain a minimum science GPA of 3.50
4. Must take MCAT and receive at least 504.
5. Completion of 2 semesters of clinical observation
6. Completion of 1 semester of team-based learning exercises
7. Must complete application to medical school through AMCAS

ALABAMA

ARKANSAS

DELAWARE

DISTRICT OF COLUMBIA

FLORIDA

GEORGIA

KENTUCKY

LOUISIANA

MARYLAND

MISSISSIPPI

NORTH CAROLINA

OKLAHOMA

SOUTH CAROLINA

TENNESSEE

TEXAS

VIRGINIA

WEST VIRGINIA

SOUTH

UNIVERSITY OF DELAWARE
BS/MD PROGRAM (8-YEAR)

Medical School: Sidney Kimmel Medical College
1025 Walnut St #100, Philadelphia, PA 19107
Undergraduate: University of Delaware
4 Kent Way, Newark, DE 19716
Program Information:
https://www.cas.udel.edu/medical-scholars/program-requirements
Request for Information Form:
https://apply.udel.edu/register/prospectivestudent
Phone: (302) 831-2793
E-Mail: *as-advise@udel.edu*
Additional Combined Programs: BS/DDS
International Students: Not listed

COST OF ATTENDANCE

In-State Tuition and Fees: $12,730
Additional Expenses with Room and Board: $17,557
Total: $30,287

Out-of-State Tuition and Fees: $34,160
Additional Expenses with Room and Board: $17,558
Total: $51,718

Financial Aid: Scholarships available. No separate application needed for merit-based scholarship consideration for first-year students.

ADDITIONAL INFORMATION

University of Delaware is a public university established in 1833. Their Medical Dental Scholars Program (MDSP) is available to current undergraduate students. Students in their second semester of freshman year may join the Interest Group. The criteria for acceptance into the Interest Group of the MDSP are as follow:

1. Minimum SAT score of 1800 (old SAT, Note: new SAT equivalent is approximately 1290)
2. B+ average in high school coursework
3. Commitment to a health-related career
4. GPA of 3.50 in science and non-science courses by the end of sophomore year at University of Delaware

Approximately 30-70 students enter the Interest Group. Only 15 may be selected from this group. Selection happens at the end of the applicant's second year.

Once accepted to the MDSP, the students are conditionally accepted to Sidney Kimmel so long as they meet the following continuing requirements

1. Minimum 3.50 GPA in sciences and non-sciences
2. Minimum score of 504 on the MCAT with no subsection score less than 126

The MDSP is open to all students at the University of Delaware, even if they are out-of-state. Non-Delaware residents are supported through the Health Professions Evaluation Committee. Delaware residents are supported through the Delaware Institute for Dental Education and Research (DIDER) and Delaware Institute of Medical Education and Research (DIMER).

Note: Their combined program with Kornberg School of Dentistry at Temple is no longer running.

THE GEORGE WASHINGTON UNIVERSITY BA/MD PROGRAM (7-YEAR)

Medical School: The George Washington University Medical School
2300 I Street, NW Washington, D.C., 20037
Undergraduate: The George Washington University
2121 I Street, NW Washington, D.C., 20037
Program Information: *https://smhs.gwu.edu/academics/md-program/admissions/dual-programs/bamd*
Request for Information Form: *https://undergraduate.admissions.gwu.edu/get-information-about-gw*
Phone: (202) 994-6040
E-Mail: *gwadm@gwu.edu*
Additional Combined Programs: N/A
International Students: Not listed

COST OF ATTENDANCE

Tuition and Fees: $58,550
Additional Expenses with Room and Board: $19,151
Total: $77,701

Financial Aid: Scholarships available. For more information, visit:
https://financialaid.gwu.edu/scholarships

ADDITIONAL INFORMATION

The George Washington University is a private university established in 1821. The GWU Columbian College of Arts and Sciences, in partnership with the GWU Medical School, offers a 7-year dual BA/MD program for high school seniors. GWU seeks high school students with competitive standardized scores, demonstrated leadership, community service, and health care experiences. Applications are sent directly to GWU via undergraduate admissions.

Continuing requirements to ensure entry into the MD program are as follows:

1. Maintain a minimum 3.60 cumulative GPA
2. No grades of C or lower in science courses
3. MCAT practice exam score
4. Participation in medically-related experiences

ALABAMA

ARKANSAS

DELAWARE

DISTRICT OF COLUMBIA

FLORIDA

GEORGIA

KENTUCKY

LOUISIANA

MARYLAND

MISSISSIPPI

NORTH CAROLINA

OKLAHOMA

SOUTH CAROLINA

TENNESSEE

TEXAS

VIRGINIA

WEST VIRGINIA

SOUTH

ALABAMA

ARKANSAS

DELAWARE

DISTRICT OF COLUMBIA

FLORIDA

GEORGIA

KENTUCKY

LOUISIANA

MARYLAND

MISSISSIPPI

NORTH CAROLINA

OKLAHOMA

SOUTH CAROLINA

TENNESSEE

TEXAS

VIRGINIA

WEST VIRGINIA

HOWARD UNIVERSITY
BS/MD PROGRAM (6-YEAR)

Medical School: Howard University College of Medicine
520 W St NW, Washington, DC 20059
Undergraduate: Howard University
2400 6th St NW, Washington, DC 20059
Program Information:
https://medicine.howard.edu/education/dual-degree-programs
Request for Information Form:
https://www2.howard.edu/admission/admissions-mailing-list
Phone: (202) 806-2755
E-Mail: *preprofessional@howard.edu*
Additional Combined Programs: N/A
International Students: Not listed

COST OF ATTENDANCE

Tuition and Fees: $26,464
Additional Expenses with Room and Board: $21,516
Total: $47,980

Financial Aid: Howard University Freshman (HUF) scholarships are available.

ADDITIONAL INFORMATION

Howard University is a private, historically black university established in 1867. The BS/MD program allows students to obtain their bachelor's degree and MD in 6 years. Students apply to this program while they are in their senior year of high school. This program is for "students who are admitted to Howard University who would matriculate into the College of Arts and Sciences in the Fall semester immediately after graduation from high school." This program is available for current Howard University students enrolled in the College of Arts and Sciences.

Students should apply via the Common App and select a Biology or Chemistry Major by the Early Action deadline (November 1). Acceptance letters are given out by December 15th. In the Spring, invitations are sent out to eligible students to apply to the BS/MD program.

Initial eligibility requirements:

1. High school GPA of 3.5 minimum
2. ACT 28 minimum
3. SAT 1300 minimum
4. 2+ years of foreign language including literature
5. High school coursework in biology, chemistry, physics, and math (including pre-calculus)

Students must then submit two hard copies of the following by March 15th:

1. Essay demonstrating interest in Medicine to help those less privileged
2. 3 Letters of Recommendation
3. high school counselor
4. science instructor
5. community/volunteer supervisor or mentor
6. Copy of updated transcript and resume

Continuing Requirements are as follow:

1. Minimum science GPA of 3.25
2. Minimum overall GPA of 3.50
3. Minimum MCAT score of 504
4. Strong interview
5. Letters of recommendation

FLORIDA ATLANTIC UNIVERSITY
BA/BS-MD PROGRAM (7-YEAR, 8-YEAR)

Medical School: Florida Atlantic University College of Medicine
777 Glades Rd, Boca Raton, FL 33431
Undergraduate: Florida Atlantic University
777 Glades Rd, Boca Raton, FL 33431
Program Information: *http://www.fau.edu/honors/future-students/*
medical-scholar-program/
Request for Information Form: *http://fau.edu/info/*
Phone: (561) 799-8646
E-Mail: *medicalpipelines@fau.edu*
Additional Combined Programs: N/A
International Students: Not listed

COST OF ATTENDANCE

In-State Tuition and Fees: $5,488
Additional Expenses with Room and Board: $20,722
Total: $26,210

Out-of-State Tuition and Fees: $19,488
Additional Expenses with Room and Board: $20,722
Total: $40,210

Financial Aid: Scholarships are available. Students admitted by December 15 eligible for the highest awards.

ADDITIONAL INFORMATION

Florida Atlantic University is a public university established in 1961. The Wilkes Medical Scholars Program provides early admission to the Charles E. Schmidt College of Medicine (a.k.a. FAU'S College of Medicine). Admission is open to incoming freshman students. Students receive admission to medical school so long as they fulfill the program requirements:

1. Finish each undergraduate semester with a minimum 3.70 GPA
2. Calculated after three years, science GPA of 3.70
3. Must participate in certain activities/experiences during each semester of enrollment
4. AMCAS application by October 15
5. MCAT composite score minimum of 510

For a complete list of the possible activities/experiences, please visit the link listed under "Program Information".

The Medical Scholars Program is "restricted", meaning students in this program are not allowed to apply to other LCME accredited medical schools.

ALABAMA

ARKANSAS

DELAWARE

DISTRICT OF COLUMBIA

FLORIDA

GEORGIA

KENTUCKY

LOUISIANA

MARYLAND

MISSISSIPPI

NORTH CAROLINA

OKLAHOMA

SOUTH CAROLINA

TENNESSEE

TEXAS

VIRGINIA

WEST VIRGINIA

SOUTH

ALABAMA

ARKANSAS

DELAWARE

DISTRICT OF COLUMBIA

FLORIDA

GEORGIA

KENTUCKY

LOUISIANA

MARYLAND

MISSISSIPPI

NORTH CAROLINA

OKLAHOMA

SOUTH CAROLINA

TENNESSEE

TEXAS

VIRGINIA

WEST VIRGINIA

NOVA SOUTHEASTERN
BS/DO PROGRAM (7-YEAR, 8-YEAR)

Medical School: Nova Southeastern College of Osteopathic Medicine
3200 S University Dr., Davie, FL 33328
Undergraduate: Nova Southeastern University
3301 College Ave, Fort Lauderdale, Florida 33314
Program Information: *https://www.nova.edu/undergraduate/ academics/dual-admission/osteopathic-medicine.html*
Request for Information Form:
https://www.nova.edu/request-info/index.html
Phone: (954) 262-8000
E-Mail: *admissions@nova.edu*
Additional Combined Programs: N/A
International Students: Not listed

COST OF ATTENDANCE

Tuition and Fees: $15,635
Additional Expenses with Room and Board: $12,185
Total: $27,820

Financial Aid: Merit-based scholarships available.

ADDITIONAL INFORMATION

Nova Southeastern University is a private university established in 1964. The dual admission program at NSU allows students to obtain a BS and DO within 7- or 8- years. If students choose the 7-year program, their bachelor's degree will be conferred upon completion of the first year of medical school. Students in this program attend the Nova Southeastern College of Osteopathic Medicine. An interview is required for both the 7year and 8-year tracks.

High school applicants must meet the following criteria to be considered:

1. Minimum 3.5 weighted
2. 7-year: ACT composite 30 or total SAT 1360 or 8-year: ACT composite 27 or total SAT 1270
3. 7-year: 4 years of Math, Science, and English or 8-year: 4 years of Math, 3 years of Science, and 4 years of English

Required courses:

1. Biology
2. Chemistry
3. Pre-Calculus or Trigonometry

Undergraduate requirements to enter the College of Osteopathic Medicine:

1. Minimum cumulative GPA of 3.5
2. Minimum science GPA of 3.5
3. Grade of "C" or better in each prerequisite course
4. MCAT 502 with a minimum 125 on each subsection, achieved on same test attempt
5. Graduate application required
6. 7-year: 90 major and GE coursework credits completed or 8-year: 120 credits required

UNIVERSITY OF MIAMI
BS/MD PROGRAM (7-YEAR, 8-YEAR)

Medical School: Miller School of Medicine
1600 NW 10th Ave #1140, Miami, FL 33136
Undergraduate: University of Miami
1320 S Dixie Hwy, Coral Gables, FL 33146
Program Information: *http://admissions.med.miami.edu/md-programs/medical-scholars-program/prerequisites*
Request for Information Form: Go to "request info" at
https://admissions.miami.edu/undergraduate/index.html
Phone: (305) 243-3234
E-Mail: *admission@miami.edu*
Additional Combined Programs:
HPME program for current undergraduates
International Students: Not considered

COST OF ATTENDANCE

Tuition and Fees: $52,080
Additional Expenses with Room and Board: $21,632
Total: $73,712

Financial Aid: All applicants are considered for merit-based academic scholarships. No separate applications required.

ADDITIONAL INFORMATION

The University of Miami is a private university established in 1925. The Medical Scholars Program is only open to current University of Miami students. Applicants must have the following:

1. Be a U.S. citizens or permanent residents
2. Be in the fourth consecutive semester of full-time academic work
3. Must have entered the University of Miami with a minimum SAT score of 1300 (CR&M), or ACT of 31

Promotion to the Miller School of Medicine is contingent upon the following factors:

1. Maintain a cumulative GPA of at least 3.70
2. Maintain a science GPA of at least 3.70
3. MCAT composite score that "at least meets equivalent average score of preceding medical school matriculating class"
4. Must participate in patient contact, volunteer experiences, research, campus/community service organizations, or study abroad
5. Must complete AMCAS

ALABAMA
ARKANSAS
DELAWARE
DISTRICT OF COLUMBIA
FLORIDA
GEORGIA
KENTUCKY
LOUISIANA
MARYLAND
MISSISSIPPI
NORTH CAROLINA
OKLAHOMA
SOUTH CAROLINA
TENNESSEE
TEXAS
VIRGINIA
WEST VIRGINIA

SOUTH

ALABAMA

ARKANSAS

DELAWARE

DISTRICT OF COLUMBIA

FLORIDA

GEORGIA

KENTUCKY

LOUISIANA

MARYLAND

MISSISSIPPI

NORTH CAROLINA

OKLAHOMA

SOUTH CAROLINA

TENNESSEE

TEXAS

VIRGINIA

WEST VIRGINIA

UNIVERSITY OF SOUTH FLORIDA
BS/MD PROGRAM (7-YEAR)

Medical School: Morsani College of Medicine
12901 Bruce B Downs Blvd, Tampa, FL 33612
Undergraduate: University of South Florida
4202 E Fowler Ave, Tampa, FL 33620
Program Information:
https://www.usf.edu/honors/prospective-students/7-year-med.aspx
Request for Information Form: *http://usfsm.edu/request-information.aspx*
Phone: (813) 974-3087
E-Mail: *admissions@usf.edu*
Additional Combined Programs: BS/PharmD
International Students: Not considered

COST OF ATTENDANCE

In-State Tuition and Fees: $5,588
Additional Expenses with Room and Board: $15,120
Total: $20,708

Out-of-State Tuition and Fees: $16,502
Additional Expenses with Room and Board: $15,120
Total: $31,622

Financial Aid: All Honors College students receive $2000 after completing three requirements. Other scholarships are available.

Note: There is no on-campus housing. USF has affiliated housing.

ADDITIONAL INFORMATION

University of South Florida (USF) is a public university founded in 1956. In partnership with the Morsani College of Medicine (MCOM), USF offers high school students the opportunity to apply for their 7-year BS/MD program. The first three years will be completed at Judy Genshaft Honors College at USF. The next four years are spent at Morsani College of Medicine. The B.S. degree is awarded following completion of the fourth year of study. Students are required to major in Biomedical Sciences. The M.D. is conferred after completion of the four-year medical program at MCOM.

Applicants must apply through undergraduate admission to USF. Students who have a 4.0 weighted high school GPA (calculated by USF admissions), will automatically be admitted to the Judy Genshaft Honors College. After this point, no additional application is required for the BS/MD program. Requirements to be admitted to the BS/MD program are as follow:

1. SAT score of 1500 minimum (may be Superscored)
2. Combined ACT score of 34 minimum (may be Superscored)
3. U.S. citizenship or permanent residency by the time of the AMCAS application (end of second year)
4. Transfer and current students not eligible

In the spring of year 1, students must submit a declaration of intent and utilize an Early Decision (EDP) timeline to submit an AMCAS application. For specific details on the EDP timeline, please visit the link under "Program Information".

Students in the BS/MD program must take the MCAT and submit an AMCAS application. A formal interview is also required. Additional requirements for a secured spot at MCOM are as follow:

1. By the end of year 1, overall and science/math GPA of 3.60
2. By end of years 2 and 3, overall and science/math GPA of 3.70
3. MCAT to be taken at least one month before EDP primary application
4. At least two semesters of health-related research
5. Successful completion of Judy Genshaft Honors College curriculum
6. Required number of contact hours for medical observation and community service
7. Interview
8. Letters of recommendation

MERCER UNIVERSITY
BS/MD PROGRAM (8-YEAR)

Medical School: Mercer University School of Medicine (MUSM)
1550 College St., Macon, GA 31207
Undergraduate: Mercer University
1501 Mercer University Dr., Macon, GA 31207
Program Information: *https://medicine.mercer.edu/admissions/
doctor-of-medicine/special-programs-admission-information/special-
consideration-program/*
Request for Information Form:
https://undergrad.mercer.edu/request-information/
Phone: (478) 301-2650
E-Mail: *admissions@mercer.edu*
Additional Combined Programs: N/A
International Students: Not considered

COST OF ATTENDANCE

Tuition and Fees: $35,130
Additional Expenses with Room and Board: $15,152
Total: $50,282

Financial Aid: Merit-based scholarships and grants are available.

ADDITIONAL INFORMATION

Mercer University is a private university founded in 1833. Their
Special Consideration Program is available for up to 18 incoming
first-year students. Eligibility depends on the following:

1. U.S. citizenship or permanent residency
2. 2Maintained Georgia residency for four years prior to
   matriculation at Mercer University
3. Accepted into undergraduate program at Mercer University
4. At least 2 confidential letters of reference

Acceptance into MUSM is given if the following conditions are met:

1. Meeting bachelor's degree requirements
2. Obtaining undergraduate degree from Mercer University
3. Completing pre-medical coursework at Mercer University
4. Attending 80% of SCP student meetings at MUSM
5. Minimum cumulative GPA and cumulative science GPA of 3.0
   at end of Year 1
6. Minimum cumulative GPA and cumulative science GPA of 3.25
   at end of Year 2
7. Minimum cumulative GPA and cumulative science GPA of 3.50
   at end of Year 3
8. 8.   At least 100 hours of volunteer work
9. MCAT minimum at 66th percentile
10. At least 50th percentile in Biological and Biochemical
    Foundations of Living Systems subsection of MCAT
11. Submit a complete application by Early Decision Program
    deadline for MUSM
12. Must submit AMCAS

ALABAMA

ARKANSAS

DELAWARE

DISTRICT OF COLUMBIA

FLORIDA

GEORGIA

KENTUCKY

LOUISIANA

MARYLAND

MISSISSIPPI

NORTH CAROLINA

OKLAHOMA

SOUTH CAROLINA

TENNESSEE

TEXAS

VIRGINIA

WEST VIRGINIA

SOUTH

AUGUSTA UNIVERSITY
BS/MD PROGRAM (7-YEAR)

Medical School: Medical College of Georgia
1120 15th St, Augusta, GA 30912
Undergraduate: Augusta University
2500 Walton Way, Augusta, GA 30912
Program Information:
https://www.augusta.edu/admissions/professionalscholars.php
Request for Information Form:
https://www.augusta.edu/admissions/request-info.php
Phone: (706) 737-1632
E-Mail: *admissions@augusta.edu*
Additional Combined Programs: BS/DMD
International Students: Not listed

COST OF ATTENDANCE

In-State Tuition and Fees: $6,892
Additional Expenses with Room and Board: $16,935
Total: $23,827

Out-of-State Tuition and Fees: $22,270
Additional Expenses with Room and Board: $21,662
Total: $43,932

Financial Aid: Scholarship application deadline is February 1.

ADDITIONAL INFORMATION

Augusta University is a public university established in 1828. Their Professional Scholars Program allows students the opportunity to obtain a BS/MD in 7 years. Students must major in Biology or Cell and Molecular Biology. Students in this program take classes together and are invited to participate in special volunteer opportunities, research, and clinical exposure.

To maintain eligibility for this BS/MD program, students must meet the following requirements:

1. Successful interview after the first year
2. Maintain minimum cumulative and science/math GPA of 3.5 (year 1), 3.6 (year 2), and 3.7 (year 3)
3. Complete 40 hours of volunteer clinical service by October of year 3
4. Minimum score no less than prior year's national mean on MCAT (must be taken before the end of September in year 3)

SPELMAN COLLEGE
BS/MD PROGRAM (8-YEAR)

Medical School: SUNY Upstate Medical University
750 E Adams St, Syracuse, NY 13210
Undergraduate: Spelman College
350 Spelman Ln SW, Atlanta, GA 30314
Program Information:
https://www.upstate.edu/com/admissions/options/bs-md.php
Request for Information Form:
https://apply.spelman.edu/register/inquiry%20
Phone: (404) 270-5193
Dr. Alayna Blash, Associate Director Health Careers Program,
E-Mail: *ablash@spelman.edu*
Additional Combined Programs: N/A
International Students: Not listed

COST OF ATTENDANCE

Tuition and Fees: $29,972
Additional Expenses with Room and Board: $14,338
Total: $44,310

Financial Aid: Merit-based scholarships awarded to select few
applicants (minimum 1330 SAT or 31 ACT and 3.8 weighted GPA).
Some scholarships cover tuition, fees, and housing. No separate
application required.

ADDITIONAL INFORMATION

Spelman College is a private, women's college established in 1881. In
partnership with SUNY Upstate, high school seniors may apply to their
Accelerated Scholars Program (ASP) Program. A goal of this program
is to encourage diversity and allow students of various academic
backgrounds a pathway to medical school. The ASP encourages
students to apply to any academic program, although the "program
chosen should contain enough flexibility in the curriculum to
incorporate the required science courses within four years."

This program is binding. Additionally, the MCAT is not required.

Students interested in applying to the ASP must meet the following
requirements:

1. Minimum 90% average OR 3.50 weighted GPA
2. SAT minimum of 1360 (CR&M) or
3. ACT minimum of 29
4. Extra-curricular activities indicating demonstrated
   commitment to community service in healthcare setting

Continuing Requirements for admission to SUNY Upstate:

1. Unofficial transcripts sent to Upstate at end of each semester
2. Complete all Spelman College major requirements
3. Complete certain medical school prerequisite courses
4. No grade lower than a "B" in the medical school prerequisites
5. Minimum 3.50 cumulative GPA and 3.50 science GPA each
   semester
6. 40 hours of volunteer service, preferably in
   direct contact with patients or physicians

ALABAMA

ARKANSAS

DELAWARE

DISTRICT OF COLUMBIA

FLORIDA

GEORGIA

KENTUCKY

LOUISIANA

MARYLAND

MISSISSIPPI

NORTH CAROLINA

OKLAHOMA

SOUTH CAROLINA

TENNESSEE

TEXAS

VIRGINIA

WEST VIRGINIA

SOUTH

ALABAMA

ARKANSAS

DELAWARE

DISTRICT OF COLUMBIA

FLORIDA

GEORGIA

KENTUCKY

LOUISIANA

MARYLAND

MISSISSIPPI

NORTH CAROLINA

OKLAHOMA

SOUTH CAROLINA

TENNESSEE

TEXAS

VIRGINIA

WEST VIRGINIA

UNIVERSITY OF LOUISVILLE G.E.M.S. BS/MD PROGRAM (8-YEAR)

Medical School: University of Louisville School of Medicine
500 S Preston St, Louisville, KY 40202
Undergraduate: University of Louisville
2301 S 3rd St., Louisville, KY 40292
Program Information:
https://louisville.edu/medicine/admissions/programs/gems
Request for Information Form: *https://louisville.edu/admissions/apply/transfer/info-request/information-packet-request*
Phone: (502) 852-6531
E-Mail: *admitme@louisville.edu*
Additional Combined Programs: N/A
International Students: Not considered

COST OF ATTENDANCE

In-State Tuition and Fees: $11,732
Additional Expenses with Room and Board: $5,380
Total: $17,112

Financial Aid: Kentucky and Southern Indiana residents who meet certain academic criteria will automatically receive a scholarship, no separate application required. Trustee's scholarship is available for students with 29 ACT or 1330 SAT and 3.5 GPA minimum.

ADDITIONAL INFORMATION

The University of Kentucky is a public university founded in 1865. The Guaranteed Entrance to Medical School (GEMS) program was established in 1988. This program is only open to Kentucky high school seniors.
Interested high school seniors must meet the following criteria to be considered for the GEMS program:

1. 31 ACT or 1390 SAT minimum
2. 3.75 GPA
3. Complete GEMS application:
    *   One essay about how you arrived at this point in your life
    *   Two letters of recommendation (high school principal or counselor and one science/math teacher)
    *   Be a KY resident
4. Submit the application by Dec 15

Guaranteed entrance to the School of Medicine is offered if GEMS students complete the following:

1. Maintain a 3.4 GPA
2. Score at or above the national mean on each section of the MCAT
3. Fully participate in program activities

GRAMBLING STATE UNIVERSITY
BS/MD PROGRAM (7-YEAR, 8-YEAR)

Medical School: Meharry Medical College
1005 Dr. DB Todd Jr Blvd, Nashville, TN 37208
Undergraduate: Grambling State University
403 Main St., Grambling, LA, 71245
Program Information: *https://www.gram.edu/academics/majors/arts-and-sciences/biology/degrees/bsmd_prog.php*
Request for Information Form:
https://www.gram.edu/admissions/requestinfo/
Phone: (318) 274-3811
E-Mail: *admissions@gram.edu*
Additional Combined Programs: N/A
International Students: Not listed

COST OF ATTENDANCE

In-State Tuition and Fees: $7,682
Additional Expenses with Room and Board: $6,949
Total: $14,631

Out-of-State Tuition and Fees: $16,706
Additional Expenses with Room and Board: $6,948
Total: $23,654

Financial Aid: Applicants are automatically considered for merit-based scholarships. For more details, visit:
https://www.gram.edu/finaid/scholarships/

ADDITIONAL INFORMATION

Grambling State University is a public, historically black university established in 1901. Their BS/MD program aims to increase the number of African American physicians. The program can be complete in 7 or 8 years. Admitted students must "attend a six-week summer academic and clinical enrichment program at MMC beginning the summer following freshman year." This program is open to current freshman students at GSU.

Eligibility requirements for this program are as follow:

1. Black/African American
2. U.S. citizen or permanent resident
3. Economically and/or educationally disadvantaged (first-gen college)
4. Express a desire to be a physician
5. Minimum cumulative GPA of 3.25
6. No grade less than "C" in science coursework
7. Minimum ACT of 20 and SAT of 900

Continuing requirements include an overall 3.25 GPA minimum and an MCAT score with no subsection less than 122. An interview is required.

ALABAMA

ARKANSAS

DELAWARE

DISTRICT OF COLUMBIA

FLORIDA

GEORGIA

KENTUCKY

LOUISIANA

MARYLAND

MISSISSIPPI

NORTH CAROLINA

OKLAHOMA

SOUTH CAROLINA

TENNESSEE

TEXAS

VIRGINIA

WEST VIRGINIA

SOUTH

ALABAMA

ARKANSAS

DELAWARE

DISTRICT OF COLUMBIA

FLORIDA

GEORGIA

KENTUCKY

LOUISIANA

MARYLAND

MISSISSIPPI

NORTH CAROLINA

OKLAHOMA

SOUTH CAROLINA

TENNESSEE

TEXAS

VIRGINIA

WEST VIRGINIA

UNIVERSITY OF OKLAHOMA
BS/MD PROGRAM (8-YEAR)

Medical School: University of Oklahoma College of Medicine
800 Stanton L Young Blvd., Oklahoma City, OK 73117
Undergraduate: University of Oklahoma
660 Parrington Oval, Norman, OK 73019
Program Information: *http://www.ou.edu/honors/specialprograms/*
MedHumanitiesScholarship
Request for Information Form:
http://www.ou.edu/coe/contact/info_request
Phone: (405) 325-2151
MHSP Director, Sarah Tracy E-Mail: *swtracy@ou.edu*
Admissions E-Mail: *admissions@ou.edu*
Additional Combined Programs: N/A
International Students: Not listed

COST OF ATTENDANCE

In-State Tuition and Fees: $12,788
Additional Expenses with Room and Board: $18,757
Total: $31,545

Out-of-State Tuition and Fees: $28,169
Additional Expenses with Room and Board: $18,757
Total: $46,926

Financial Aid: Scholarships available. Apply by December 15 to receive priority consideration.

ADDITIONAL INFORMATION

The University of Oklahoma is a public university founded in 1890. Their Medical Humanities Scholars Program (MHSP) is an 8-year BS/MD opportunity for five incoming freshmen. MHSP students may take electives such as "medicine and spirituality" or "literature and medicine" in their first two years. A Medical Humanities Minor is available as well, where students can learn about the history of sports medicine, or the politics of AIDS vaccine development. Medical humanities are strongly emphasized in this program, where students "[explore] medicine through the lenses of the historian, the ethicist, the sociology, the anthropologist, the write, and the visual artist" so they may "gain insights into the nature of the human condition, human suffering, personhood, and the responsibilities of individuals to one another..."

FISK UNIVERSITY
BA/MD PROGRAM (7-YEAR, 8-YEAR)

Medical School: Meharry Medical College
1005 Dr. DB Todd Jr Blvd, Nashville, TN 37208
Undergraduate: Fisk University
1000 17th Ave N, Nashville, TN 37208
Program Information:
https://www.fisk.edu/academics/pre-professional-programs/
Request for Information Form:
Go to "Request Information", *https://www.fisk.edu/contact/contact-us*
Phone: (615) 329-8666
Pre-Health Coordinator, Dr. Phyllis Freeman E-Mail:
pfreeman@fisk.edu
Additional Combined Programs: BA/DDS
International Students: Not listed

COST OF ATTENDANCE

Tuition and Fees: $20,220
Additional Expenses with Room and Board: $13,024
Total: $33,244

Financial Aid: Merit-based scholarships available. No separate application.

ADDITIONAL INFORMATION

Fisk University is a private, historically black university founded in 1866. The BA to MD pathway is open to Fisk University students. Acceptance happens in the second semester of the first year at Fisk. The MCAT is required.

Students can spend three years at Fisk and obtain their bachelor's degree after their first year at medical school, or they can transition to medical school after four years at Fisk University with their completed bachelor's degree.

The application process has two stages. Stage 1 includes the personal statement and transcript from Fisk University. These materials must be submitted in early January. Stage 2 requires three letters of recommendation from Fisk faculty members and other application materials. Students are interviewed in February after this second stage is complete.

ALABAMA

ARKANSAS

DELAWARE

DISTRICT OF COLUMBIA

FLORIDA

GEORGIA

KENTUCKY

LOUISIANA

MARYLAND

MISSISSIPPI

NORTH CAROLINA

OKLAHOMA

SOUTH CAROLINA

TENNESSEE

TEXAS

VIRGINIA

WEST VIRGINIA

SOUTH

ALABAMA

ARKANSAS

DELAWARE

DISTRICT OF COLUMBIA

FLORIDA

GEORGIA

KENTUCKY

LOUISIANA

MARYLAND

MISSISSIPPI

NORTH CAROLINA

OKLAHOMA

SOUTH CAROLINA

TENNESSEE

TEXAS

VIRGINIA

WEST VIRGINIA

BAYLOR UNIVERSITY
BS/MD PROGRAM (8-YEAR)

Medical School: Baylor College of Medicine
1 Baylor Plaza, Houston, TX 77030
Undergraduate: Baylor University
1311 S 5th St, Waco, TX 76706
Program Information:
https://www.baylor.edu/admissions/index.php?id=872132
Join Mailing List Form: *https://apply.baylor.edu/register/mailinglist*
Ask a Question Form:
https://www.baylor.edu/admissions/index.php?id=872103
Phone: (254) 710-3435
E-Mail: *admissions@baylor.edu*
Additional Combined Programs: N/A
International Students: Not considered

COST OF ATTENDANCE

Tuition and Fees: $44,544
Additional Expenses with Room and Board: $17,384
Total: $61,928

Financial Aid: Two of the six admitted students receive a scholarship total of $40,000 ($10,000 per year). The other four will receive a $12,000 scholarship ($3,000 per year). Once entering the program, another two students will be eligible to earn the $40,000 scholarship ($10,000 per year).

ADDITIONAL INFORMATION

Baylor University is a private, Baptist university established in 1845. This 8-year program offers students conditional acceptance to Baylor College of Medicine. Six students are admitted to the Baylor2 Medical Track Program. Students are required to take the MCAT and receive scores in the range of 501-507 with no section lower than 125. Finalists to the program must attend an on-campus event. Following this event, finalists write an essay on their experience. This essay is used to determine scholarship amounts.

A committee selects finalists for the program that are invited to campus. On campus, the students go on a Baylor student-led tour, eat lunch in the dining halls, and learn more about Baylor traditions. Students also have the opportunity to hear a lecture by a faculty member and attend informational sessions on financial aid. After this experience, students must write an essay about the event. Scholarship consideration is based on this essay.

For more information on deadlines and important dates, please visit: *https://www.baylor.edu/admissions/index.php?id=872132*

RICE UNIVERSITY WITH BAYLOR UNIVERSITY BS/MD PROGRAM (8-YEAR)

Medical School: Baylor College of Medicine
1 Baylor Plaza, Houston, TX 77030
Undergraduate: Rice University
6100 Main St, Houston, TX 77005
Program Information:
https://admission.rice.edu/apply/freshman/ricebaylor-medical-scholars
Request for Information Form:
https://riceadmission.rice.edu/register/request-info
Phone: (713) 348-7423
E-Mail: *admission@rice.edu*
Additional Combined Programs: N/A
International Students: Considered

COST OF ATTENDANCE

Tuition and Fees: Typically $50,310
Additional Expenses with Room and Board: $19,247
Total: $69,557

Financial Aid: Rice is a need-based institution. Under the Rice Investment, all demonstrated need is met without loans. Students whose family income is less than 65,000 receive full tuition, fees, and housing. For more information, visit: *https://financialaid.rice.edu/*

ADDITIONAL INFORMATION

Rice University is a private university established in 1912. The Medical Scholars Program is available to 6 incoming freshmen. Medical Scholars receive conditional acceptance to Baylor College of Medicine. There is no SAT/ACT or GPA minimum requirement to apply. Additionally, the MCAT and AMCAS are not required.

Application Information:

1. Students submit an admission application and the Rice/Baylor application, due December 1
2. Students may choose Early or Regular Decision
3. Early Decision applicants submit Rice application materials by November 1, but Rice/Baylor application is due December 1
4. Baylor College of Medicine notifies finalists of interview by late January
5. Interviews are held at Baylor College of Medicine in February
6. Rice/Baylor Scholars notified of acceptance by April 1

ALABAMA

ARKANSAS

DELAWARE

DISTRICT OF COLUMBIA

FLORIDA

GEORGIA

KENTUCKY

LOUISIANA

MARYLAND

MISSISSIPPI

NORTH CAROLINA

OKLAHOMA

SOUTH CAROLINA

TENNESSEE

TEXAS

VIRGINIA

WEST VIRGINIA

SOUTH

TEXAS JAMP BS/MD PROGRAM
(6-YEAR, 7-YEAR, 8-YEAR)

Medical School: N/A (9 medical schools)
Joint Admission Medical Program, P.O. Box 2175, Austin, TX, 78768
Undergraduate: N/A (67 undergraduate institutions)
Joint Admission Medical Program, P.O. Box 2175, Austin TX, 78768
Program Information: *http://www.texasjamp.org/ProspectiveStudents/become-a-JAMPer.html*
Request for Information Form:
https://www.texasjamp.org/Become-A-JAMPer/Homepage.aspx
Phone: (512) 499-4352
E-Mail: *info@texasjamp.org*
Additional Combined Programs: N/A
International Students: Not considered

COST OF ATTENDANCE

Tuition and Fees: N/A
Additional Expenses with Room and Board: N/A
Total: N/A

Financial Aid: Scholarships and summer stipends available.

ADDITIONAL INFORMATION

The Joint Admission Medical Program (JAMP) is "a unique partnership between nine Texas medical schools and sixty-seven public and private four-year undergraduate institutions." This program aims to support economically disadvantaged students. Students are only eligible if they have an Estimated Family Contribution up to 8000. Applicants must be a U.S. citizen or permanent resident with Texas residency.

There is an Early Admission Track and a Regular Admission Track. The Early Admission Track allows students to complete their undergraduate degree in 3 years. Eligible applicants for the Early Admission Track are students who have completed 27+ college credits during high school, including two semesters of general chemistry and relevant labs with a minimum "C" grade. The Regular Admission Track requires students to complete 27+ college credits in their first year of college. The MCAT is required.

For a complete list of participating undergraduate institutions and medical schools, visit: *http://www.texasjamp.org/AboutJAMP/participating-schools.htm*

TEXAS TECH UNIVERSITY
BS/MD PROGRAM (8-YEAR)

**Medical School: Texas Tech University Health Sciences Center
School of Medicine**
3601 4th Street, Lubbock, TX 79430
Undergraduate: Texas Tech University
2500 Broadway, Lubbock, TX 79409
Program Information: *https://www.ttuhsc.edu/medicine/admissions/
undergraduate-to-medical-school-initiative.aspx*
Request for Information Form:
http://www.ttu.edu/about/contact.php
**Ashley Hanson, Assistant Director of Recruitment and Special
Programs Phone:** (806) 743-2297
Ashley Hanson, E-Mail: *ashley.hanson@ttuhsc.edu*
Additional Combined Programs: N/A
International Students: Not considered

COST OF ATTENDANCE

In-State Tuition and Fees: $11,320
Additional Expenses with Room and Board: $15,392
Total: $26,712

Out-of-State Tuition and Fees: $23,770
Additional Expenses with Room and Board: $15,392
Total: $39,162

Financial Aid: Merit-based and need-based scholarships available.
TTU recommends applying as early as possible since many of their
scholarships are on a first-come, first-served basis.

ADDITIONAL INFORMATION

The Undergraduate to Medical School Initiative (UMSI) program is
offered by Texas Tech University (TTU) and Texas Tech University
Health Sciences Center School of Medicine (TTUHSC). This program is
not an accelerated program. It must be completed in 8 years, however
students who complete their undergraduate degree in 3 years may
request for early entrance into TTUHSC. Applicants to the UMSI
program must be U.S. citizens or permanent residents with Texas
residency. It is only open to high school seniors in a Texas high school.

Students in the UMSI program must complete Honors College
requirements. The MCAT is not required. Students are encouraged
to take on internships or study abroad. For more information on the
continuing program requirements, visit: *https://www.ttuhsc.edu/
medicine/admissions/documents/umsi-program-guidelines.pdf*

ALABAMA

ARKANSAS

DELAWARE

DISTRICT OF COLUMBIA

FLORIDA

GEORGIA

KENTUCKY

LOUISIANA

MARYLAND

MISSISSIPPI

NORTH CAROLINA

OKLAHOMA

SOUTH CAROLINA

TENNESSEE

TEXAS

VIRGINIA

WEST VIRGINIA

SOUTH

UNIVERSITY OF TEXAS – RIO GRANDE VALLEY BS/MD PROGRAM (8-YEAR)

Note: This program has been discontinued. It is no longer available to future students.
Medical School: University of Texas Medical Branch at Galveston (UTMB)
School of Medicine – 301 University Blvd., Galveston, TX 77555
Undergraduate: University of Texas Rio Grande Valley (UTRGV)
1201 W University Dr., Edinburg, TX 78539
Program Information: *https://www.utrgv.edu/biology/academics/programs/health-oriented/ems-acceptance-program/index.htm*
Request for Information Form:
https://www.utrgv.edu/campus-tours/request-information/index.htm
Phone: (844) 288-8748
E-Mail: *admissions@utrgv.edu*
Additional Combined Programs: Dental Early Acceptance Program (DEAP) for UTRGV first-year students
International Students: Not considered
Note: Must be Texas Resident with U.S. citizenship or permanent residency

COST OF ATTENDANCE

In-State Tuition and Fees: $8,132
Additional Expenses with Room and Board: $12,814
Total: $20,946

Out-of-State Tuition and Fees: $20,792 Additional Expenses with Room and Board: $12,814
Total: $33,606

Financial Aid: Scholarships available. Applicants must apply for scholarships.

ADDITIONAL INFORMATION

The Early Medical School Acceptance Program (EMSAP) is a combined degree opportunity for high school students provided by the University of Texas Rio Grande Valley (UTRGV). This program only considers U.S. citizens (Texas residency) who are financially and/or educationally disadvantaged. Educationally disadvantaged students are those who are first-generation college students. This program is no longer open to new applicants.

UTRGV also offers a Dental Early Acceptance Program (DEAP) for first-year UTRGV students who have completed their first semester. For more information on the DEAP program, visit: *https://www.utrgv.edu/biology/academics/programs/health-oriented/programs-in-dentistry/index.htm*

UNIVERSITY OF TEXAS HEALTH SAN ANTONIO
BS/MD PROGRAM (7-YEAR)

Note: This program has been discontinued. It is no longer available to future students.

Medical School: University of Texas Health San Antonio
7703 Floyd Curl Dr., San Antonio, TX 78229
Undergraduate: University of Texas San Antonio
1 UTSA Circle, San Antonio, TX 78249
Program Information: *https://www.utsa.edu/about/pdfLibrary/ pdf/13-27904%20FAME%20Brochure%202014-lo_res.pdf*
Request for Information Form: *https://future.utsa.edu/requestinfo/*
Phone: (210) 458-8000
E-Mail: N/A
Additional Combined Programs: N/A
International Students: Not listed

COST OF ATTENDANCE

In-State Tuition and Fees: $10,154
Additional Expenses with Room and Board: $15,020
Total: $25,174

Out-of-State Tuition and Fees: $25,125
Additional Expenses with Room and Board: $15,020
Total: $40,145

Financial Aid: Scholarships available. Need to apply through a separate scholarship application.

ADDITIONAL INFORMATION

The Facilitated Acceptance to Medical Education (FAME) Program was established in 2013.

ALABAMA

ARKANSAS

DELAWARE

DISTRICT OF COLUMBIA

FLORIDA

GEORGIA

KENTUCKY

LOUISIANA

MARYLAND

MISSISSIPPI

NORTH CAROLINA

OKLAHOMA

SOUTH CAROLINA

TENNESSEE

TEXAS

VIRGINIA

WEST VIRGINIA

SOUTH

ALABAMA

ARKANSAS

DELAWARE

DISTRICT OF COLUMBIA

FLORIDA

GEORGIA

KENTUCKY

LOUISIANA

MARYLAND

MISSISSIPPI

NORTH CAROLINA

OKLAHOMA

SOUTH CAROLINA

TENNESSEE

TEXAS

VIRGINIA

WEST VIRGINIA

HAMPTON UNIVERSITY
BS/MD PROGRAM (8-YEAR)

Medical School: SUNY Upstate Medical University
750 E Adams St, Syracuse, NY 13210
Undergraduate: Hampton University
100 E Queen St, Hampton, VA 23669
Program Information:
https://www.upstate.edu/com/admissions/options/bs-md.php
Request for Information Form:
http://www.hamptonu.edu/about/contact.cfm
Phone: (757) 727-5328
Medical Science/Pre-Health Coordinator, Michael Druitt, E-Mail:
Michael.druitt@hamptonu.edu
Additional Combined Programs: N/A
International Students: Not listed

COST OF ATTENDANCE

Tuition and Fees: $26,198
Additional Expenses with Room and Board: $16,420
Total: $42,618

Financial Aid: Need-based scholarships and educational grant awards are available.

ADDITIONAL INFORMATION

Hampton University is a private, historically black university founded in 1868. In partnership with SUNY Upstate, high school seniors may apply to their Upstate Accelerated Scholars (UAS) Program. A goal of this program is to encourage diversity and allow students of various academic backgrounds a pathway to medical school. The UAS encourages students to apply to any academic program, although the "program chosen should contain enough flexibility in the curriculum to incorporate the required science courses within four years."

This program is binding. Additionally, the MCAT is not required.

Students interested in applying to the UAS must meet the following requirements:

1. Minimum 90% average
2. SAT minimum of 1360 (CR&M) or
3. ACT minimum of 31
4. Extra-curricular activities indicating demonstrated commitment to community service in healthcare setting

Continuing Requirements for admission to SUNY Upstate:

1. Unofficial transcripts sent to Upstate at end of each semester
2. Complete all Hampton University major requirements
3. Complete certain medical school prerequisite courses
4. No grade lower than a "B" in the medical school prerequisites
5. Minimum 3.50 cumulative GPA and 3.50 science GPA each semester
6. 40 hours of volunteer service, preferably in direct contact with patients or physicians

VIRGINIA COMMONWEALTH UNIVERSITY
BS/MD PROGRAM (8-YEAR)

Medical School: Virginia Commonwealth University School of Medicine
1201 E Marshall St #4-100, Richmond, VA 23298
Undergraduate: Virginia Commonwealth University
907 Floyd Ave, Richmond, VA 23284
Program Information:
https://honors.vcu.edu/admissions/guaranteed-admission/gmed-app/
Request for Information Form: *https://www.vcu.edu/admissions/*
contact-admissions/ugrad-interest-form/
Phone: (804) 828-1222
E-Mail: *honors@vcu.edu*
Additional Combined Programs:
BS/DDS, BS/OTD, BS/PharmD, BS/DPT
International Students: Not listed

COST OF ATTENDANCE

In-State Tuition and Fees: $14,596
Additional Expenses with Room and Board: $16,764
Total: $31,360

Out-of-State Tuition and Fees: $35,904
Additional Expenses with Room and Board: $17,488
Total: $53,392

Financial Aid: Honors College merit-based and need-based scholarships available.

ADDITIONAL INFORMATION

Virginia Commonwealth University (VCU) is a public university founded in 1838. VCU offers a variety of combined degree programs. The BS/MD program with the VCU School of medicine is only open to high school students. Current VCU Honors College premedical students may apply through the Preferred Applicant Track for medicine at the end of their sophomore year.

Once admitted as an undergraduate, some of the continuing requirements to enter VCU School of Medicine are as follow:

1. Must graduate with University Honors
2. Maintain 3.50 GPA in pre-medical science courses; all taken at VCU
3. Cumulative 3.50 GPA minimum at end of 4th-7th semesters
4. Complete certain coursework requirements
5. No grade below a C
6. MCAT score minimum of 508
7. Minimum 120 hours of health care experience during summers in first three years
8. Complete 60-hour semester clinical mentorship
9. Complete 50 hours of non-clinical community service
10. Register with AMCAS by May 15 of year prior to starting medical school

ALABAMA

ARKANSAS

DELAWARE

DISTRICT OF COLUMBIA

FLORIDA

GEORGIA

KENTUCKY

LOUISIANA

MARYLAND

MISSISSIPPI

NORTH CAROLINA

OKLAHOMA

SOUTH CAROLINA

TENNESSEE

TEXAS

VIRGINIA

WEST VIRGINIA

SOUTH

ALABAMA

ARKANSAS

DELAWARE

DISTRICT OF COLUMBIA

FLORIDA

GEORGIA

KENTUCKY

LOUISIANA

MARYLAND

MISSISSIPPI

NORTH CAROLINA

OKLAHOMA

SOUTH CAROLINA

TENNESSEE

TEXAS

VIRGINIA

WEST VIRGINIA

MARSHALL UNIVERSITY
BS/MD PROGRAM (7-YEAR)

Medical School: Marshall University Joan C. Edwards School of Medicine
1600 Medical Center Dr., Huntington, WV 25701
Undergraduate: Marshall University
1 John Marshall Dr., Huntington, WV 25755
Program Information:
https://jcesom.marshall.edu/students/bsmd-program/
Request for Information Form:
https://www.marshall.edu/admissions/request-info/
Phone: (304) 696-3160
E-Mail: *BSMDProgram@marshall.edu*
Additional Combined Programs: N/A
International Students: Not considered

COST OF ATTENDANCE

In-State Tuition and Fees: $8,532
Additional Expenses with Room and Board: $14,103
Total: $22,635

Out-of-State Tuition and Fees: $18,734
Additional Expenses with Room and Board: $13,908
Total: $32,642

Financial Aid: Merit-based scholarships available.
Note: Students will receive a tuition waiver for their four years at medical school. Undergraduate tuition and fees are still paid by the student.

ADDITIONAL INFORMATION

Marshall University is a public university founded in 1837. In their accelerated BS/MD program, students spend their first three years at Marshall University, and their four years of medical school at Marshall University School of Medicine. This program is only open to West Virginia high school students.

Continuing requirements as an undergraduate are as follow:

1. Declared biology major
2. Cumulative GPA at least 3.50 by the end of the first three years
3. Successful completion of at least 26 credit hours each undergraduate year
4. Participation in enrichment programs
5. AMCAS required
6. MCAT not req.

In this program, students will receive their bachelor's degree after completion of their first year of medical school. For more information on the program policy, visit: *https://jcesom.marshall.edu/media/43479/Program-Policy.pdf*

REGION FOUR
WEST

ALASKA

ARIZONA

CALIFORNIA

COLORADO

HAWAII

IDAHO

MONTANA

NEVADA

NEW MEXICO

OREGON

UTAH

WASHINGTON

WYOMING

5 *Programs* | **13** *States*

1. *CA - California Northstate University BS/MD (6-year)*
2. *CA – Pitzer College BS/DO (7-year)*
3. *CO – University of Colorado – Denver BA/MD, BS/MD (8-year)*
4. *NM – University of New Mexico BA/MD (8-year)*
5. *NV – University of Nevada BS/MD (7-year)*

UNIVERSITY	PROGRAM/DEADLINE	MIN SAT, ACT, GPA	OTHER REQUIREMENTS
CA NORTHSTATE UNIV. COLLEGE OF HEALTH SCIENCES 2910 PROSPECT PARK DR. RANCHO CORDOVA, CA 95670	*2+4, 3+4, 4+4 BS/MD Pathways *Aug. 1 - App opens *Oct. 31 – Priority Deadline *Materials must be rec. by Oct. 31 or postmarked by Oct. 17	Min SAT ERW+M - 1400 for 2+4; 1350 for 3+4; 1250 for 4+4 Min ACT - 31 for 2+4; 29 for 3+4; 27 for 4+4 (Superscored) Min GPA - 3.75 for 2+4, 3.60 for 3+4; 3.50 for 4+4 No SAT II Req.	*Maintain 3.5 GPA *Volunteer *Score 510+ on MCAT *AMCAS req.
PITZER COLLEGE 1050 N MILLS AVE, CLAREMONT, CA 91711	*BS/DO (7-year) *Apply through Common App *Interviews in late Feb/ early Mar	Competitive SAT/ACT scores Competitive GPA	*Six students accepted *Must demonstrate community involvement and motivation for primary care medicine career
UNIV. OF CO, DENVER UG HEALTH PROF. PROG. 1200 LARIMER ST. N. CLASSROOM BLDG, SUITE 3002 DENVER, CO 80204	*8-year (incl. 4 summers) *Apply to CU-Denver by Oct. 28 *Apps open Aug. 1 (rolling) *Suppl app. req. after admission to CU-Denver	Min SAT ERW+M – 1185 Min ACT – 27 Min GPA - 3.50 No SAT II req.	*Students must be CO res. *Diversity high priority *10 students chosen *CCHE index no longer used *Students complete 2 apps
UNIV. OF NM BA/MD PROG. HEALTH SCIENCES & SERVICES BLDG, SUITE 102, 2500 MARBLE AVE. ALBUQUERQUE, NM 87131	*8-year (1 req. summer) *Apps open Aug 1. *Deadline - 1st Th. of Nov. 5 pm (MST). *Interviews: Nov. – Feb. *Decision/Notification: April 1 *Commitment: May 1	SAT ERW+M – 1307 (avg. 2019) ACT – 28 (avg. 2019) GPA – 4.31 (avg. 2019) SAT II not req.	*Applicants must attend NM H.S. or be a tribal member living on the Navajo Nation *Students must commit to a medical career in NM rural or medically underserved areas. *28 students admitted
UNIV. OF NEVADA COLLEGE OF A & S 1664 NORTH VIRGINIA ST. RENO, NV 89557	*7-year *Apply in mid-Sept. *Non-binding EA deadline is Nov. 15 *Separate BS-MD app open Nov. 15 *Supporting docs req. by Jan. 12	Min SAT ERW+M – 1320 Min Act – 28 Min GPA - 3.65 unwt Top 10% of grad class	*15 students accepted from 75-100 *Must be a Nevada H.S. senior

ALASKA

ARIZONA

CALIFORNIA

COLORADO

HAWAII

IDAHO

MONTANA

NEVADA

NEW MEXICO

OREGON

UTAH

WASHINGTON

WYOMING

CALIFORNIA NORTHSTATE UNIVERSITY BS-MD PATHWAYS PROGRAM (6-YEAR, 7-YEAR, 8-YEAR)

Medical School: California Northstate University College of Medicine
9700 West Taron Drive, Elk Grove, Ca 95757
Undergraduate: College of Health Sciences
College of Health Sciences, 2910 Prospect Park Drive, Rancho Cordova, CA 95670
Program Information: *http://healthsciences.cnsu.edu/programs-offered/bs-md-combined-program/about*
Request for Information Form: *https://californianorthstateuniversity.formstack.com/forms/chs_request_information*
Phone: (916) 686-7300
E-Mail: *Admissions.CHS@cnsu.edu*
Additional Combined Programs:
BS-MD, BS-PharmD, BS- PsyD, BS-DMD, BS-MPS
International Students: Considered

COST OF ATTENDANCE

Tuition and Fees: $45,925
Additional Expenses w/Room & Board: $35,489
Total: $81,414

Financial Aid: California Northstate does not participate in Federal Aid programs but does offer scholarships and support for student applicants.

ADDITIONAL INFORMATION

California Northstate University College of Medicine (CNUCOM) is a private, for-profit school in Elk Grove, California that started its process to attain full WASC accreditation in 2013. Summer training is required.

The university is in the process of building a new hospital that is getting pushback from the community as of spring 2020. Research this school first before applying since there are concerns about its BS-MD Pathway program. This situation may change one way or another after the coronavirus pandemic is over. CNUCOM is unranked by U.S. News & World Report.

PITZER COLLEGE BS/DO PROGRAM (7-YEAR)

Medical School: Western University of Health Sciences' College of Osteopathic Medicine
615 E 3rd St, Pomona, CA 91766
Undergraduate: Pitzer College
1050 N Mills Ave, Claremont, CA 91711
Program Information: *https://www.pitzer.edu/admission/admission/apply/joint-medical-program-applicants/*
Request for Information Form:
Phone: (909) 621-8000
E-Mail: *admission@pitzer.edu*
Additional Combined Programs: N/A
International Students: Not listed

COST OF ATTENDANCE

Tuition and Fees: $55,734
Additional Expenses w/Room & Board: $20,116
Total: $75,850

Financial Aid: Merit-based scholarships available.

ADDITIONAL INFORMATION

Pitzer College is a private liberal arts college established in 1963. The Joint Medical Program (JMP) is a partnership between Pitzer College and Western University of Health Sciences' College of Osteopathic Medicine. High school students are welcome to apply. Students in this program obtain their bachelor's degree and their DO degree at the end of the 7-year program. Each student has two faculty advisors, one from Pitzer and the other from the College of Osteopathic Medicine. A maximum of six students are selected for this program.

To ensure continuation to the College of Osteopathic Medicine, students must do the following:

1. Minimum GPA of 3.2 in non-science courses
2. Minimum GPA of 3.3 in science courses
3. Minimum total of 24 on sub-tests of MCAT (Note: 498 on new MCAT)

ALASKA

ARIZONA

CALIFORNIA

COLORADO

HAWAII

IDAHO

MONTANA

NEVADA

NEW MEXICO

OREGON

UTAH

WASHINGTON

WYOMING

SOUTH

ALASKA

ARIZONA

CALIFORNIA

COLORADO

HAWAII

IDAHO

MONTANA

NEVADA

NEW MEXICO

OREGON

UTAH

WASHINGTON

WYOMING

UNIVERSITY OF COLORADO – DENVER BA/BS-MD (8-YEAR)

Medical School: University of Colorado School of Medicine (CUSOM), University of Colorado Anschutz Medical Campus
Fitzsimmons Building, 13001 East 17th Place, Aurora, CO 80045
Undergraduate Health Professions Programs: CU-Denver College of Liberal Arts and Sciences
1200 Larimer Street, North Classroom Building, Suite 3002, Denver, CO 80204
Program Information: *https://clas.ucdenver.edu/health-professions-programs/babs-md-program-information*
Request for Information Form: *https://application.admissions.ucdenver.edu/register/UGRDRequestInformation*
Health Professions Phone: (303) 315-7536
Medical School Phone: 303-724-5000
E-Mail: *info@cuanschutz.edu*
Additional Combined Programs: N/A
International Students: Not considered
Note: Students MUST be residents of Colorado; preference goes to educationally/financially or otherwise disadvantaged students

COST OF ATTENDANCE

Tuition and Fees: $9,782
Additional Expenses w/Room & Board: $19,575
Total: $29,357

Financial Aid: Most students receive some form of financial aid and scholarships. Students are encouraged to apply for outside scholarships. Students receive a stipend for the 4-year required summer program attendance.

ADDITIONAL INFORMATION

The goal of this program is to prepare students who seek to practice medicine in Colorado as a primary care physician. CU-Denver provides medical training to Colorado high school students who are from rural/frontier communities, under-represented ethnic groups (African American, Hispanic/Latino, Native American, Pacific Islander, Vietnamese, or first-generation college students.)

The application process requires completing two separate applications.

1. Apply and be accepted to the University of Colorado Downtown Denver Campus.
2. Complete the Supplemental Application for the BA/BS-MD Program

CU Denver considers a student's academic record, community/ volunteer service, extracurricular activities, honors/awards, full/part-time jobs, characteristics/capabilities that will make the student an excellent physician, leadership, diversity, and academic potential.

Interviews are conducted in-person on the Anschutz Medical Campus. There are no phone or Skype interviews. The interview process lasts from approximately 8:00 – 4:00 pm. Candidates will have two separate 30-minute interviews.

Accepted students to the BA/BS-MD program must complete academic, non-academic, and professional requirements, including a 3.5 GPA and no less than a B in required classes. However, this enables them to earn a reserved spot while exploring other interests and completing a degree of their choice during their 4-year undergraduate experience at CU-Denver.

The following course work is required:

1. 8 semester hours - human biology (with lab),
2. 8 semester hours - general chemistry (with lab),
3. 8 semester hours - organic chemistry (with lab),
4. 8 semester hours - general physics (with lab)
5. 6 semester hours - English literature/composition
6. 6 semester hours - College level mathematics (algebra and above).

Students are encouraged to consider additional coursework in biochemistry, computer sciences, genetics, humanities, and social sciences.

Note: Colorado Commission for Higher Education (CCHE) stopped using the CCHE index for admissions in fall 2019.

BA/BS-MD students live in Campus Village Apartments during their freshman year and participate in the Pre-Health Learning Community with students in the program. Students participate in paid summer programs each year as an undergraduate, including a 3-day bridge program in June before their freshman year and a week-long boot camp before classes begin in August. The MCAT is required as is a CU School of Medicine interview before entering medical school.

See *https://clas.ucdenver.edu/health-professions-programs/babs-md-program-information/how-it-works* for more information.

ALASKA

ARIZONA

CALIFORNIA

COLORADO

HAWAII

IDAHO

MONTANA

NEVADA

NEW MEXICO

OREGON

UTAH

WASHINGTON

WYOMING

SOUTH

ALASKA

ARIZONA

CALIFORNIA

COLORADO

HAWAII

IDAHO

MONTANA

NEVADA

NEW MEXICO

OREGON

UTAH

WASHINGTON

WYOMING

UNIVERSITY OF NEW MEXICO COMBINED BA/MD PROGRAM (8-YEAR)

Medical School: University of New Mexico School of Medicine
915 Camino de Salud, NE, Albuquerque, NM 87106
Undergraduate: UNM College of Arts & Sciences
Health Sciences and Services Building, Suite 102, 2500 Marble Avenue, Albuquerque, NM 87131
Program Information: *https://hsc.unm.edu/school-of-medicine/ education/md/bamd/admission-requirements.html*
Request for Information Form: *https://hsc.unm.edu/school-of-medicine/education/md/bamd/request-information.html*
Combined BA/MD Phone: (505) 925-4500 or (505) 277-2128
UNMSOM Phone: (505) 272-2321
E-Mail: *HSC-Combinedbamd@salud.unm.edu*
Additional Combined Programs: BS/MD is available to students who graduate with science degrees.
International Students: Considered. Contact Karen McGillvray regarding separate UNM paperwork.

COST OF ATTENDANCE

Tuition and Fees: $0
Room & Board: $0
Personal Expenses/Travel: about $3,000
Total: $3,000.00

Financial Aid: During the 4-year undergraduate education, BA/MD students have their basic educational costs (tuition, student fees, course fees up to $119, books up to $515/semester, housing allowance, and meal plan) covered by the BA/MD Undergraduate Scholarship, which is applied after all other scholarships and work study awards.

ADDITIONAL INFORMATION

Applicants must be: (1) a current high school senior, (2) live in and attend a high school in N.M. or be a tribal member living on the Navajo Nation, (3) commit to pursuing medicine in one of N.M.'s rural or medically underserved areas. Students must sign a Statement of Commitment to help alleviate the physician shortage in N.M.'s rural and medically underserved communities by practicing medicine in areas with the greatest need.

Cohort Data from 2006 – 2019: *https://hsc.unm.edu/school-of-medicine/education/md/bamd/docs/ba-md-demographics.pdf*

The UNM Combined BA/MD Degree Program at the University of New Mexico is designed to prepare students who will practice medicine in New Mexico as a primary care physician. Factors considered in the admissions process in addition to GPA and test scores include: AP/IB courses, community involvement, volunteer service, honors/awards, extracurricular activities, letters of recommendation, personal statement, and 2 interviews.

BA/MD students are required to take an MCAT preparatory course at no cost, take the MCAT, and either meet or exceed the minimum score required by the UNM School of Medicine admissions. A second-year summer experiential learning practicum in rural or medically underserved New Mexico communities is required along with five seminars.

Students can choose any Arts & Sciences or Health major that emphasizes the liberal arts while completing core classes required for UNM's School of Medicine. Core classes have a low student-teacher ratio and use research-based, active-learning to apply knowledge to situations.

Twenty-eight students are admitted into the BA/MD program with an active waitlist maintained until the first day of UNM fall semester. In order to graduate 28 students to support N.M. underserved communities with the greatest need, UNM has a MERGE program. At academic milestones, students may drop out due to academics or change of heart. Those spots (if available) are filled with cohort waitlist students who complete a secondary application and have a 3.5 GPA in the second semester of their second year with (General Chemistry, Molecular and Cell Biology, and Genetics)

Students who accept the University of New Mexico Combined BA/MD Degree Program are required to attend UNM School of Medicine and may not apply to any other medical schools. To facilitate this, UNMSOM has an Early Decision for BA/MD students through AMCAS. Students are admitted contingent upon successful completion of all coursework.

229

ALASKA

ARIZONA

CALIFORNIA

COLORADO

HAWAII

IDAHO

MONTANA

NEVADA

NEW MEXICO

OREGON

UTAH

WASHINGTON

WYOMING

SOUTH

PART 5

LISTS AND WORKSHEETS

LISTS AND GUIDES

ALPHABETIZED LIST OF B/MD, B/DO, EAP, AND DIRECT MED BY STATE/CITY

UNIVERSITY/PROGRAM	CITY	STATE
University of Alabama at Birmingham	Birmingham	AL
University of South Alabama	Mobile	AL
California Northstate Univ.	Rancho Cordova	CA
Univ. of Colorado, Denver	Denver	CO
University of Connecticut	Storrs	CT
George Washington University	NW Washington	D.C.
Howard University	Washington	DC
University of Delaware	Newark	DE
Florida Atlantic Univ	Boca Raton	FL
University of Miami	Coral Gables	FL
University of South Florida	Tampa	FL
Spelman College	Atlanta	GA
Augusta University	Augusta	GA
Mercer University	Macon	GA
St. George's University	Saint George's	Grenada
Loyola University Chicago	Chicago	IL
Northwestern University	Chicago	IL
University of Illinois Chicago	Chicago	IL
Grambling State University	Grambling	LA
Tufts University Early Assurance	Medford	MA
Wayne State University Med-Direct Program	Detroit	MI
University of Missouri, Kansas City	Kansas City	MO
St. Louis University Medical Scholar Program	St. Louis	MO
Washington University in St. Louis Med Scholars	St. Louis	MO
Caldwell University w/ St. George's University	Caldwell	NJ
Montclair University	Montclair	NJ
Rutgers University	Newark	NJ
New Jersey Inst. of Tech. w/ St. George's	Newark	NJ

UNIVERSITY/PROGRAM	CITY	STATE
Monmouth University	West Long Branch	NJ
University of New Mexico	Albuquerque	NM
University of Nevada	Reno	NV
Albany College of Pharmacy and Health Sciences	Albany	NY
University at Albany - SUNY	Albany	NY
Brooklyn College BA/MD	Brooklyn	NY
Adelphi University with Upstate	Garden City	NY
Hofstra University BS-BA/MD	Hempstead	NY
Siena College with Albany Medical College	Loudonville	NY
CUNY/CCNY Sophie Davis	New York	NY
Yeshiva University	New York	NY
Purchase College	Purchase	NY
Rochester University REMS	Rochester	NY
Rochester Institute of Technology	Rochester	NY
Union College Leadership in Medicine with Albany Medical College	Schenectady	NY
SBU-George Washington University Medical School	St Bonaventure	NY
Stony Brook BA/MD Scholars Program	Stony Brook	NY
Rensselaer Polytechnic Institute	Troy	NY
SUNY Polytechnic Institute	Utica	NY
University of Cincinnati	Cincinnati	OH
Case Western Reserve University	Cleveland	OH
Kent State University (discontinued)	Kent	OH
University of Toledo	Toledo	OH
University of Oklahoma	Norman	OK
Lehigh University	Bethlehem	PA
Drexel University	Philadelphia	PA
Temple University Health Scholars	Philadelphia	PA
University of the Sciences with Cooper Medical	Philadelphia	PA
Duquesne University	Pittsburgh	PA

UNIVERSITY/PROGRAM	CITY	STATE
University of Pittsburgh, Guaranteed Admissions	Pittsburgh	PA
Rosemont College Dual Degree	Rosemont	PA
Penn State University Accelerated Med	University Park	PA
Washington and Jefferson College	Washington	PA
West Chester University	West Chester	PA
Brown College PLME	Providence	RI
Fisk University	Nashville	TN
Texas JAMP	Austin	TX
Rice/Baylor Medical Scholars Program (MSP)	Houston	TX
Texas Tech University	Lubbock	TX
Baylor University	Waco	TX
Hampton University	Hampton	VA
Virginia Commonwealth University	Richmond	VA
Marshall University	Huntington	WV

BS/MD STATE RESIDENCY REQUIRED LIST

UNIVERSITY/PROGRAM
Chadron State College
Indiana State University
Marshall University
Mercer University
Montclair University
Texas JAMP
Texas Tech University
Univ. of Colorado, Denver
University of Evansville
University of Illinois Chicago
University of Louisville
University of Minnesota
University of Nevada
University of New Mexico

BS/MD STATE RESIDENCY NOT REQUIRED LIST

UNIVERSITY/PROGRAM
Adelphi University with Upstate
Albany College of Pharmacy and Health Sciences
Augusta University
Baylor University
Brooklyn College
Brown University PLME
Caldwell University
California Northstate University
Case Western Reserve University
CUNY/CCNY Sophie Davis
Drexel University
Duquesne University
Fisk University
Florida Atlantic University
George Washington University
Grambling State University
Hampton University
Hofstra University
Howard University
Illinois Institute of Technology
Lehigh University
Loyola University Chicago
Monmouth University
New Jersey Institute of Technology
New York Institute of Technology
Northwestern University
Nova Southeastern University
Penn State University Accelerated Med
Pitzer College
Purchase College

LISTS AND GUIDES

UNIVERSITY/PROGRAM
Rensselaer Polytechnic Institute
Rice/Baylor Medical Scholars Program (MSP)
Rochester Institute of Technology
Rosemont College
Rutgers University
Siena College with Albany Medical College
Spelman College
St. Bonaventure University w/ GWU
St. George's University
St. Louis University
Stevens Institute of Technology
Stockton University
Stony Brook Scholars Program
SUNY Geneseo
SUNY New Paltz
SUNY Old Westbury
SUNY Polytechnic Institute
Temple University Health Scholars
Tufts University Early Assurance
University of Missouri, Kansas City
Union College Leadership in Medicine Program
University at Albany
University of Alabama
University of Cincinnati
University of Connecticut
University of Delaware
University of Miami
University of Oklahoma
University of Pittsburgh, Guaranteed Admissions
University of Rochester REMS
University of South Alabama
University of South Florida

UNIVERSITY/PROGRAM
University of the Sciences with LECOM
University of Toledo
Virginia Commonwealth University
Washington and Jefferson College
Washington University in St. Louis Med Scholars
Wayne State University Med-Direct Program
West Chester University
Yeshiva University

BS/MD LENGTH OF PROGRAM LIST

6-YEAR PROGRAMS

UNIVERSITY/PROGRAM
California Northstate University
Cleveland State University
Howard University
Loyola University Chicago
Texas JAMP
University of Missouri, Kansas City

7-YEAR PROGRAMS

UNIVERSITY/PROGRAM
Augusta University
Caldwell University
California Northstate University
CUNY/CCNY Sophie Davis
Fisk University
Florida Atlantic University
George Washington University
Grambling State University
Lehigh University
Marshall University
Montclair University

LISTS AND GUIDES

UNIVERSITY/PROGRAM
New Jersey Institute of Technology
New York Institute of Technology
Northwestern University
Nova Southeastern University
Penn State University Accelerated Med
Pitzer College
Rensselaer Polytechnic Institute
Rosemont College
Rutgers University
Siena College with Albany Medical College
St. George's University
Stevens Institute of Technology
Stockton University
SUNY Geneseo
SUNY New Paltz
SUNY Old Westbury
Temple University Health Scholars
Texas JAMP
University of Miami
University of Minnesota
University of Nevada
University of South Florida
University of the Sciences with LECOM

8-YEAR PROGRAMS

UNIVERSITY/PROGRAM
Adelphi University with Upstate
Albany College of Pharmacy and Health Sciences
Baylor University
Brooklyn College
Brown University PLME
California Northstate University

UNIVERSITY/PROGRAM
Case Western Reserve University
Chadron State College
College of St. Elizabeth
Drexel University
Duquesne University
Fisk University
Florida Atlantic University
Grambling State University
Hampton University
Hofstra University
Illinois Institute of Technology
Indiana State University
Mercer University
Monmouth University
Montclair University
Northwestern University
Nova Southeastern University
Purchase College
Rice/Baylor University
Rochester Institute of Technology
Rosemont College
Siena College with Albany Medical College
Spelman College
St. Bonaventure University w/ GWU
St. Louis University
Stony Brook Scholars Program
SUNY Polytechnic Institute
Temple University Health Scholars
Texas JAMP
Texas Tech University
Tufts University Early Assurance

LISTS AND GUIDES

UNIVERSITY/PROGRAM
Union College Leadership in Medicine Program
University of Colorado, Denver
University at Albany - SUNY
University of Alabama
University of Cincinnati
University of Connecticut
University of Delaware
University of Evansville
University of Illinois Chicago
University of Louisville
University of Miami
University of New Mexico
University of Oklahoma
University of Pittsburgh, Guaranteed Admissions
University of Rochester REMS
University of South Alabama
University of the Sciences with LECOM
University of Toledo
Virginia Commonwealth University
Washington and Jefferson College
Washington University in St. Louis Med Scholars
Wayne State University Med-Direct Program
West Chester University
Yeshiva University

BS/MD MCAT NOT REQUIRED LIST

UNIVERSITY/PROGRAM
Adelphi University with Upstate
Albany College of Pharmacy and Health Sciences
Brown University PLME
Case Western Reserve University
Chadron State College
Hampton University
Loyola University Chicago
Marshall University
Northwestern University
Purchase College
Rensselaer Polytechnic Institute
Rochester Institute of Technology
Siena College with Albany Medical College
Spelman College
SUNY Polytechnic Institute
Texas Tech University
Tufts University Early Assurance
University of Missouri, Kansas City
Union College Leadership in Medicine Program
University at Albany - SUNY
University of Pittsburgh, Guaranteed Admissions
University of Rochester REMS
University of the Sciences with LECOM
University of Toledo
Yeshiva University

MEDICAL SCHOOLS ALPHABETIZED

UNIVERSITY/PROGRAM
Albany Medical College
Albert Einstein College of Medicine
Baylor College of Medicine
Boonshoft School of Medicine Wright State University
Boston University School of Medicine
California Northstate University College of Medicine
California University of Science and Medicine – School of Medicine
Carle Illinois College of Medicine
Case Western Reserve University School of Medicine
Central Michigan University College of Medicine
Charles E. Schmidt College of Medicine at Florida Atlantic University
Chicago Medical School at Rosalind Franklin University of Medicine and Science
Columbia University Vagelos College of Physicians and Surgeons
Cooper Medical School of Rowan University
Creighton University School of Medicine
CUNY School of Medicine
David Geffen School of Medicine at UCLA
Donald and Barbara Zucker School of Medicine at Hofstra/Northwell
Drexel University College of Medicine
Duke University School of Medicine
East Tennessee State University James H. Quillen College of Medicine
Eastern Virginia Medical School
Emory University School of Medicine
Florida International University Herbert Wertheim College of Medicine
Frank H. Netter MD School of Medicine at Quinnipiac University
Geisel School of Medicine at Dartmouth
Geisinger Commonwealth School of Medicine
Georgetown University School of Medicine
Hackensack-Meridian School of Medicine at Seton Hall University
Harvard Medical School

UNIVERSITY/PROGRAM
Howard University College of Medicine
Icahn School of Medicine at Mount Sinai
Indiana University School of Medicine
Jacobs School of Medicine and Biomedical Sciences at the University at Buffalo
John A. Burns School of Medicine University of Hawaii at Manoa
Johns Hopkins University School of Medicine
Kaiser Permanente School of Medicine
Keck School of Medicine of the University of Southern California
Lewis Katz School of Medicine at Temple University
Loma Linda University School of Medicine
Louisiana State University School of Medicine in Shreveport
Loyola University Chicago Stritch School of Medicine
LSU Health Sciences Center School of Medicine in New Orleans
Marshall University Joan C. Edwards School of Medicine
Mayo Clinic Alix School of Medicine
McGovern Medical School at The University of Texas Health Science Center at Houston
Medical College of Georgia at Augusta University
Medical College of Wisconsin
Medical University of South Carolina College of Medicine
Meharry Medical College School of Medicine
Mercer University School of Medicine
Michigan State University College of Human Medicine
Morehouse School of Medicine
New York Medical College
New York University Grossman School of Medicine
New York University Long Island School of Medicine
Northeast Ohio Medical University College of Medicine
Northwestern University Feinberg School of Medicine
Nova Southeastern University Dr. Kiran C. Patel College of Allopathic Medicine
Oakland University William Beaumont School of Medicine
Oregon Health & Science University School of Medicine

UNIVERSITY/PROGRAM
Paul L. Foster School of Medicine Texas Tech University Health Sciences Center
Penn State College of Medicine
Ponce Health Sciences University School of Medicine
Renaissance School of Medicine at Stony Brook University
Rush Medical College of Rush University Medical Center
Rutgers New Jersey Medical School
Rutgers, Robert Wood Johnson Medical School
Saint Louis University School of Medicine
San Juan Bautista School of Medicine
Sidney Kimmel Medical College at Thomas Jefferson University
Southern Illinois University School of Medicine
Stanford University School of Medicine
State University of New York Downstate Medical Center College of Medicine
State University of New York Upstate Medical University College of Medicine
TCU and UNTHSC School of Medicine
Texas A&M University Health Science Center College of Medicine
Texas Tech University Health Sciences Center School of Medicine
The Brody School of Medicine at East Carolina University
The Florida State University College of Medicine
The George Washington University School of Medicine and Health Sciences
The Ohio State University College of Medicine
The Raymond and Ruth Perelman School of Medicine at the University of Pennsylvania
The Robert Larner, M.D. College of Medicine at the University of Vermont
The University of Arizona College of Medicine – Phoenix
The University of Arizona College of Medicine – Tucson
The University of Texas at Austin Dell Medical School
The University of Texas Health Science Center at San Antonio Joe R. and Teresa Lozano Long School of Medicine
The University of Texas Medical Branch at Galveston School of Medicine
The University of Texas Rio Grande Valley School of Medicine
The University of Texas Southwestern Medical School
The University of Toledo College of Medicine and Life Sciences

UNIVERSITY/PROGRAM
The Warren Alpert Medical School of Brown University
Tufts University School of Medicine
Tulane University School of Medicine
Uniformed Services University of the Health Sciences, F. Edward Hébert School of Medicine
Universidad Central del Caribe School of Medicine
University of Alabama School of Medicine
University of Arkansas for Medical Sciences College of Medicine
University of California, Davis School of Medicine
University of California, Irvine School of Medicine
University of California, Riverside School of Medicine
University of California, San Diego School of Medicine
University of California, San Francisco School of Medicine
University of Central Florida College of Medicine
University of Chicago Division of the Biological Sciences, The Pritzker School of Medicine
University of Cincinnati College of Medicine
University of Colorado School of Medicine
University of Connecticut School of Medicine
University of Florida College of Medicine
University of Houston College of Medicine
University of Illinois College of Medicine
University of Iowa Roy J. and Lucille A. Carver College of Medicine
University of Kansas School of Medicine
University of Kentucky College of Medicine
University of Louisville School of Medicine
University of Maryland School of Medicine
University of Massachusetts Medical School
University of Miami Leonard M. Miller School of Medicine
University of Michigan Medical School
University of Minnesota Medical School
University of Mississippi School of Medicine
University of Missouri-Columbia School of Medicine

LISTS AND GUIDES

UNIVERSITY/PROGRAM
University of Missouri-Kansas City School of Medicine
University of Nebraska College of Medicine
University of Nevada, Las Vegas School of Medicine
University of Nevada, Reno School of Medicine
University of New Mexico School of Medicine
University of North Carolina School of Medicine
University of North Dakota School of Medicine and Health Sciences
University of Oklahoma College of Medicine
University of Pittsburgh School of Medicine
University of Puerto Rico School of Medicine
University of Rochester School of Medicine and Dentistry
University of South Alabama College of Medicine
University of South Carolina School of Medicine, Columbia
University of South Carolina School of Medicine, Greenville
University of South Dakota Sanford School of Medicine
University of Tennessee Health Science Center College of Medicine
University of Utah School of Medicine
University of Virginia School of Medicine
University of Washington School of Medicine
University of Wisconsin School of Medicine and Public Health
USF Health Morsani College of Medicine
Vanderbilt University School of Medicine
Virginia Commonwealth University School of Medicine
Virginia Tech Carilion School of Medicine
Wake Forest School of Medicine of Wake Forest Baptist Medical Center
Washington State University Elson S. Floyd College of Medicine
Washington University in St. Louis School of Medicine
Wayne State University School of Medicine
Weill Cornell Medicine
West Virginia University School of Medicine
Western Michigan University Homer Stryker M.D. School of Medicine
Yale School of Medicine

D.O. SCHOOLS LIST

UNIVERSITY/PROGRAM
A. T. Still University Kirksville College of Osteopathic Medicine (ATSU-KCOM)
A.T. Still University, School of Osteopathic Medicine in Arizona (ATSU-SOMA)
Alabama College of Osteopathic Medicine (ACOM)
Arkansas College of Osteopathic Medicine (ARCOM)
Burrell College of Osteopathic Medicine (BCOM)
California Health Sciences University College of Osteopathic Medicine (CHSU-COM)
Campbell University Jerry M. Wallace School of Osteopathic Medicine (CUSOM)
Des Moines University College of Osteopathic Medicine (DMU-COM)
Edward Via College of Osteopathic Medicine (VCOM - Auburn Campus)
Edward Via College of Osteopathic Medicine (VCOM-Virginia Campus)
Edward Via College of Osteopathic Medicine-Carolinas Campus (VCOM - Carolinas Campus)
Edward Via College of Osteopathic Medicine-Monroe Campus (VCOM - Monroe Campus)
Idaho College of Osteopathic Medicine (ICOM)
Kansas City University of Medicine and Biosciences College of Osteopathic Medicine (KCU-COM-Joplin)
Kansas City University of Medicine and Biosciences College of Osteopathic Medicine (KCU-COM)
Lake Erie College of Osteopathic Medicine - Elmira (LECOM-Elmira)
Lake Erie College of Osteopathic Medicine - Seton Hill (LECOM-Seton Hill)
Lake Erie College of Osteopathic Medicine-Bradenton (LECOM-Bradenton)
Lake Erie College of Osteopathic Medicine-Erie (LECOM)
Liberty University College of Osteopathic Medicine (LUCOM)
Lincoln Memorial University DeBusk College of Osteopathic Medicine - Knoxville (LMU-DCOM Knoxville)
Lincoln Memorial University DeBusk College of Osteopathic Medicine (LMU-DCOM)
Marian University College of Osteopathic Medicine (MU-COM)
Michigan State University College of Osteopathic Medicine (MSUCOM-DMC)
Michigan State University College of Osteopathic Medicine (MSUCOM-MUC)
Michigan State University College of Osteopathic Medicine (MSUCOM)
Midwestern University Arizona College of Osteopathic Medicine (MWU/AZCOM)
Midwestern University Chicago College of Osteopathic Medicine (MWU/CCOM)
Minnesota College of Osteopathic Medicine
New York Institute of Technology College of Osteopathic Medicine (NYITCOM)

LISTS AND GUIDES

UNIVERSITY/PROGRAM
New York Institute of Technology College of Osteopathic Medicine at Arkansas State (NYITCOM)
Noorda College of Osteopathic Medicine
Nova Southeastern University Dr. Kiran C. Patel College of Osteopathic Medicine (NSU-KPCOM-Clearwater)
Nova Southeastern University Dr. Kiran C. Patel College of Osteopathic Medicine (NSU-KPCOM)
Ohio University Heritage College of Osteopathic Medicine (OU-HCOM)
Ohio University Heritage College of Osteopathic Medicine in Cleveland (OU-HCOM-Cleveland)
Ohio University Heritage College of Osteopathic Medicine in Dublin (OU-HCOM-Dublin)
Oklahoma State University Center for Health Sciences College of Osteopathic Medicine - Tahlequah (OSU-COM Tahlequah)
Oklahoma State University Center for Health Sciences College of Osteopathic Medicine (OSU-COM)
Pacific Northwest University of Health Sciences College of Osteopathic Medicine (PNWU-COM)
Philadelphia College of Osteopathic Medicine (PCOM)
Philadelphia College of Osteopathic Medicine Georgia (PCOM Georgia)
Philadelphia College of Osteopathic Medicine South Georgia (PCOM South Georgia)
Rocky Vista University College of Osteopathic Medicine (RVUCOM-SU Campus)
Rocky Vista University College of Osteopathic Medicine (RVUCOM)
Rowan University School of Osteopathic Medicine (RowanSOM)
Sam Houston State University College of Osteopathic Medicine
Touro College of Osteopathic Medicine (TouroCOM-Harlem)
Touro College of Osteopathic Medicine (TouroCOM-Middletown)
Touro University College of Osteopathic Medicine-California (TUCOM)
Touro University Nevada College of Osteopathic Medicine (TUNCOM)
University of New England College of Osteopathic Medicine (UNECOM)
University of North Texas Health Science Center Texas College of Osteopathic Medicine (UNTHSC/TCOM)
University of Pikeville Kentucky College of Osteopathic Medicine (UP-KYCOM)
University of the Incarnate Word School of Osteopathic Medicine (UIWSOM)
West Virginia School of Osteopathic Medicine (WVSOM)
Western University of Health Sciences College of Osteopathic Medicine of the Pacific (WesternU/COMP)
Western University of Health Sciences College of Osteopathic Medicine of the Pacific-Northwest (WesternU/COMP-Northwest)
William Carey University College of Osteopathic Medicine (WCUCOM)

DENTAL SCHOOLS LIST

DENTAL SCHOOLS
Arizona School of Dentistry & Oral Health
Boston University Henry M. Goldman School of Dental Medicine
California North State College of Dental Medicine
Case Western Reserve University School of Dental Medicine
Columbia University College of Dental Medicine
Creighton University School of Dentistry
Dental College of Georgia at Augusta University
East Carolina University School of Dental Medicine
Harvard School of Dental Medicine
Herman Ostrow School of Dentistry of USC
Howard University College of Dentistry
Indiana University School of Dentistry
Lake Erie College of Osteopathic Medicine School of Dental Medicine
Loma Linda University School of Dentistry
Louisiana State University Health New Orleans School of Dentistry
Marquette University School of Dentistry
Medical University of South Carolina James B. Edwards College of Dental Medicine
Meharry Medical College School of Dentistry
Midwestern University College of Dental Medicine-Arizona
Midwestern University College of Dental Medicine-Illinois
Missouri School of Dentistry & Oral Health
Nova Southeastern University College of Dental Medicine
NYU College of Dentistry
Oregon Health & Science University School of Dentistry
Roseman University of Health Sciences College of Dental Medicine – South Jordan, Utah
Rutgers, The State University of New Jersey, School of Dental Medicine
Southern Illinois University School of Dental Medicine
Stony Brook University School of Dental Medicine
Texas A&M College of Dentistry
Texas Tech University Health Sciences Center El Paso Woody L. Hunt School of Dental Medicine

DENTAL SCHOOLS
The Maurice H. Kornberg School of Dentistry, Temple University
The Ohio State University College of Dentistry
The University of Iowa College of Dentistry & Dental Clinics
The University of Texas School of Dentistry at Houston
Touro College of Dental Medicine at New York Medical College
Tufts University School of Dental Medicine
University at Buffalo School of Dental Medicine
University of Alabama at Birmingham School of Dentistry
University of California, Los Angeles, School of Dentistry
University of California, San Francisco, School of Dentistry
University of Colorado School of Dental Medicine
University of Connecticut School of Dental Medicine
University of Detroit Mercy School of Dentistry
University of Florida College of Dentistry
University of Illinois at Chicago College of Dentistry
University of Kentucky College of Dentistry
University of Louisville School of Dentistry
University of Maryland School of Dentistry
University of Michigan School of Dentistry
University of Minnesota School of Dentistry
University of Mississippi Medical Center School of Dentistry
University of Missouri-Kansas City School of Dentistry
University of Nebraska Medical Center College of Dentistry
University of Nevada, Las Vegas, School of Dental Medicine
University of New England College of Dental Medicine
University of North Carolina at Chapel Hill Adams School of Dentistry
University of Oklahoma College of Dentistry
University of Pennsylvania School of Dental Medicine
University of Pittsburgh School of Dental Medicine
University of Puerto Rico School of Dental Medicine
University of Tennessee Health Science Center College of Dentistry
University of the Pacific Arthur A. Dugoni School of Dentistry
University of Utah School of Dentistry

DENTAL SCHOOLS
University of Washington School of Dentistry
UT Health San Antonio School of Dentistry
Virginia Commonwealth University School of Dentistry
West Virginia University School of Dentistry
Western University of Health Sciences College of Dental Medicine

PHARMD SCHOOLS LIST

PHARMD SCHOOLS
Albany College of Pharmacy and Health Sciences School of Pharmacy and Pharmaceutical Sciences
American University of Health Sciences School of Pharmacy
Appalachian College of Pharmacy
Auburn University Harrison School of Pharmacy
Belmont University College of Pharmacy
Binghamton University State University of New York School of Pharmacy and Pharmaceutical Sciences
Butler University College of Pharmacy and Health Sciences
California Health Sciences University College of Pharmacy
California Northstate University College of Pharmacy
Campbell University College of Pharmacy and Health Sciences
Cedarville University School of Pharmacy
Chapman University School of Pharmacy
Chicago State University College of Pharmacy
Concordia University Wisconsin School of Pharmacy
Creighton University School of Pharmacy and Health Professions
D'Youville College School of Pharmacy
Drake University College of Pharmacy and Health Sciences
Duquesne University School of Pharmacy
East Tennessee State University Bill Gatton College of Pharmacy
Fairleigh Dickinson University School of Pharmacy
Ferris State University College of Pharmacy
Florida Agricultural & Mechanical University College of Pharmacy and Pharmaceutical Sciences
Hampton University School of Pharmacy
Harding University College of Pharmacy

LISTS AND GUIDES

PHARMD SCHOOLS
High Point University Fred Wilson School of Pharmacy
Howard University College of Pharmacy
Husson University School of Pharmacy
Idaho State University College of Pharmacy
Keck Graduate Institute (KGI) School of Pharmacy and Health Sciences
Lake Erie College of Osteopathic Medicine School of Pharmacy
Larkin University College of Pharmacy
Lipscomb University College of Pharmacy and Health Sciences
Loma Linda University School of Pharmacy
Long Island University Arnold and Marie Schwartz College of Pharmacy and Health Sciences
Manchester University College of Pharmacy, Natural and Health Sciences
Marshall B. Ketchum University College of Pharmacy
Marshall University School of Pharmacy
MCPHS University School of Pharmacy - Boston
MCPHS University School of Pharmacy - Worcester
Medical College of Wisconsin School of Pharmacy
Medical University of South Carolina College of Pharmacy
Mercer University College of Pharmacy
Midwestern University Chicago College of Pharmacy
Midwestern University College of Pharmacy-Glendale
North Dakota State University College of Health Professions School of Pharmacy
Northeast Ohio Medical University College of Pharmacy
Northeastern University Bouvé College of Health Sciences School of Pharmacy
Notre Dame of Maryland University School of Pharmacy
Nova Southeastern University College of Pharmacy
Ohio Northern University Raabe College of Pharmacy
Ohio State University College of Pharmacy
Oregon State University College of Pharmacy
Pacific University School of Pharmacy
Palm Beach Atlantic University Lloyd L. Gregory School of Pharmacy
Philadelphia College of Osteopathic Medicine - Georgia School of Pharmacy

PHARMD SCHOOLS
Presbyterian College School of Pharmacy
Purdue University College of Pharmacy
Regis University Rueckert-Hartman College for Health Professions School of Pharmacy
Roosevelt University College of Pharmacy
Rosalind Franklin University of Medicine and Science College of Pharmacy
Roseman University of Health Sciences College of Pharmacy
Rutgers, the State University of New Jersey Ernest Mario School of Pharmacy
Samford University McWhorter School of Pharmacy
Shenandoah University Bernard J. Dunn School of Pharmacy
South Carolina College of Pharmacy
South College School of Pharmacy
South Dakota State University College of Pharmacy and Allied Health Professions
South University School of Pharmacy
Southern Illinois University Edwardsville School of Pharmacy
Southwestern Oklahoma State University College of Pharmacy
St. John Fisher College Wegmans School of Pharmacy
St. John's University College of Pharmacy and Health Sciences
St. Louis College of Pharmacy
Sullivan University College of Pharmacy
Temple University School of Pharmacy
Texas A & M University Health Science Center Irma Lerma Rangel College of Pharmacy
Texas Southern University College of Pharmacy and Health Sciences
Texas Tech University Health Sciences Center Jerry H. Hodge School of Pharmacy
Thomas Jefferson University Jefferson College of Pharmacy
Touro New York College of Pharmacy
Touro University - California College of Pharmacy
Union University College of Pharmacy
University at Buffalo The State University of New York School of Pharmacy & Pharmaceutical Sciences
University of Arizona College of Pharmacy
University of Arkansas for Medical Sciences College of Pharmacy
University of California, San Diego Skaggs School of Pharmacy & Pharmaceutical Sciences

LISTS AND GUIDES

PHARMD SCHOOLS
University of California, San Francisco School of Pharmacy
University of Charleston School of Pharmacy
University of Cincinnati James L. Winkle College of Pharmacy
University of Colorado Anschutz Medical Campus Skaggs School of Pharmacy and Pharmaceutical Sciences
University of Connecticut School of Pharmacy
University of Findlay College of Pharmacy
University of Florida College of Pharmacy
University of Georgia College of Pharmacy
University of Hawaii at Hilo Daniel K. Inouye College of Pharmacy
University of Houston College of Pharmacy
University of Illinois at Chicago College of Pharmacy
University of Iowa College of Pharmacy
University of Kansas School of Pharmacy
University of Kentucky College of Pharmacy
University of Louisiana at Monroe College of Pharmacy
University of Maryland Eastern Shore School of Pharmacy and Health Professions
University of Maryland School of Pharmacy
University of Michigan College of Pharmacy
University of Minnesota College of Pharmacy
University of Mississippi School of Pharmacy
University of Missouri-Kansas City School of Pharmacy
University of Montana College of Health Professions and Biomedical Sciences Skaggs School of Pharmacy
University of Nebraska Medical Center College of Pharmacy
University of New England College of Pharmacy
University of New Mexico College of Pharmacy
University of North Carolina Eshelman School of Pharmacy
University of North Texas Health Science Center UNT System College of Pharmacy
University of Oklahoma College of Pharmacy
University of Pittsburgh School of Pharmacy
University of Puerto Rico Medical Sciences Campus School of Pharmacy
University of Rhode Island College of Pharmacy

PHARMD SCHOOLS
University of Saint Joseph School of Pharmacy and Physician Assistant Studies
University of South Carolina College of Pharmacy
University of South Florida Health Taneja College of Pharmacy
University of Southern California School of Pharmacy
University of Tennessee Health Science Center College of Pharmacy
University of Texas at Austin College of Pharmacy
University of Texas at El Paso School of Pharmacy
University of Texas at Tyler Ben and Maytee Fisch College of Pharmacy
University of the Incarnate Word Feik School of Pharmacy
University of the Pacific Thomas J. Long School of Pharmacy
University of the Sciences Philadelphia College of Pharmacy
University of Toledo College of Pharmacy and Pharmaceutical Sciences
University of Utah College of Pharmacy
University of Washington School of Pharmacy
University of Wisconsin-Madison School of Pharmacy
University of Wyoming School of Pharmacy
Virginia Commonwealth University at the Medical College of Virginia Campus School of Pharmacy
Washington State University College of Pharmacy and Pharmaceutical Sciences
Wayne State University Eugene Applebaum College of Pharmacy and Health Sciences
West Coast University School of Pharmacy
West Virginia University School of Pharmacy
Western New England University College of Pharmacy
Western University of Health Sciences College of Pharmacy
Wilkes University Nesbitt School of Pharmacy
William Carey University School of Pharmacy
Wingate University School of Pharmacy
Xavier University of Louisiana College of Pharmacy

VET SCHOOLS LIST

VET SCHOOLS
Auburn University College of Veterinary Medicine
Colorado State University College of Veterinary Medicine and Biomedical Sciences
Cornell University College of Veterinary Medicine
Iowa State University College of Veterinary Medicine
Kansas State University College of Veterinary Medicine
Lincoln Memorial University College of Veterinary Medicine
Louisiana State University School of Veterinary Medicine
Michigan State University College of Veterinary Medicine
Midwestern University College of Veterinary Medicine
Mississippi State University College of Veterinary Medicine
North Carolina State University College of Veterinary Medicine
Oklahoma State University College of Veterinary Medicine
Oregon State University College of Veterinary Medicine
Purdue University College of Veterinary Medicine
Texas A&M University College of Veterinary Medicine & Biomedical Sciences
The Ohio State University College of Veterinary Medicine
Tufts University School of Veterinary Medicine
Tuskegee University School of Veterinary Medicine
University of California, Davis School of Veterinary Medicine
University of Florida College of Veterinary Medicine
University of Georgia College of Veterinary Medicine
University of Illinois College of Veterinary Medicine
University of Minnesota College of Veterinary Medicine
University of Missouri - Columbia College of Veterinary Medicine
University of Pennsylvania School of Veterinary Medicine
University of Tennessee College of Veterinary Medicine
University of Wisconsin-Madison School of Veterinary Medicine
Virginia Tech Virginia-Maryland College of Veterinary Medicine
Washington State University College of Veterinary Medicine
Western University of Health Sciences College of Veterinary Medicine

BS/MD TESTING PLAN

NORTHWESTERN UNIVERSITY'S HONORS PROGRAM IN MEDICAL EDUCATION (HPME) REQUIRES:

SAT or ACT, SAT II Subject Tests required in Math 2 and Chemistry
Average Scores for 2018-2019
SAT R&W – 762, Math 792; ACT 35, Writing 12
SAT II Chemistry: 777, Math 2: 790

BROWN UNIVERSITY'S PROGRAM IN LIBERAL MEDICAL EDUCATION (PLME)

SAT or ACT w/writing; SAT II Subject Tests - 2 recommended (one should be a science)
Average Scores:
SAT ERW: 742; SAT Math: 770; ACT Composite: 34

RICE/BAYLOR MEDICAL SCHOLARS PROGRAM

SAT or ACT; SAT II Subject Tests – 2 recommended (Math 2 and a Science)
There are no minimums, although Rice's average SAT is 1540 and ACT is 34

ST. BONAVENTURE/GWU SCHOOL OF MEDICINE AND HEALTH SCIENCES

SAT or ACT; SAT II Subject Test in a science (Biology-M preferred, Chemistry is acceptable)

Note: If you complete the requirements for these schools, you are set. Although many programs do not require or recommend subject tests, BS/MD programs are extremely competitive. Finalists often demonstrate the highest academic credentials.

What tests and scores do you need for the schools to which you are applying?

BS/MD PROGRAM	TESTS REQUIRED	SCORE RANGE

What tests and scores do you need for the schools to which you are applying?

YOUR TESTS	DATE TAKEN	SCORES & SUBSCORES

LISTS AND GUIDES

BS/MD TIMELINE

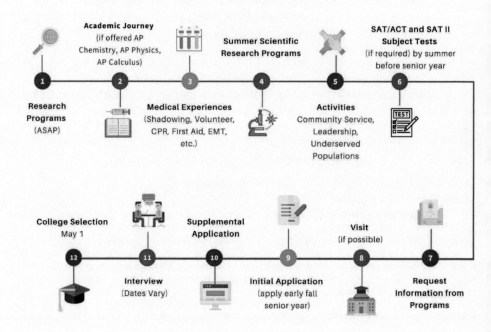

BS/MD PROGRAMS	INITIAL APPLICATION DATES	BS/MD SUPPLEMENTAL APPLICATION DATES	INTERVIEW DATES

INDEX

A

B

C

E

F

G

H

I

J

K

L

M

N

O

268

S

T

U

V

W

Y

Z

Made in the USA
Monee, IL
10 June 2024

59715783R00171